FOR MY PARENTS
Ruth and Jesse Lebow

ALL ABOUT
SOCCER

by
Jared Lebow

NEWSWEEK BOOKS, New York

Copyright © 1978 by Jared Lebow

All rights reserved. No part of this book may be reproduced or utilized in any form or by any means, electronic or mechanical, including photocopying, recording or by an information storage and retrieval system, without permission in writing from the publisher. Inquiries should be addressed to Newsweek Books, 444 Madison Avenue, New York, N.Y. 10022. Published simultaneously in Canada by Prentice-Hall of Canada Ltd., 1870 Birchmount Road, Scarborough, Ontario.

Printed in the United States of America

First Edition 1978

Library of Congress Cataloging in Publication Data

Lebow, Jared

All about soccer.

1. Soccer. I. Title

GV943.L395 796.33'42 77-99208

ISBN o-88225-256-9

Book Design: Eugene Milbauer

Contents

Appendices

1. HISTORY OF THE GAME

On a hot and humid evening in the summer of 1975, Edson Arantes de Nascimento climbed from a helicopter before 7,000 people in New York's old and decrepit Downing Stadium on Randall's Island. As he walked across a field of freshly trimmed grass the crowd began to chant his nickname, "Pelé, Pelé," over and over again. He had been lured here, drawn out of retirement in his native Brazil, by two things; one guaranteed, the other purely speculative. The initial reason was a three-year contract worth $4.7 million. The second was something many skeptics had already relegated to the impossible dream category—an opportunity to popularize soccer in the United States.

Two summers later, on a hot and humid August evening in New Jersey's new and sparkling Giants Stadium, Pelé walked across a field of shiny artificial turf and gazed up at a crowd of 77,691 cheering spectators. They had come, some paying scalpers as much as fifty dollars for a single ticket, to watch Pelé's team, the Cosmos, play the Ft. Lauderdale Strikers in a North American Soccer League playoff game. The impossible dream had come true.

That it had should not be all that surprising, for whether it is called football, *voetbal, fussball, fotball,* or *futbol,* soccer is *the* international game played everywhere from Argentina to Zanzibar. No matter if the field of play be in Moscow or Paris, the rules are the same, and the fans are as excitable under gray English skies as they are under the brilliant South American sun.

The Most Popular Game

The world's one truly international game, the sport is governed by the Fédération Internationale de Football Association (FIFA). Headquartered in Zurich, Switzerland, the

There were no sportswriters in the seventeenth century, but here is an example of how soccer inspired one poet.

Fourteenth-century soccer was such a rough-and-tumble affair that King Edward II banned the game.

organization has, at the moment, 142 nations listed on its membership rolls.

About 20 million people play organized soccer, and as a spectator sport the game is in a class by itself. Rio de Janeiro's Maracana Stadium is capable of holding over 200,000 cheering Cariocans for a single game, while throngs in excess of 100,000 are commonplace at Mexico City's Aztec Stadium and London's Wembley.

With the aid of satellite-beamed television signals, an estimated 750 million people watched West Germany defeat Holland 2–1 in the final game of the 1974 World Cup competition. The 1978 edition of this quadrennial soccer festival was staged in Argentina, where the sixteen national teams that survived two years of rugged elimination matches battled for international football supremacy. In 1982 this traveling tournament will move to Spain, and in 1986 it will return to South America to be staged in Colombia.

How did it all begin? The answer is still shrouded in the shadows of antiquity. A sporting event similar to soccer was played by the Chinese some 2,500 years ago. It was called *tsuchu,* which roughly translates into "kick a leather ball with the foot." The ancient Greeks and Romans played a kicking game using an inflated cow bladder for a ball. Rome's conquering legions took the game with them, and according to one theory introduced it to the British Isles during the third century A.D.

A Rough-and-Tumble Affair

The British have a somewhat different version. According to them, the first real soccer games were played in the ninth century when Denmark invaded and tried to make England part of Scandinavia. The English thought the idea bloody awful, so they lopped off the heads of Danish prisoners and kicked them around to show their contempt for the plan. Idle kicking of inanimate objects soon developed into organized games, with whole towns taking part in the fun.

Whether or not this legend is true matters little. It is known that a kicking game making use of an inflated ball was played in the walled city-states of northern Italy during the early Renaissance, but the game of soccer as we know it had its real roots in the British Isles.

At first it was a rough-and-tumble affair, so rough as a matter of fact that in 1314 Edward II issued the following proclamation: "Forasmuch as there is great noise in the city caused by hustling over large balls, from which many evils may arise, which God forbid, we command and forbid on behalf of the King, on pain of imprisonment, such game to be used in the city in future."

Royal acceptance or not the game persisted, becoming, over the centuries, no less violent. In the 1570's Sir Thomas Elyot wrote that "foote balle was a pastime to be utterly objected by all noble men, the game giving no pleasure, but beastlie furie and violence."

The Playing Fields of Eton

By the early nineteenth century, the game had become popular at England's famous public schools, Eton and Harrow, institutions that began to formalize the game by adding some rules and regulations. Not that this made soccer any less a rough-and-tumble sport. In one contest, A.W. Alcock of Harrow crashed into Alcock Lubbock of Eton. "If you do that again," thundered Lubbock, "I'll hack off your legs."

Public schools were not public at all, being in fact private institutions for the upper classes, but their graduates joined athletes from all walks of life as more and more teams were formed and various leagues organized. Some refinements were added, but the violence remained. The wife of Lord Kinnaird, an old Etonian and one of soccer's first stars, feared her husband might come home from a game with a broken leg. "Don't worry," a friend assured her, "if he does, it won't be his own."

Something had to be done, and it was. Soccer's first complete set of official rules was written at Cambridge University in 1846, but the basic rules of the game as it is played today were not established until 1863, when the Football Association was organized and held its first meeting in London. The new organization's rules were based on the Cambridge dictates, with several important refinements.

Holding, tripping, and hacking(kicking an opponent's legs), once universally accepted tactics, were disallowed, and their advocates withdrew in a huff to develop a sport that has evolved into the modern game of rugby.

England Sticks to Tradition

It is interesting to note here that while everywhere else in the world football associations have a national designation, such as the Federación Mexicana de Futból Asociación or the Deutscher Fussball-Bund, the British organization is still known simply as the Football Association. The word "soccer" is, incidentally, derived from association, first shortened to Assoc., then corrupted to soccer.

When the British Empire was at its zenith in the late nineteenth century the game was quickly spread around the globe by English colonists, sailors, and merchants. One of the most powerful clubs in the Soviet Union, Moscow Dynamo,

was formed in the 1890's by English industrialists who, under a contract with the czar, had established a cotton mill in Moscow and organized a soccer team for the workers. Times have changed, and today Moscow Dynamo receives its financial support from Russia's security services, including the infamous KGB.

One of Italy's great teams, AC Milan, many times Italian national champions, was originally the Milan Cricket and Football Club, organized by a group of British businessmen who wanted to play their native games while overseas. During World War II, Mussolini renamed the club AC Milano, but soon after he was overthrown the traditional Anglicized spelling was reinstated.

After the First World War the various nations that had adopted the game began to add their own refinements and to develop distinctive national styles. By the early 1950's England, although still a soccer power to be reckoned with, was no longer the dominant force in the game.

America's Day in the Sun

The great turning point came in 1953, when a visiting Hungarian team defeated the English national squad 6–3 before over 100,000 shocked spectators in Wembley Stadium. It was the first time England had ever been defeated at home by an overseas team. Proving that the outcome was no fluke, Hungary won again, 7–1, a few months later in Budapest.

Three years earlier, the English had suffered an even more humiliating defeat during the 1950 World Cup tournament in Brazil. England drew the United States in a preliminary round and expected to cruise to an easy victory over a team that had already been easily defeated, 3–1, by Spain. The match was to be played in Belo Horizonte and the American squad, a half and half mixture of native and foreign-born players, was given no chance of victory by the scores of soccer writers who had come to cover the event.

Unsurprisingly, some members of the American team seemed to share that assessment, and spent the night before the game partying until 2:00 A.M. When game time arrived, the English took to the field relaxed and laughing, but their attitude soon changed when attack after attack was repulsed by the suddenly stubborn American squad and the brilliant play of goalkeeper Frank Borghi. Then, a few minutes before the first half ended, Joe Gaetjens, who had been born in Haiti, headed in a goal and the U.S. led 1–0 at the half.

In the second half, their confidence growing with each passing minute, the American team played their highly rated British opponents dead even, and when the final gun sounded the score was still 1–0. It could have been the beginning of mass interest in American soccer, but in their next game the team reverted to form, lost to Chile 5–2, and the sport remained dormant in the U.S. until the mid-1960's.

As for Gaetjens, the man who fired the shot heard round the soccer world, he became an enigma by returning to his native Haiti and simply vanishing from the face of the earth. There is some speculation that he ran afoul of dictator François "Papa Doc" Duvalier and was eliminated by his secret police, the dreaded *Tontons Macoute*. A few years ago, the NASL's Cosmos staged a benefit game to raise funds to sponsor a search for Gaetjens. Several thousand dollars were raised but no new information was uncovered and the fate of Joe Gaetjens still remains a mystery.

In the mid-nineteenth century, soccer was still a very rugged sport, as this sketch of a game played at Kingston on Thames illustrates.

The Sunderland "Team of All Talents" won four English League titles between 1892 and 1902.

Millions Watched Thriller

American interest in the game received its greatest boost when England defeated West Germany for the 1966 World Cup. The game was televised in the U.S., allowing millions of viewers their first glimpse of top-flight soccer in a contest that had all the ingredients of first-rate melodrama.

Queen Elizabeth was among the crowd in Wembley Stadium that witnessed the seesaw contest that sustained nail-biting tension from start to finish. West Germany scored first, England tied, took the lead, and then, with less than a minute left, the game was tied at 2–2, which is how the score read when regulation time ran out.

Physically exhausted and emotionally drained after ninety minutes of nonstop action, the two teams were forced to play a thirty-minute overtime period. Ten minutes had elapsed when England's Alan Ball dribbled through West Germany's defense and booted a perfect pass to teammate Geoff Hurst, who knocked in a go-ahead goal that is still a subject of disputation among soccer aficionados. Hurst's shot struck the underside of the crossbar and ricocheted almost straight down. In English eyes the ball fell just behind the goal line, in German eyes just in front. The final decision rested with a Russian linesman who ruled that a goal had been scored.

A demoralized German team was unable to mount a successful scoring drive after that and as the overtime's last seconds ticked away Hurst scored again, his third goal of the game. The final tally read England 4, West Germany 2.

Lord Kinnard (above), one of soccer's first superstars, appeared in nine F.A. Cup finals. West Germany's Luther Emmerich (white jersey) shoots the ball past England's George Cohen (left) and Martin Peters during the 1966 World Cup championship game.

The Game Gains New Fans

The excitement of the 1966 World Cup introduced millions of Americans, who had previously been oblivious to soccer, to a fast-paced game that required a minimum of equipment and placed the emphasis on skill rather than size. The arrival of Pelé in 1975 gave soccer the extra push it needed to become an important part of the American sports scene. Some facts and figures demonstrate the sport's incredible growth in a relatively short period of time.

In 1966, when the England–West Germany World Cup final was televised, there were 277 college soccer teams. By 1977, the game was being played at the varsity level by 429 colleges and hundreds of junior colleges. Membership gains in youth soccer leagues were even more spectacular. In 1967, there were 50,000 registered players in youth leagues. A decade later that figure was close to one million.

Professional soccer also began to gain public acceptance, and the North American Soccer League finally began to record some profits after operating in the red for years. Teams whose nicknames were once no more than sports-trivia quiz items—like the Rowdies of Tampa and the Whitecaps of Vancouver—sold a record number of tickets as overall attendance in 1977, when the league had 18 teams, totaled 3,674,638. In 1974 B.P. (Before Pelé), the league attendance figure was just slightly over one million.

Fans were attracted by such international stars as Italy's Giorgio Chinaglia and Germany's Franz Beckenbauer, both of whom joined Pelé on the Cosmos, and England's George Best, who plays for the Los Angeles Aztecs. Attendance figures soared wherever Pelé and the Cosmos played, and his very presence in a league city was a boon for soccer.

Native-Born Players Improve

Also helping to draw spectators was the improved play of such American players as Shep Messing, the Cosmos' Brooklyn-born, Harvard-educated goalie. After the 1977 championship game, which the Cosmos won 2–1 over the Seattle Sounders before an S.R.O. crowd of 35,548 in Portland, Oregon, Pelé symbolically acknowledged the improvement of U.S. players by giving the Sounders' defensive star Jim McAlister, a Seattle native who was the league's Rookie of the Year, a souvenir any player would treasure—the Great One's jersey.

After his final game, an exhibition match between the Cosmos and Santos, the team he had played for in Brazil, Pelé issued the following letter addressed to his fans in America:

The three years I have spent in America have been among the finest of my life. I came here to help make soccer famous to Americans and no one is more happy than I that this dream has been fulfilled. To see the youngsters and the teenagers playing soccer everywhere I go is a thrill to me and shows me once again that this sport—soccer—is the finest game in the world.

2. HOW THE GAME IS PLAYED

occer begins with a ball and two teams, each with eleven players. The ball has a circumference of 27 to 28 inches and, when inflated, weighs 14 to 16 ounces. The overall dimensions of the soccer field, or pitch, may vary from 100 to 130 yards in length and 50 to 100 yards in width. All other dimensions (see diagram) remain fixed, regardless of the field's overall size.

Soccer is a game of constant motion with one basic objective: to propel the ball into an opponent's goal. Any part of a player's body—head, chest, legs—except the hands may be used to control and propel the ball. For soccer purposes the hand extends from shoulder to fingertips. Only one player on each team, the goalkeeper, may use his hands within the field of play, and only within the confines of the penalty area, which is always 44 yards wide and extends 18 yards into the field of play. To distinguish them from their teammates, goalies must wear a distinctive jersey in a color recognizably different from those worn by their own team and the opposition.

One referee has complete control of play and, although assisted by two linesmen on opposite sides of the pitch, is the only official allowed onfield during the course of a game. Unless otherwise agreed upon, a regulation game has two forty-five-minute halves separated by a five-minute halftime period. The referee has power to extend each half for time lost as a result of injuries or other events that may have delayed the game. In some championship contests there is, if needed, an overtime period of two fifteen-minute halves.

Substitution Rules

Depending on the type of competition, usually only one or two substitutes are permitted, and they must be identified before a game begins. If a player has been substituted, the original player may not return unless local rules specify otherwise. The NASL allows three substitutes, with no reentry permitted. U.S. college rules permit seven substitutes, who may enter and leave without limitation. High school rules allow unlimited substitution. In international competition, a player who is ejected by the referee (usually for a flagrant foul) may not be replaced. In such instances a team is obliged to continue the game short-handed.

A coin flip decides which team kicks off. Unlike American football, a team kicks off to itself, not to its opponent. Each team must remain in its own half of the field before the kickoff, and no player on the defending team may be within ten yards of the ball.

After each goal the team scored upon kicks off. Following a half of play the teams switch ends of the field, and the team that did not kick off to open the game now kicks off. A goal cannot be scored directly from a kickoff; the ball must first be touched by at least one other player.

Once a ball crosses a touchline (sideline) it is considered out of bounds, but a ball on the touchline is considered to be in

THE FIELD OF PLAY

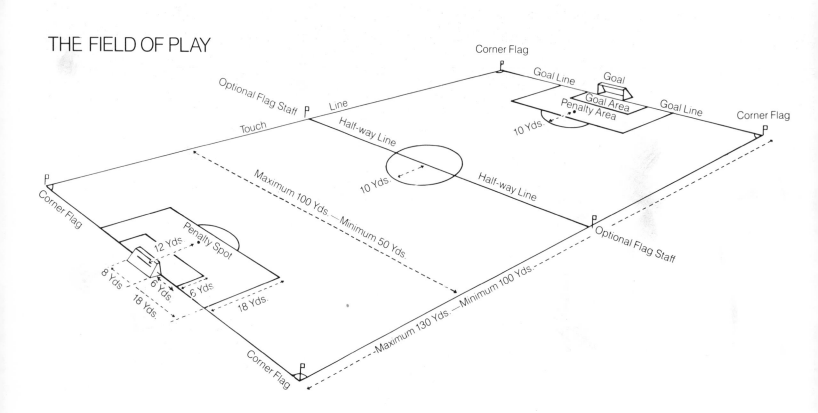

bounds. The team kicking the ball out of bounds loses possession and the other team puts it back into play by means of a throw-in.

A goal is scored when a ball passes completely over the goal line, between the goalposts, and under the crossbar.

The Offside Rule

One of the more complicated rules or "laws" (the complete FIFA Official Laws of the Game are given in Appendix A) is that governing offside. A player is considered to be offside if he is in his opponent's half of the field and the ball is played to him when there are fewer than two defenders between him and the goal. For all practical purposes, the goalie is one of these defenders so in actual practice the offside line moves back and forth with the rearmost defensive player. In the United States, the North American Soccer League has altered this law somewhat by drawing a "blue line" across the field thirty-five yards in front of each goal. Only when an attacking player is inside this line can he be whistled offside if the ball is played to him with fewer than two opponents between him and the goal.

A player is not offside if the ball was last touched or played by an opponent or if a player receives the ball directly from a goal kick, a corner kick, a throw-in, or when dropped by the referee.

A goal kick is awarded the defending team when the attacking team propels the ball across the goal line. This kick is taken within the goal area, on the same side of the goal where the ball went out of play.

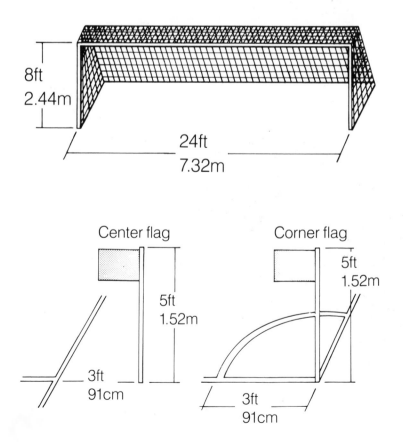

8ft
2.44m

24ft
7.32m

Center flag

Corner flag

5ft
1.52m

5ft
1.52m

3ft
91cm

3ft
91cm

The Corner Kick

If the ball is propelled over the goal line by a defender, the attacking team is given a corner kick from the corner of the field nearest to the spot where the ball went out of play. The corner kick is a powerful offensive weapon, and whenever one is awarded both teams, attackers and defenders, mass near the goal. A point can be scored directly from a corner kick, but the kicker may not play the ball again until it has been touched by another player. Opponents must remain ten yards away until a corner kick is taken.

Free Kicks

There are nine major violations (described in the Referees section) for which a direct free kick is awarded. If one of these fouls occurs in the penalty area, a penalty kick is awarded. Free kicks are divided into two categories, "direct" and "indirect." On a direct free kick the ball need not touch another player before going into the goal. On an indirect free kick the ball must touch at least one other player before a goal can be scored. Indirect free kicks are awarded for violations that include offsides, dangerous plays (kicking a ball directly at an opponent's head from close range), obstructing an opponent while not attempting to play the ball (in order to prevent the opponent from reaching it), and for charging an opponent fairly, as with a shoulder, when the ball is not within playing distance.

For all free kicks, direct or indirect, players on the offending team must be at least ten yards from the ball until it is kicked.

Penalty Kicks

Penalty kicks are direct free kicks taken from the penalty mark (see diagram), a white spot located exactly twelve yards in front of each goal. The player fouled does not have to take the kick himself; it can be booted by a teammate. All players, except the kicker and the goalkeeper, must stay outside the penalty area and at least ten yards from the ball. This is the reason for the arc at the penalty area's front edge. A classic game of cat and mouse takes place between kicker and goalie. Since the goalkeeper must stand on the goal line without moving his feet until the ball is kicked, he must guess if the ball is going to be booted to the left, right, or straight ahead. The goalkeeper usually makes this decision at the moment of contact between foot and ball. If he guesses correctly he has a chance for a save. Guessing wrong means losing that chance and an almost certain goal for the opposition. The kicker can only boot the ball once. If he touches it twice, the defending side is awarded an indirect free kick.

Equipment and Systems

One of the virtues of soccer is that not very much equipment is needed in order to play the game. All a team needs, besides a field, are a ball, shorts and jerseys, shoes and knee-length socks. Some players tuck light shinguards inside their socks, but many prefer to run the risk of scraped shins rather than carry any extra weight.

Soccer differs from other team sports in that there are very few set plays, and as the game has developed in recent years there has been a lessening of specialization in favor of more mobility, thus allowing players to change position to deal with changing situations.

In place of set plays there are "systems," basic formations upon which players improvise. One of the systems most frequently seen is the 4–3–3 (see diagram at right). In all systems there are three general positions not, of course, counting the goalkeeper. First there are the defenders, or fullbacks; then the midfielders, or linkmen; and the attackers, also known as forwards, wingers, or strikers.

Play evolves from these systems (which will be discussed in greater detail later on) in a free-flowing manner, so that a defender may suddenly find himself in an attacker's role while a few seconds later the forwards may be forced to race back to take up defensive positions.

Since soccer is a relatively low-scoring game, goals are a precious commodity, often achieved as much through one player's error as through another's outstanding effort. For this reason all eleven players on both teams must play the game all-out for ninety minutes, for a momentary lapse can spell disaster in a sport where more often than not one goal means the difference between victory and defeat.

Now let's take a closer look at the specific duties of the four different types of soccer players: defenders, midfield players, attackers, and goalkeepers.

4–3–3

Goalkeeper

4 Defenders
(2,4,5,3)

3 Midfielders or
linkmen (6,8,10)

3 Attackers or
forwards (7,9,11)

When two players are in direct competition for the ball, a shoulder charge (below) is a perfectly legal maneuver. But ramming an elbow into an opponent's chest (right) is a foul and will result in a direct free kick.

Pushing an opponent from behind (above) will attract the referee's whistle and a foul call. Grabbing an attacker's jersey (left) is an effective but illegal defensive tactic.

THE DEFENDERS

It is precisely because soccer is a relatively low-scoring game that defense plays such an important role in the success or failure of any team. Although squads are divided into groups of players with specific titles—defenders, midfielders, and forwards—soccer is above all else a team sport. Simply stated this means all ten outfielders (that is, everyone except the goalie) work in concert to score and, of equal importance, to prevent their opponents from scoring.

It was not always thus. Until the 1960's it was still a common practice for a defender to concentrate his efforts on the third of the field nearest his goal line. It was his job to stop an attack, gain possession of the ball, and then kick it upfield to an attacking teammate. All that has changed. The way soccer is played today a defender must be prepared to become an attacker the moment he captures the ball, just as attackers must take on the defensive role the moment they lose the ball.

Most soccer teams keep four defensive players in the rear as a kind of human screen to protect their goal. This is a moving screen, traveling up and downfield as teams trade possession of the ball. A blackboard diagram would show these four players arranged in one of two formations; either in a line with two fullbacks (defenders) covering the center of the field while the other two cover their flanks on the left and right, or in a line with one player in the center (sometimes called a midstopper) and two on the flanks backed up by a *libero,* or sweeper, who stands between them and the goal, ready to plug any holes opened by the offense.

That is how it would look on a blackboard, but of course soccer is played with athletes not chalk figures, and as it is with all positions in this sport, none of these defenders is frozen in place. Each player is required to adjust to rapidly changing situations and to coordinate his efforts with the actions of his teammates.

In a well-executed front-block tackle (opposite page), the defender (dark shirt) stops the attacker with a shoulder charge and maneuvers for the ball. A perfect side-block tackle (above) by the defender (white shorts) allows him to place his foot in front of the attacker and behind the ball.

The whole concept of team offense and team defense (a philosophy that has been given the rather all-inclusive title of "total football") requires genuine teamwork on the part of defenders, midfielders, and forwards whenever ball control is gained or lost.

There are really only two principal methods of team defense—zone and man-to-man—which can be employed separately or in combination, as events require.

The Two Basic Defenses

Let us say, for example, that in a game between the Blues and the Reds, a Blue forward has the ball taken away from him near the Red penalty area. He immediately tries to regain control by closely marking (guarding) the Red player, but his efforts fail and the Red team begins to advance upfield.

Members of the Blue team, suddenly no longer on the attack, begin to move back toward midfield, occupying differ-

ent areas or zones. Each Blue player is now responsible for an area rather than an individual opponent. Should a Red player enter a Blue defender's territory he will be closely marked, man-to-man, until he moves on to the next zone where he will be picked up by another Blue defender.

These tactics delay and hinder the Red attack while preventing any through passes that would send the ball from the Red half of the field into the Blue half. Meanwhile the Blue rear line has had a chance to organize itself into a solid defensive screen.

Once the Red attackers reach the third of the field around the Blue penalty area, zone defenses are often abandoned in favor of a close-marking man-to-man defense, as each Blue defender moves to within a yard or two of every Red attacker.

The Sweeper

The last line of the Blue defensive screen is the sweeper. He floats along behind the rest of his team, adding depth to its defense by standing ready to challenge any attacker who breaks through toward his goal. If the sweeper is beaten in this instance his goalkeeper may be left in the uncomfortable position of trying to stop the shot of an unguarded attacker, which is almost as difficult as trying to reject a penalty shot. For this reason teams that use a sweeper usually assign one of their finest players to this position. Franz Beckenbauer, who helped make Bayern Munich the best team in Europe and was capped* 103 times for the West German national team before joining the NASL's Cosmos, revolutionized the role of the sweeper.

Playing at times behind his fullbacks and at times in front, he doubled as an attacker, bursting through from the defensive end of the field to strike at the opponent's goal. It is an aggressive kind of play that has added a new dimension to soccer.

The One-Man Screen

When playing in front of the fullbacks, the sweeper serves as a one-man screen. He threatens any possible through pass, challenges any opponent who manages to slip between two zones, and is prepared to attack should one of his teammates suddenly regain possession of the ball.

An individual defender's most potent weapon in trying to regain ball possession is the tackle. Unlike American football, soccer rules require defenders to tackle the ball, not the person with the ball, although some body contact is allowed.

There are four basic tackles in soccer: front block, side block (both of which may be augmented with a shoulder charge), back tackle, and sliding tackle.

The Front-Block Tackle

As an attacker approaches the defender he must judge the precise instant when the ball will be within reach and temporarily out of his opponent's control. A front-block tackle made too early or too late will cause the tackler to miss the ball and possibly result in a collision between the two players and a foul call from the referee. When attempting a frontal assault, the defender should be in a well-balanced crouching position and prepared to absorb any impact caused by body contact.

*Players receive a symbolic cap every time they are chosen to play for their country in an international match.

Tackling from behind is a dangerous and delicate maneuver, which in this case resulted in a foul when the defender's foot missed the ball and kicked the attacker.

Franz Beckenbauer (above) in action for Bayern Munich. Four nervous members of Tottenham Hotspur (right) form a wall to try and block a direct free kick.

The defender's tackling foot (the one going after the ball) should be placed at an angle that presents the largest possible target for the ball. Obviously timing is all-important in this maneuver, for the tackler must make his move just as his opponent is attempting to play the ball. He must either kick the ball past the attacker or take it off his foot. If he is close enough the tackler may jar his opponent with a shoulder charge—making sure his elbow is close to his body, because the contact must be shoulder to shoulder. If the defender pushes with his arm, a foul may be called and a free kick awarded.

The purpose of a shoulder charge is to knock the attacker off balance. If the ball is wedged between attacker and defender the player in best control of his body will probably gain possession by dragging the ball over the other player's foot or knocking it off to one side.

The Side-Block Tackle

If a tackler cannot confront his opponent head-on, he may challenge from the side, pivoting to place his outer foot in contact with the ball and then ramming the defender with a shoulder charge. Here again, timing is of the utmost impor-

tance; since both players are moving, the tackler is required to make his pivot at precisely the right moment or risk missing the ball completely. A missed tackle leaves the defender off balance, allowing the attacker to easily brush him aside and continue his advance.

The Back Tackle

If the defender is approaching an attacker from the rear he may attempt to swing a leg in front of the ball from behind. This is a delicate maneuver, for should the pursuing player trip the attacker while his leg is not clearly in position to take the ball a foul may be called. Even when there is no foul committed the man losing the ball may attempt to instigate one by falling to the ground and giving a short, dramatic performance for benefit of the referee.

The Sliding Tackle

This is both the most exciting and, by the same token, the most dangerous tackle from a defensive point of view—it should only be attempted if no other tackle is possible. It is usually employed as a desperation move, when the attacker

is running free with the ball, dribbling toward the goal. Once the defender commits himself to a sliding tackle he is off his feet and must make contact with the ball. If he fails, he finds himself sprawled on the ground and effectively out of play while the attacker continues downfield.

The sliding tackle is most effective near a touchline or goal line, where the defender can either push the ball to a teammate or destroy an attack's momentum by sending the ball out of play. A defender usually goes into his slide eight to ten feet from his target, aiming just ahead of the ball rather than exactly for it, for he will lose a split second between the time he goes into the slide and the moment he makes contact with the ball.

Corner-Kick Defense

When a member of the defensive team knocks a ball over his own goal line the attacking team is awarded a corner kick. Most goalies will take a position at the goalpost farthest from the kicker, a spot that provides a better angle for judging the ball's flight. One fullback will stand at the near post, ready to both clear a kick curving into the goal or prevent the ball from passing across the goalmouth, where it might easily be deflected in for a score. Meanwhile the other defenders will be closely marking any opponents within or near the penalty area. Once the kick has been taken, the defending team will try to clear the ball away from its penalty area as quickly as possible.

Bobby Moore (dark shirt), one of soccer's all-time great defenders, is shown here clearing the ball upfield for West Ham United.

Free-Kick Defense

The referee signals a direct free kick by pointing his arm in the direction the kick will be taken. An indirect free kick is signaled by holding one arm straight up. If a free kick is awarded at a point more than thirty-five yards from their goal, defenders will concentrate on close, man-to-man marking, their main interest being to keep the ball and their opponents out of the penalty area.

Tactics change drastically when a free kick is awarded at close range. Now the defenders will form a human wall of four or more players between the kicker and their goal. Manning this barrier requires a degree of physical courage, for on a direct free kick the attacker may decide to try and blast the ball right through this wall of flesh and blood. Once the kick is taken the wall immediately disbands and its members reas-

sume their regular defensive assignments.

If a foul that calls for a direct free kick is committed in the penalty area, a penalty shot is awarded. But if an indirect free kick is awarded within ten yards of the goal line, a wall may be established between the goalposts. Since the ball must be touched by two players before a goal can be scored on an indirect free kick, the members of this wall will charge forward as soon as the ball is touched in order to block any possibility of a shot on goal.

Often when a member of the team on defense gains possession of the ball near his penalty area he will pass it back to the goalie, who will then start his team's attack with a well-aimed pass or kick. The ball is then carefully advanced upfield to the players who link the offensive and defensive halves of the field together; the midfielders.

One of soccer's most spectacular moves is the perfectly timed sliding tackle, executed here by an Argentine defender (striped jersey) against England's star forward, Kevin Keegan.

THE MIDFIELDERS

Since control of the midfield area more often than not means control of the game, midfield players (also referred to as halfbacks and linkmen) must possess a variety of talents. On defense their chief responsibility is to destroy the opposition's attack before it really gets underway, while on offense they are responsible for initiating and supporting their team's attack. In addition they have to be ready, should the opportunity arise, to go on the attack and score goals themselves.

Although the midfielder's primary task is control of the area twenty-five yards on either side of the center line—on one hand taking pressure off the rear defensive line and on the other providing extra power to the forward attacking line—his position is an elastic one, not rigidly defined. Midfielders go where the action takes them. Outstanding halfbacks can, whenever the need arises, operate effectively from goal line to goal line, plugging holes on defense and exploiting opportunities on offense.

Midfielders are sometimes referred to as the distance runners of soccer because they must be capable of a high work rate, a term that means they must almost always be on the move. In top-flight competition midfielders will often run ten or more miles in a single match, so for them the ability to keep going for a full ninety minutes is much more important than flat-out speed.

Most modern soccer systems place three players in the midfield area, although some use as many as four here and others as few as two. Whatever the system, the role a midfielder fills remains relatively constant.

Basic Midfield Tactics

When a team gains ball control in the midfield area it normally does one of two things. It launches a quick counterattack, plunging into the opponent's half of the field, or it slowly builds an attack in the midfield area with a series of short passes that probe and exploit the defense.

Perhaps the easiest way to understand how an attack can be slowly constructed is to visualize a soccer field divided into three distinct sections: an offensive third, a midfield area, and a defensive third.

When midfielders pass the ball amongst themselves in the middle area they draw the opposition fullbacks out of their rear guard positions. When these fullbacks come upfield to challenge for the ball they create gaps in the defensive third of the field, openings the attacking team can exploit.

The Defensive Midfielder

One of the midfielders is usually assigned a primary role as a defender, detailed to the area where the defensive third and midfield areas blend together. Should the opposition suddenly gain ball control in the midfield area he is in position to act as the first line of defense, to slow the counterattack and prevent through passes.

When his team is on the attack this midfielder will act in a supporting role for the forwards and other midfielders in the offensive third of the field. He also serves as a link between his goalkeeper and fullbacks and the rest of his team, taking passes from the defensive third and then dribbling or passing the ball into the midfield area.

Roberto Rivelino (right) threads the ball between four Argentine defenders.

Johnny Giles (white shirt), an outstanding midfielder for
Leeds United in the late 1960's, joined the NASL's Philadel-
phia Fury in 1978. He also manages the Republic of
Ireland's national team.

The Great Giles

Johnny Giles, who when teamed in midfield with Billy Bremner helped make Leeds United the most successful team in English soccer during the second half of the 1960's, was an outstanding example of a defensive midfielder. Sweeping his area like a human radar screen, he had an uncanny ability to track and destroy an attacking team's advance before it could develop and probe deeply into his team's defensive third of the field.

A pinpoint passer and a superb feeder, he was also capable of instantly making the switch from defense to offense, able to steal the ball with a perfect tackle and then send it soaring downfield to an unmarked forward.

The Playmaker

This player performs much the same function as a play-making guard in basketball, often acting as the "brains" of his team, organizing play in the midfield area, directing the attack, and controlling the tempo of the game. In addition to athletic ability, this player must also have the kind of take-charge personality necessary to assume a leadership role both on offense and defense.

Such a player is Brazilian international star Roberto Rivelino. A combination of talent and seemingly boundless self-confidence, he makes dozens of split-second decisions during the course of a game. A master of the short pass, he can also boot the ball with remarkable accuracy to a teammate

A summit meeting of superstars: Franz Beckenbauer (left) and Brazil's brilliant midfielder, Roberto Rivelino.

fifty yards away. He is the player others look to in tight situations, relying on his ability to read the action and quickly detect changes in the flow of play and then orchestrate the actions of his teammates to deal with defensive problems and offensive opportunities.

The Attacking Midfielder

Just as the defensive midfielder serves as a link between the defensive third of the field and midfield, this player serves as the connection between midfield and the offensive third. On defense he is the first barrier an attacking team must penetrate in the midfield area and on offense he is often the spearhead of his team's initial thrust toward the opponent's defensive third of the field.

This player attempts to place himself in dangerous attacking positions where he can back up the efforts of his team's forwards and deliver the pass that will set up a goal or, if the opportunity arises, break through to score the goal himself.

It is this ability to lurk behind the first line of attackers and then suddenly appear as if from nowhere to surprise and befuddle the defenders that makes an offensive midfielder such a valuable and potent weapon. He is the player who tries to be in the right place at the right time to take advantage of opportunities that last for only a moment.

Midfield Techniques

The modern soccer player must be capable of performing effectively in any position on the field. Most importantly, he

Mark Lindsay, in 1977 a midfielder with the Tampa Bay Rowdies, gets ready to pass the ball.

Billy Bremner (light shirt), shown here playing for Leeds United, captained Scotland's 1974 World Cup team and was one of soccer's all-time great midfielders.

must understand what actions are required in any area on the field during the different stages through which a game passes. If a midfielder is operating near his own penalty area his actions will differ from those that would be employed in the opponent's half of the field. Risks that are prohibitively dangerous near one's own goal—such as moving out of position to try for an interception—involve less chance when attempted farther upfield, since there will be time and space enough to recover from a mistake.

Ball Control and Passing

Quickness in bringing the ball under control is an important technique for players in all parts of the field, but it is vital for midfield players since they usually operate in a congested area of the field and are more often than not surrounded by opponents. The best midfielders are able to receive a pass and control the ball with one movement, and then pass the ball off to a teammate with the next. There are several basic principles that must be mastered in order to bring the ball under instant and close control. These include:

● Making certain the part of the body being used to bring the ball under control is in line with the flight of the ball. Whenever possible, good players will move their feet rather than reaching with their head or a leg.

● Relaxing the part of the body being used to stop the ball. If the ball is being stopped with the foot, the ankle should be relaxed. If it is the head doing the "catching," the neck should be relaxed.

● Cushioning the ball's impact by drawing the stopping surface away from the ball just before it strikes. This prevents a hard pass from bouncing off and out of the receiver's control. Good players are able to stop the ball with any part of their bodies, except, of course, the hands and arms.

Volley Passes

One pass that can be made after the ball has been stopped is the short volley, a pass that is given before the ball even touches the ground. Another is the half volley, made just as the ball touches the ground.

The short volley can be made in different ways, with different parts of the foot. The short-volley lob is employed to lift the ball delicately over the heads of nearby players. The ball is struck with the instep on a kick that is powered from the knee rather than the hip. To volley a pass directly to a teammate's foot, the ball is chopped downward with the inside of the passing foot. The direction of a volley pass (or any pass for that matter) can be disguised if the pass is flicked, using only the ankle to direct the ball. In this technique the ankle is bent inwards and the foot is flicked outwards at the ball to knock it in the desired direction. The ankle is relaxed as much as possible to produce the flicking action.

The half-volley pass is struck in much the same manner as any other pass, the difference being that most passes are hit when the ball is rolling on the ground, while the half volley is kicked just as the ball makes contact with the ground. This means the foot must make contact with the ball at a point slightly higher on its surface than would be the case for a normal ground pass.

A midfield player should always move with speed and determination toward the ball whenever he has a chance of possession, for the team controlling the ball controls the game.

Screening the Ball

Midfield is often like a commuter highway at rush hour. It is where a great deal of a game's action takes place and a large number of players are usually in this area. Therefore midfield players must be adept at creating time and space for themselves when there does not appear to be much of either commodity available. The technique of controlling the ball while keeping one's body between it and an opponent gives a midfielder some operating room and time to make a move. If a midfielder skillfully screens the ball with his body, his opponent will have a difficult time tackling for it without committing a foul.

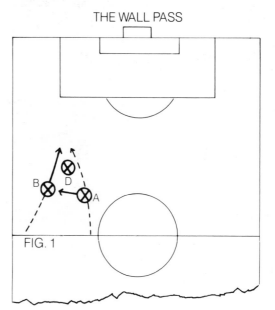

THE WALL PASS

FIG. 1

The Wall Pass: Player A advances toward the defender (D), threatening to dribble by on the right, while his teammate (B) has taken up a position facing A, who passes the ball to B who immediately sends the ball toward an open area A is running towards. In other words, A has bounced the ball off B as if the latter were a wall.

The Wall Pass

How to advance the ball toward an opponent's goal once possession is gained is a problem an offensive midfielder is often called upon to solve. One of the most commonly used methods is the wall pass (Figure 1), a soccer variation of basketball's give and go. It is a relatively simple maneuver. The player with the ball moves toward the man guarding him and threatens to dribble by, let's say on the right side. Meanwhile, a teammate has taken up a position where he can, for a moment, stand still facing the player with the ball. The player with the ball passes to the stationary teammate and then breaks downfield behind his opponent to a point where, in full stride, he takes a return pass from his stationary teammate, who has served as a "wall" off of which the ball has been bounced.

Now the ball is in the offensive third of the field where a team's primary attacking force, the forwards, operate.

FORWARDS

Pelé, who during his twenty-two-season career scored 1,281 goals, celebrates here after scoring against Italy in the 1970 World Cup championship game.

f there is a single point to be garnered from the previous sections, it is that soccer is above all else a team sport. Nevertheless, it is still true that in this game, as in all other team games, those players who score points tend to be the ones who attract the most attention. Ask someone who knows nothing about soccer to name one of the game's great players and the answer will invariably be Pelé, one of the most prolific goal scorers of all time.

If the person being questioned knows just a tad more about the game, the answer might include such names as George Best, Eusebio, Gerd Müller, and Kevin Keegan. If it is an American being questioned, players like Giorgio Chinaglia and Steve David might be mentioned. These are the players who score the goals and, as they say in the newspaper business, "get the ink." They all have one thing in common and that is, in a relatively low-scoring sport they score the most points because as forwards they, more often than their teammates, are in a position to score.

A Special Kind of Player

Modern defenses, which keep three fullbacks and a sweeper in the rear to protect their goal, make the forward's job tougher than it has ever been. He must be the kind of player who can function effectively in a position where there is

Dennis Tueart, who joined the Cosmos in 1978, uses a spectacular overhead scissors kick to give Manchester City the goal it needed to win, 1–0, the 1976 English League Cup final against Newcastle United.

always constant pressure—from teammates, coaches, fans, and the press—to produce goals.

Such an athlete is Steve David, twice, in 1975 and 1977, the North American Soccer League's scoring champion. When asked by *Soccer Corner* magazine to describe what qualities were required to be effective in a forward's position this is what he had to say. "My strength as a player is my speed and my ability to take defenders on one-on-one. Also, I can put the ball where I want to. I don't have to use power or kick very hard, I can place the ball where I want it to go.

"Scoring goals is a lot of pressure. You get inside the penalty box and that's where all the pressure is. That's where opponents are going to kill you, because you're not supposed to be in the box."

Like all great forwards, David's ability appears to be instinctual. He says, "I think it's something I've just inherited. It's natural. Since I've been playing soccer I've always played up front and I've always been the leading scorer on any team I've ever played for. There's no other player on the team that outscored me. It's like it's built in."

Wingers and Strikers

Basically there are two kinds of forwards, those who operate along the sideline, the outside forwards or wingers, and those who operate in the middle, the inside forwards or strikers. One cannot function without the other since they must work together, complementing each other's actions to create space in today's tight defensive systems.

These defensive systems have sealed the area around the penalty box to all but the most powerful or cleverest attacks. It is the function of the winger, operating along the touchlines, to exploit a defense's flanks, spread the opposition, and create openings in the middle.

Because of his position in the middle on a team's attacking line, the striker is usually the highest scorer. He is also the most closely marked player on a team and must expect to operate in close quarters while being buffeted by defenders trying to either prevent him from getting the ball or attempting to take it away once he gets it.

Both wingers and strikers have important defensive functions if the ball is taken away. They must immediately try to get it back and, failing that, delay its advance back upfield to give their defense a chance to get organized.

Wing Tactics

Today's wingers must be prepared to deal with frustration, for no sooner will they get past the fullback marking them than they will be met by a sweeper moving up to plug the newly created gap in his defense. Instead of simply crossing the ball blindly toward the middle, the winger must now take advan-

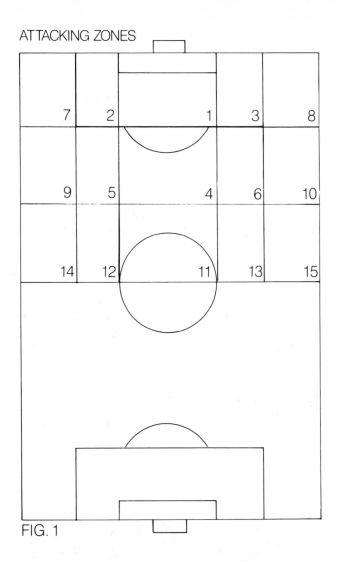

FIG. 1

tage of the space created when the sweeper moves out to mark him. A team that has a coordinated offense will have a striker or midfielder moving into this newly created open space to receive a well-placed pass from the wing.

Or, instead of passing to the open space, the winger may combine for a wall pass (give-and-go) with the properly positioned teammate. This will allow the winger to pass, run by the man marking him, and get the ball back in an open area. The primary object of this exercise being to create a situation where a shot on goal can be taken.

Some wing forwards, like George Best, have been great scorers, while others, like England's Stanley Matthews, have been exceptional in creating opportunities for others to score. The player who usually benefits most from a winger's activities is the striker.

Tactics for Strikers

Consider the attacking half of the field as a grid (see Figure 1, above) divided into fifteen areas. The number of each area indicates how important it is to the attacking team. The lower the number, the better the position for scoring a goal.

Strikers will try to spend most of their time on offense in the low-numbered areas. If a winger or midfielder succeeds in drawing a defender out of one of these spaces, a striker should quickly move into the open area, and whenever possible attempt to be in position to take a pass behind defenders instead of in front of them.

If a striker cannot take up a threatening position he will try to allow a teammate to move into one of these areas, moving in

support of a player who either has the ball or is about to receive it. Above all, strikers try to insure that their team will maintain possession in this area, because controlling the ball means controlling the game. A team can't shoot unless it has the ball to shoot with.

Shooting

All forwards must have the ability to put the ball into the net. This is not only a matter of skill in kicking or heading the ball; it is also a matter of courage, control, and optimism. Forwards must be positive thinkers. The possibility of missing should be ignored, because scoring opportunities develop so suddenly they must be seized instantly or they will just as suddenly disappear.

Scoring is seldom a matter of just banging the ball. Good forwards rarely boot the ball unnecessarily hard. Their shots represent controlled power rather than force. Most importantly, a missed shot must be taken in stride. So few goals are scored in a soccer game it must be expected there will be more failures than successes. The important thing is that pressure be continually applied and that no shooting opportunities be passed up.

Kicking

In American football, kicks are almost always made for distance; the long punt sailing downfield, or the fifty-yard field goal booted by a converted soccer player. A forward in soccer who kicks like this is destroying his team, for in the attacking area such long kicks are useless.

Johann Cruyff, one of the world's premier forwards, in action for Barcelona, a club that gave him a $1 million "signing-on" bonus in 1973.

One of soccer's all-time great wing forwards, George Best, shown here playing for the Los Angeles Aztecs.

Forwards must be capable of shooting accurately when the ball is bouncing crazily and approaching at different heights and angles. This means they must be adept at volleying the ball, especially when turning. Sometimes a forward will try to get additional power into his kick by turning his back to the goal, and then moving his whole body around and into the ball. The main kicking power comes as the knee is straightened when the foot makes contact with the ball.

Fowards are almost always tightly marked and therefore must be able to control the ball and shoot or pass with a single movement. The ball is kicked with the instep or the inside or outside of the foot, not with the toes.

The Instep Kick

Kicks made with the instep usually travel straight to where they are aimed. This kick is made with the laced part of the shoe with the kicker's toes pointing downward. It is made with a flexed knee as if the kicker were running at full speed.

When the ball is on the ground this kick can be kept low by placing the nonkicking foot alongside the ball. All the kicker's weight now rests on that foot while the kicking foot swings down into the ball and strikes it at its midpoint. Swinging the leg through after contact is made is important, for most of the kick's power results from this follow-up action.

To loft the ball off the ground, the kicker places the nonkicking foot behind and to one side of the ball. Contact is made with the ball's lower half, allowing the foot to pick it up and lift it into the air.

Steve David, the NASL's scoring champion in 1977, heads goalward in a game against the Cosmos. When asked about his ability to collect goals David said, "I think it's something I just inherited. I've always been the leading scorer on any team I've played for."

The Outside Kick

Made with the outside of the foot and not as powerful as an instep kick, this kick is most often used to pass the ball to a player running to the kicker's side, and is also quite effective when employed in a wall pass. A clever forward can also use the kick as a feint, faking a pass but just putting the ball off to one side, eluding an opponent and then regaining ball control.

The Inside Kick

Most passes are made with the inside of the foot, since it is the easiest and most reliable method of sending the ball to a teammate. It is accomplished with the foot turned outward so that the inside of the kicking shoe makes contact while the kicking foot clears the ground by about an inch. The other foot is placed slightly behind and to the side, allowing the kicking leg to swing by freely.

The Chipped Kick

Like a chip shot in golf, this kick is used to make the ball rise steeply into the air to clear a nearby opponent. It should rise no more than about ten feet and land without bouncing away from the teammate it is intended to reach. The kick is made with the lower part of the instep, which lifts the ball off the ground.

The Banana Kick

One of the most difficult to master, this kick is particularly effective on corner kicks because the ball's curving flight serves to confuse the goalkeeper and draw him out of position.

To swerve the ball from right to left the kicker must make contact with the right side of the ball with part of his instep and part of his toes, almost wrapping this portion of his foot around the ball. To swerve the ball from left to right, contact is made with the ball's left side.

The Scissors Kick

This is a spectacular but dangerous method for volleying the ball backward or over a kicker's head. Contact is made at waist level or a little higher, with the basic technique the same as a volley kick, the exception being that the toes are pulled back, allowing the ankle joint to become a right angle that directs the ball backwards.

To make this kick successful the kicker must fall backward in the direction he intends the ball to be kicked. A really powerful scissors kick, usually taken in a shooting situation, often involves a kick made in mid-air after the kicker has jumped. This is a dangerous maneuver, for if other players are nearby it may result in a foul.

A forward must be able to use his head as well as his feet, as Kevin Keegan, England's Player of the Year in 1976, demonstrates here.

Heading

A forward must expect to receive passes at all angles and at different heights, so one who is as adept at using his head as he is at using his feet will be at a tremendous advantage. All shots or passes made with the head require determination to beat all opponents to the ball and a well-timed run or jump that will enable a player to reach the ball first.

When a winger makes a high crossing pass into the penalty area, the ball is usually aimed for a part of the area, not for a particular player's head. It is generally the area that will cause the greatest difficulty for the goalkeeper and the defenders.

A player heading the ball, either toward the goal or toward another player, must strike the ball, not let the ball strike him. The most effective headers are made with the forehead, since this is the flattest part of a player's head and affords the greatest control over the direction the ball will take.

Throw-Ins

When one team kicks the ball out of bounds over a sideline, the other team will put it back in play with a throw-in. When made within twenty yards of the goal line a throw-in can be a potent offensive weapon, since the ball can be tossed into the penalty area where it may result in a header or shot on goal.

The player making the throw-in must have both feet on the ground and must not cross the touchline until after the ball has been released. The ball must be thrown into play with both hands, from behind and over the head. The throw-in may be made from either a standing position or following a short running start, but when a run is used the thrower must make sure both feet remain on the ground when the ball is thrown.

Dribbling

Although all players must be able to dribble, it is usually the forwards who are called upon to advance the ball this way— all the while being closely marked by a defender who is constantly trying to take the ball away. The great dribblers, like Pelé and George Best, have been able to develop this technique into a minor art form, faking and feinting around defenders as they work their way toward the goalmouth to apply tremendous pressure to that last line of defense, the goalkeeper.

THE GOALKEEPERS

No single player carries as much responsibility for a team's success or failure as its goalkeeper. Defenders, midfielders, and forwards can all make mistakes with the knowledge that for the most part their errors can be rectified as play progresses. A forward who muffs a chance to score knows there will be other chances, but a goalkeeper who misjudges a shot sees his mistake go up on the scoreboard where it cannot be erased.

This is such a key position that a poor goalkeeper can destroy the confidence of a good team, just as a good goalkeeper can make a poor team look much better than it actually is. To perform effectively a goalkeeper must possess a variety of talents and skills. For openers, he must be capable of catching the ball cleanly whenever it comes within range or, if a catch is impossible, he should have the ability to knock the ball over the crossbar or around a post where it will bounce harmlessly out of bounds. He must be able to stop shots that come from all angles, no matter how viciously they have been booted toward the net or how crazily they may bounce and swerve.

Stopping shots on goal is, however, just a small part of a goalkeeper's job. Being able to intelligently read the game so that problems may be anticipated and shots foiled before they are attempted is as important to a team's success or failure as

a spectacular save. Goalkeepers must be willing to dominate the eighteen-yard-long, forty-four-yard-wide penalty area. This is a goalie's territory, and he must stake out a symbolic "no trespassing" sign opponents will be instantly aware of once they enter this area.

Protecting this territory means the goalkeeper must be willing to contest forwards for high-crossing passes and be courageous enough to dive and snatch the ball away from an attacker's foot just before it is about to be kicked.

First Line of Attack

In addition to being the last line of defense, goalkeepers are their team's first line of attack. When they have the ball, goalies must be able to think like a playmaking midfielder, ready and prepared to exploit any opportunity by instigating counterattacks with accurate passes, either thrown or kicked, to the feet of unmarked teammates.

For those long stretches of time when play is at the opposite end of the field, a goalkeeper is more than a spectator. He is a careful observer and schemer, analyzing what is happening upfield, spotting flaws in his defense, and preparing to make the necessary changes and corrections.

While there is no special size for a goalkeeper—some of the greatest have been short, others tall—all the outstanding goalies have shared certain characteristics.

The most difficult decision a goalkeeper must make is which way to dive on a penalty kick. Pat Jennings of Tottenham Hotspur guessed correctly on this one, diving to his left to make a save against Liverpool's Tommy Smith.

Dino Zoff, who guards the nets for Juventus of Turin, dives to snatch the ball away from an attacker's feet.

Five Important Qualities

Courage: A goalkeeper should have the nerve to go into positions where there will be a possibility of hard physical contact. At these times a goalie must be prepared to absorb some hard knocks, for there will be scant opportunity for self-protection when diving toward a forward's kicking foot or leaping in the air to challenge two onrushing attackers for a header. Perhaps most importantly, he must not flinch away from kicked balls that can rip through the air toward him at speeds as high as 80 m.p.h.

Confidence: In many situations, a goalkeeper will have only a fraction of a second in which to make a decision. Should he dive to the left or right on a penalty shot? Should he move out to cut down on a forward's shooting angle? Should he leave his position in the goalmouth to challenge for a header? Questions like these will arise over and over during the course of a game and must be answered quickly and with determination. Once a goalie commits himself to a course of action, he must rely upon his own judgment. Nothing undermines the confidence of his teammates more than a goalie who is indecisive and hesitant in playing his position.

Agility: Great goalkeepers move with a catlike grace both on the ground and in the air, twisting and turning their bodies to intercept or knock away balls careening toward their net.

Strength: Often a goalkeeper has to counter physical challenges while in an exposed position. When going for a loose ball he must be prepared to move other players out of his path by the power and determination of his actions.

Anticipation: To be successful in their role as a team's last line of defense, goalies must be able to correctly predict what will happen before it actually does. Some of the best maintain detailed records of how certain opponents will react in particular situations, knowing in advance which players prefer kicking with their left foot, or which tend to fake one way before shooting in the opposite direction. Knowledge of such seemingly minor details can often mean the difference between victory and defeat.

Positional Play

All other elements being equal, goalkeepers have a tremendous advantage over attackers in that only the goalie may use his hands on the ball. In order to fully exploit this advantage goalies will roam all over their penalty area, moving up from and back to the goal line as play moves toward or away from them.

When the action is taking place at the other end of the field a goalie will usually stand on the outer edge of his penalty area, drifting back as play draws nearer. When the ball is in his half of the field the goalie can most often be found somewhere around the penalty spot, usually about twelve yards in front of his goalmouth.

It is important that he not be a stationary figure, waiting for an opponent to take a shot on goal. He must move with the flow of play, providing depth to his team's defense and attempting to snuff out attacks before a shot can even be taken. There is one important restriction on a goalie's actions. Once he leaves the penalty area, he is treated just like any other player and may not use his hands. If he does, the other team will be awarded a direct free kick from the spot where the ball was touched.

Playing the Angles

The goalmouth is twenty-four feet wide and eight feet high, quite a tempting target for an attacker who breaks away with the ball and races downfield unmarked. What a goalie must do in a situation like this is transform a seemingly easy shot into a difficult one. He does this by moving out to meet the attacker and reducing his target, forcing him to take his shot at an angle.

His actions may also force the attacker to hesitate and enter into a game of cat and mouse. The attacker feints one way and tries to go another, but the goalie now has the advantage, for by watching the attacker's feet he can tell which way the ball will go, and, using his hands, the goalie can dive toward the ball and snatch it away. Of course, the attacker can foil this move by lobbing a shot over the goalie or

passing to a teammate. Cooperation between a goalkeeper and his defensive backs is vital in these situations. Each must have an understanding of the other's actions, so that when the goalie moves out and leaves his net exposed a teammate will move quickly to provide temporary coverage.

Once the goalie has moved out to challenge an attacker, his primary responsibility is to keep the ball away from his goal. If possible he will try to pick it up or, failing that, to dive on it in an effort to prevent any possible shot. Should both those actions prove impossible, he will try to kick the ball away with a sliding tackle, or punch or slap it away with his hands.

At times like these the safest route is always the best, so if a goalie cannot gain complete control of the ball he will try to knock it out of bounds, for there are few things more dangerous to a goalie than a ball that has rebounded to bounce freely in the penalty area while he is away from his net.

Goalkeeping at its best: Iribar of Spain flies through the air and knocks a corner kick over the crossbar during a 1966 World Cup match against Argentina.

Special Situations

About half the goals in soccer arise out of dead-ball opportunities, that is, when a team has free play of the ball from a free kick, corner kick, penalty kick, or throw-in.

When a free kick is awarded within scoring range it is the goalkeeper who supervises the deployment of a defensive wall consisting of four or more teammates, none of whom may stand within ten yards of the ball. The wall will cover the corner of the net nearest to the kicker, while the goalkeeper will take up a position that affords him an unobstructed view of the ball.

In a free-kick situation the goalkeeper will try to catch any shot or, failing that, knock it back over the top of his goal cage, because if he attempts to punch it out the ball may be kicked right back by an opponent who has come into the penalty area. The main problem here is to remove the ball from near the goalmouth as quickly as possible, for anything can happen when a dozen or so players are milling about in front of the net. Remember, a goal is scored any time the ball crosses the goal line, even if it is knocked across accidentally by a teammate. Better to tip the ball over the crossbar and surrender a corner kick than to give up an easy goal.

Corner Kicks

On a corner kick the goalie will position himself near the far post of his goal, about two-thirds of the way across the goalmouth from the corner where the kick is being taken. One or more of his teammates should be at the opposite post.

The goalie must be able to judge where his opponents are while watching the ball's flight, and should not commit himself until he has some idea of where it is going. If possible he will try to catch the ball, but if this cannot be done safely he will attempt to punch it out of the danger zone, either toward a teammate or out of bounds.

Peter Bonetti, one of England's finest goalkeepers, gets ready to stop a shot being fired at him from point-blank range.

Gordon Banks, goalkeeper for England's 1966 World Cup champions, leaps high to punch the ball away from an attacker's head. In 1977, Banks joined the Ft. Lauderdale Strikers of the NASL.

Whenever a high cross is sent floating into the six-yard box in front of his net, the goalie must go right for it, for a ball bouncing freely in this area can very easily be nudged over the goal line.

Penalty Kicks

The most difficult moment for a goalkeeper comes when an opponent has been awarded a kick from the white spot twelve yards directly in front of the goalmouth. The rules state that the goalkeeper must stand with both feet stationary until the kicker has made contact with the ball.

Some will try to deceive the kicker by leaning one way and then diving the other once the ball is booted. Sometimes scouting reports will reveal that a kicker tends to favor one side of the goalmouth in these situations, but for the most part whatever the goalkeeper does on a penalty shot is a gamble, for it is the kicker's option to boot the ball left, right, or straight ahead.

Goalkeeping Techniques

Above all else the goalkeeper must be able to stop the ball safely and surely. In order to do this he should place as much of his body as possible behind the ball. This rule applies whether he is standing, jumping, diving, or falling, for while the ball may slip through his hands or between his feet it cannot roll through his chest.

When stopping the ball with his chest the goalie will draw it back from the ball, giving with the force of the shot so that the ball does not bounce out of control. Experienced goalkeepers never reach for the ball by bending sideways or diving if they can move their feet and place their whole body in front of it. The better the goalie, the easier he will make his job look by avoiding unnecessary risks with speedy footwork.

In all instances it is better to catch the ball than punch it. Punching or slapping the ball may be necessary in desperate situations, but given a choice it is always preferable to gain complete control of the ball.

Launching the Attack

The goalkeeper is responsible for setting up attacking movements as soon as he has possession of the ball. The rules permit him to take *four steps* while holding the ball, bouncing it, or tossing it in the air. If more are taken, the opposition will be awarded an indirect free kick.

The goalie has a choice. He may use the ball quickly, within four steps of the spot where he gained control, or he may alternate his steps by dribbling or rolling the ball, or he may momentarily release the ball to a teammate and then pick it up again for another four steps. Whichever option he selects, the goalie may be challenged by an opponent.

Once he has decided to get rid of the ball, he can send it toward the other end of the field with a long kick, or he can throw or kick the ball to a nearby teammate who will begin the drive upfield toward the opponent's goal. In both cases, the choice is usually dictated by tactical considerations and by the placement of the opposition. If they are drawn up close to the penalty area, he will try to send the ball booming downfield behind them. If they are spread out, he will drop the ball off to a teammate to avoid any possibility of an interception.

When a goalkeeper makes a mistake everyone knows about it. Here Dundee's Ally Donaldson slams the turf in frustration after muffing a shot during a Scottish League game against Glasgow Celtic.

REFEREES & LINESMEN

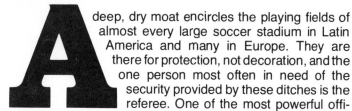

A deep, dry moat encircles the playing fields of almost every large soccer stadium in Latin America and many in Europe. They are there for protection, not decoration, and the one person most often in need of the security provided by these ditches is the referee. One of the most powerful officials in all of sports, the soccer referee has complete control of a match from start to finish and is the final arbiter of all decisions made during the course of a game.

The referee is assisted by two linesmen, one on each sideline, who move up and downfield, following the flow of play. One is designated the senior linesman and carries a red flag, while the other carries a yellow flag. These are used to signal corner kicks, goal kicks, throw-ins, and offside violations. In all instances a referee can overrule a linesman's decision.

The referee keeps the official time and only he can start and stop play. He can also add time to the regulation forty-five-minute halves to make up for halts due to injuries or if he decides one team is stalling to run out the clock.

Calling Fouls

The referee decides what is and what is not a foul. For every foul committed, a free kick is awarded. A direct free kick, one on which a goal can be scored directly by the kicker, will be given if one of the following nine fouls is committed:

1. Kicking or attempting to kick an opponent. (The key word here is "attempting," for even if one player tries to kick another and misses, the referee will award a direct free kick.)
2. Tripping an opponent.
3. Jumping at an opposing player.
4. Charging at an opponent in a violent or dangerous manner.
5. Charging an opponent from behind if he is not obstructing one's path.

"He did it," says one player. "No, you did it," insists the referee, who always wins arguments like this one.

6. Striking or attempting to strike an opponent.

7. Holding an opponent with any part of one's arm or hand.

8. Pushing an opponent with any part of one's arm or hand.

9. Using one's arm or hand to touch the ball, advance it, slow it down, or propel it in any direction (this does not, of course, include a goalie inside of his penalty area or a player awarded a throw-in).

When any of these fouls are committed by a team inside its own penalty area, the attacking team is awarded a penalty kick.

Other Infractions

Five fouls or violations will result in the award of an indirect free kick, one on which a player other than the kicker must touch the ball before a goal can be scored. These are a bit more complicated than fouls that result in a direct free kick and are often judgment calls on the part of referees and linesmen. Briefly, they are:

Yugoslavia's Enver Hadziabdic voices an emotional protest to the referee during a 1974 World Cup match against Scotland.

Life can sometimes be dangerous for a referee. Such was the case after England defeated Argentina in a 1966 World Cup quarterfinal match and police had to rescue the ref from an angry mob of Argentinians.

England's Jack Taylor, who was the referee for the 1974 World Cup championship game, flashes the yellow caution card to warn a player.

1. Playing in a manner considered dangerous by the referee. For example, an attempt by an attacker to kick the ball out of a goalkeeper's hands.

2. Charging into an opponent with a shoulder when the ball is not within playing distance.

3. Intentionally obstructing an opponent when not playing the ball.

4. Charging into the goalkeeper when he is holding the ball.

5. If a goalkeeper takes more than four steps while holding or bouncing the ball.

Booking a Player

Referees carry a small notebook and two cards, one yellow, the other red. If a referee decides a player is flagrantly violating the rules, he will caution him with the yellow card or order him off the field with the red card. A player ejected in this manner may not be replaced, and his team must continue the game without a player in what could be a crucial position.

All serious infractions are recorded in the referee's notebook and included in his game report to the league or governing association. Information contained in these reports can result in a player being fined or suspended for one or more games.

Other Powers

The referee will check to make sure a field is properly marked and that the goal nets are secure before a game begins. If he discovers any irregularities he will order them corrected. The referee is the only official who can permit a substitute to enter a match. He can allow an injured player to leave the field and later return if that player is fit to continue. While the injured player is being treated he may not be substituted for if it is expected that he will return.

The referee can order a game canceled if he feels that

Referee Norman Burtenshan is on a peacemaking mission as he moves to break up potential trouble between an angry Dave McKay of Tottenham Hotspur and a somewhat nonplussed Billy Bremner of Leeds United.

weather conditions will make it too dangerous to play, and he can call the game if he is attacked by fans—which has happened several times in Latin American and European contests.

Unusual Situations

If a player goes down with an injury it is up to the referee to decide if play will stop or continue. For minor injuries he may wait until the ball goes out of play before calling a halt.

If a team wishes to have its goalkeeper switch places with another player, the referee will allow the change provided that he is informed before it happens. In such cases, the two players involved will exchange jerseys.

If the ball strikes the referee within the field of play, he will allow the game to continue uninterrupted.

If a goalkeeper is detected moving his feet while awaiting a penalty shot, the referee will wait until the kick is taken and then, if no goal is scored, will allow the kick to be retaken.

Restarting Play

If play is halted because of an injured player or abnormal playing conditions—such as fans on the field—the referee will restart the game with a drop ball. This is similar to a jump ball in basketball or a face-off in hockey. The referee will drop the ball between two players from each team. As soon as the ball hits the ground, play has begun.

The Advantage Rule

The referee will not halt play when a foul is committed if the team fouled has possession of the ball and is able to continue play despite the foul. Play will be stopped only after the team has lost possession of the ball. At this point, play will stop and the team that was fouled will receive a free kick.

Guess who is going to win this argument between Johnny Giles and referee T.E. Dawes?

SOCCER SYSTEMS

T o England's public school elite who inadvertently popularized soccer midway through the nineteenth century, sophisticated defensive alignments with such foreign-sounding titles as *catenaccio* and *verrou* were as far from the realm of imagination as intricate attacks developing from formations referred to numerically as 4-2-4 or 4-3-3.* These and all the other strategic paraphernalia of modern soccer would have been viewed with alarm by young gentlemen who thought tactics and strategy were best left to war and politics. Sport was a straightforward and open affair. To perform in a manner that bespoke of deviousness or cunning would not only be unsportsmanlike, it would be, worst sin of all, unmanly.

Because of this attitude soccer was not only rugged, it was essentially a selfish game. Concepts such as teamwork were given the barest of lip service, and the elementary tactic of passing had yet to be invented. Teams played with seven or eight forwards and only two or three backs, who remained behind keeping the goalkeeper company while everyone else was upfield with the ball. This was the so-called "dribbling game" of the 1860's and 1870's—an era when players controlled the ball for as long as possible, never dreaming of kicking it to a teammate when they got in trouble. Forwards would simply dribble the ball around opponents until they either lost it or scored, and that was that.

Backing Up

The closest thing to tactical thought was the idea of backing up a teammate who had the ball. C.W. Alcock, secretary of England's Football Association in the 1870's, expounded on this theory when he wrote about: "The grand and essential principle of backing up. By 'backing up' of course I shall be understood to mean the following closely on a fellow-player to assist him, if required, or to take on the ball in case of his being

attacked, or otherwise prevented from continuing his onward course."

So much for teamwork. No one had yet thought of passing off to a player "backing up." Of course, this style of play did develop some athletes who were spectacularly adept dribblers. R.W.S. Vidal was such a player. In one match he scored three successive goals right from the kickoff, wending a tortuous path through the opposition without having a single defender so much as touch the ball and earning for himself the sobriquet "Prince of Dribblers."

It fell to someone as talented at dribbling as Vidal to complete the first recorded pass in English football. The historic event occurred during the 1872 F.A. Cup final between Vidal's team, the Wanderers, and the Royal Engineers. The match was drawing to a close with neither team having scored when Vidal broke with tradition and actually kicked the ball to a teammate, one A.H. Chequer,* who took advantage of everyone's momentary shock and scored.

The Scottish Game

While Vidal's pass may have been an isolated incident within English football, there was, to the north, a revolution of sorts taking place. Dubbed, to honor its inventors, "the Scottish game," it was based upon short passes made along the ground. This method of play proved so successful for Scotland in an international match against England that soccer was never the same again. The dribbling game was gone, teamwork had been discovered.

With teamwork came tactics and with tactics strategy, designed both to exploit and defend against this new style of play. It was not long before the first sophisticated system was developed. The 2-3-5 (see Figure 1), or pyramid formation, was a radical departure from past alignments in that only half the outfielders were assigned attacking positions. The remaining five were employed as defenders.

---

*Defenders are always listed first in these formulations, goalkeepers are excluded.

*Actually a nom de guerre for one M.P. Betts. The initials stood for "A Harrow Chequer," that is one who had played for the Harrow old boys' club. Don't ask why the charade, just accept the fact the English are like that.

There was another major evolution that occurred in the nineteenth century and that was the development of the long-passing game to complement the short-passing game. Once again it was northerners, this time from the north of England, who led the revolution. In the 1883 F.A. Cup final, Blackburn Olympic dazzled the Old Etonians with long, floating wing-to-wing passes. With the high pass came new skills, and heading and trapping soon became as important as kicking. It was, indeed, the end of an era in more ways than one. The Old Etonians, who had reached the cup final six times in ten years, lost the game 2–1 and never reached such heights again.

The pyramid formation was to survive for another fifty years, and although seldom used, still forms the basic pattern from which other, newer systems have evolved. The English finally abandoned it not because of any improvement in strategy or tactics, but because of a change in the rules.

The Offside Trap

Until 1925 an attacker had to have at least three defenders (one of whom was the goalkeeper) in front of him whenever the ball was played to him in his opponent's half of the field. If there were less than three, he was whistled offside.

It was complicated but did not unnecessarily hinder play until the early 1920's when a pair of enterprising fullbacks playing for New Castle United invented the offside trap. Waiting for the precise moment a pass was about to be made, one of them would sneak upfield behind the unsuspecting attackers, who only realized they had been trapped when the whistle blew. If something went wrong with the plan, there was still one fullback left behind to assist his goalie.

The tactic, which proved remarkably effective, spread quickly and was soon honed to such a fine edge that some games were being played almost entirely in the midfield area.

Something had to be done and soccer's ruling powers decided it should be the reduction by one of the number of defenders that had to be in front of an attacker receiving a pass. The offside trap was still possible, but now it became a very risky maneuver, for if it failed no one stood between the attacker and the goalkeeper.

The rule change had an immediate effect as the number of goals scored in the English First Division increased from 1,192 in 1925 to 1,703 in 1926. In both years, the same number of teams played the same number of games.

THE 2-3-5 OR PYRAMID FORMATION

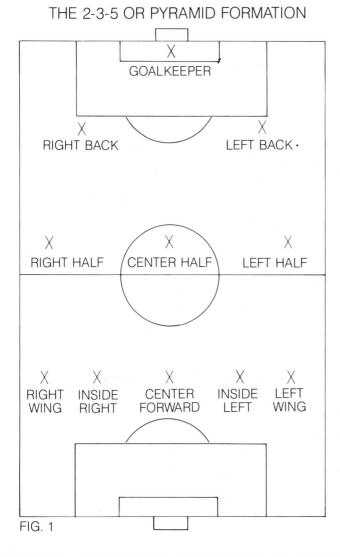

FIG. 1

THE M-W FORMATION

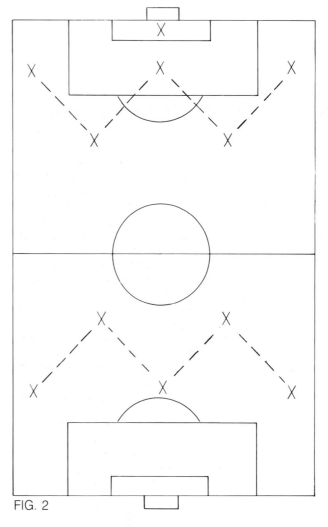

FIG. 2

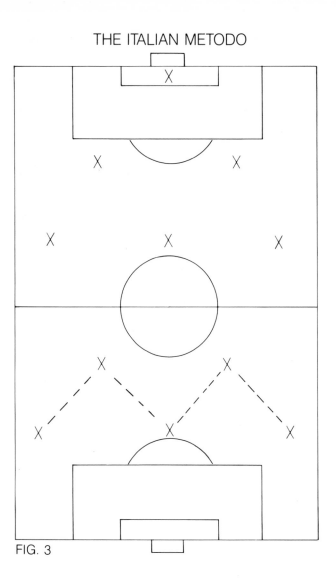

THE ITALIAN METODO

FIG. 3

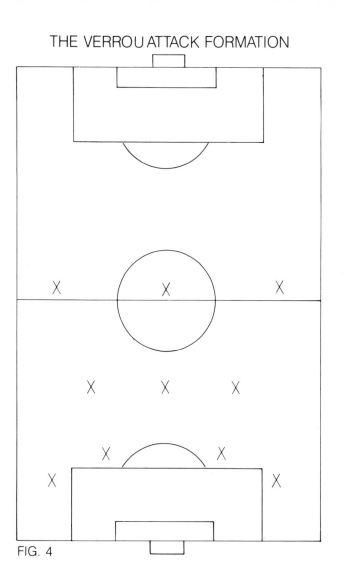

THE VERROU ATTACK FORMATION

FIG. 4

The M and W Formations

In soccer as in physics, for every action there is a reaction, and the reaction to the rule change was the creation of the M and W formations (Figure 2). Developed by Herbert Chapman, manager of the London club Arsenal, and his team captain Charlie Buchan, this new formation employed three fullbacks fronted by two halfbacks. If they remained stationary, which under actual game conditions they never did, they would, if connected by straight lines, form the letter "W" facing away from their goal. On the opposite end of the field the attacking half of their team consisted of three forwards supported by two halfbacks. Joined together they would form an "M" facing their opponent's goal.

In the old pyramid formation the key player had been the center halfback, who had organized and guided his team's attack. In this new formation, the center halfback was pulled back to become a center fullback, transferred from a positive or offensive role to a negative or defensive role. He now became his team's stopper, charged with patrolling the area in front of his team's goal and marking the opponent's center forward.

In many respects these new alignments represented a new era of negative thought in soccer, a view of the game which placed not losing on equal footing with actually winning. In fact it was the system's co-inventor, Herbert Chapman, who would tell his teams that they went out on the field with one point,* and if they did not give up a goal they would return with at least one point. It must be said that this philosophy worked well for Arsenal, which was the dominant team in English football during the 1930's, winning the First Division championship five times during that decade.

On offense the two outside prongs of the M, the wing forwards, would attempt to race downfield along the sidelines and then cut in toward the middle for a shot on goal. The center forward was usually a tall and burly fellow who would try to kick or head the ball to one of the wing forwards cutting toward the middle.

Of course with five men back clogging the area around their goal it was often difficult to get the ball either to or from the center forward, and soccer in England tended to be a much lower scoring affair than the game being played elsewhere in the world.

The Italian Variation

Italy, which won the World Cup in 1934 and 1938, used a variation of the M-W formation called the *metodo* (Figure 3). Devised by their national coach Vittorio Pozzo, this system used the 2–3 of the pyramid formation, complete with the attacking center halfback, plus the two halfback, three forward alignment of the M formation. Elsewhere around the

*In English league play a team is awarded one point for a tie and two for a victory.

globe, in Europe and South America, the old pyramid remained the most popular of soccer systems prior to World War II.

All these systems tended to limit players to specific functions in contrast to today's style of total football in which players are expected to operate on both offense and defense. Rarely, if ever, would a fullback venture upfield and, conversely, forwards would seldom drop back to their team's half of the field to retrieve the ball or tackle an attacking opponent.

The Verrou or Swiss Bolt

There was one formation developed in the 1930's that indicated the present trend in soccer, but because it was perfected in Switzerland, hardly a dominant power in international competition, it received, at the time, little attention.

It was originated by Karl Rappan, an Austrian who coached in Switzerland. His aim in creating this system was to devise a method by which his team would outnumber the opposition both on offense and defense. He therefore created a system with two permutations, one for attack, the other for defense. To make both work players could not be specialists, but instead had to be capable of quickly switching from offensive roles to defensive assignments and vice versa.

When attacking, this formation would take on a 3–3–4 alignment (Figure 4) that included an attacking center half and three fullbacks who would move upfield in close support of the attackers. If the other team gained ball possession everyone would retreat, with the four forwards acting to harass and slow the attack while the halfbacks and fullbacks raced toward their own goal to take up defensive positions.

The center halfback now became the center fullback, while the former center fullback moved to a deep position behind his teammates. From here he could move laterally across the field covering the three fullbacks and becoming the "bolt" in the Swiss Bolt (Figure 5).

The Swiss Bolt required physically fit players capable of running throughout a game and able to function both as defenders and attackers. It never caught on in the 1930's, but many of the ideas that were originated with this formation are employed by teams throughout the world today.

The Attacking W

During the early 1950's, Hungary fielded a team that was one of the greatest of all time. In addition to many talented athletes, the Hungarians also developed a new system that often confused and befuddled opponents coming up against it for the first time. The idea behind it was a simple one—reverse the attacking M and transform it into an attacking W (Figure 6).

In this system the center forward was withdrawn to operate as a deep center forward while the two deep men in the M were pulled toward the penalty area to act as twin center forwards. The two wingers now operated in positions between the one deep and two up forwards.

The new formation had many advantages. Teams using it were better able to control the vital midfield area since there

THE SWISS BOLT

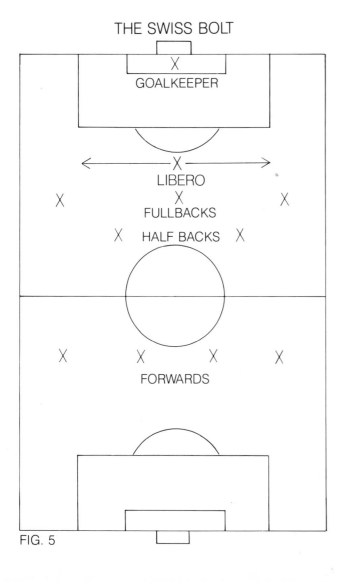

FIG. 5

THE ATTACKING W FORMATION

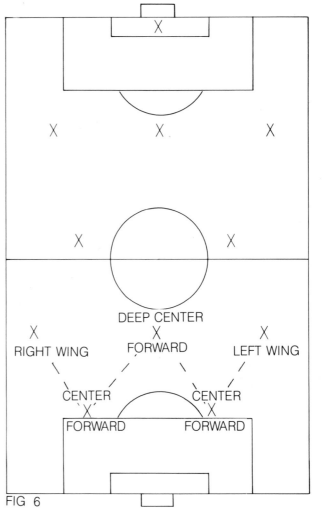

FIG 6

were three forwards in a position where they could swiftly drop back and provide assistance to the midfielders, who in turn could fall back and aid the defense.

One of the drawbacks in this formation was that it required outstanding center forwards, especially the two nearest the penalty area, in order to be really effective. With only two attackers near the opponent's goal, the three other forwards had to be accurate passers or else the ball would be easily picked off by a defender. For Hungary, with such outstanding center forwards as Ferenc Puskas and Sandor Kocsis, the system worked to perfection. For other teams, with less talented attackers, it often did not.

The 4–2–4

In 1958, Brazil came up with a quartet of brilliant forwards: Garrincha, Vava, Zagalo, and Pelé. To exploit their varied talents, the Brazilians developed a system that would allow all four to function as attackers, with Garrincha and Zagalo on the wings, while Pelé and Vava operated in the center. In support were two midfielders and four fullbacks (Figure 7).

This is one of the most offensive-minded systems ever developed, the thinking behind it being that the forwards would always score more than enough goals to make up for whatever the defenders surrendered. Because it detailed so many players to the attack this system was very vulnerable to counterattack, and because of this weakness the Brazilians converted to a 4–3–3 in the 1962 World Cup, pulling Zagalo back to a midfield position while Garrincha functioned as the team's only winger (Figure 8).

The Catenaccio

While the Brazilians were developing their exciting wide-open offensive systems, the Italians were perfecting one of the most negative defensive formulations ever seen in soccer. It took all the negative aspects of the Swiss Bolt and none of the positive. The prevention, not the scoring, of goals was the main objective of the *catenaccio* ("great chain"). Developed by the weaker teams in the Italian league, it was soon adopted by the more powerful clubs and used to the greatest effectiveness by Inter-Milan, which under the guidance of Helenio Herrera won the European Cup in 1964 and 1965.

The key to the *catenaccio* (Figure 9), was the *libero,* or sweeper, who played behind a wall of three and sometimes four fullbacks, plugging any holes that might be opened by the attacking team. It was almost impossible to score against this defense, but conversely it was almost as difficult for the team employing the *catenaccio*, which at times used only two forwards, to get any goals. The defending team often just waited for their opponents to make a mistake, hoping to capitalize on the error by quickly breaking downfield to score.

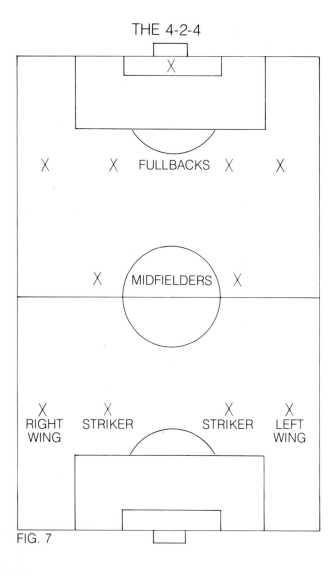

FIG. 7

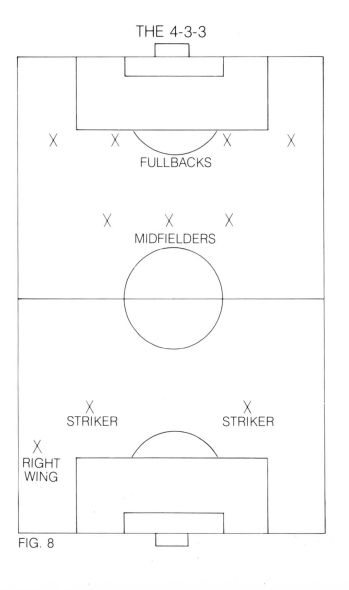

FIG. 8

While some teams had great success using the *catenaccio* it at times has been disastrous for the Italian national team.

Modern Systems

Because of the manner in which soccer has evolved over recent years, numerical systems that can be diagramed seldom bear any relevance to what is happening on the field.

The concept of "total football" expounded so brilliantly by West Germany and the Netherlands during the 1974 World Cup requires that players function effectively both on offense and defense. Gone are the forwards who would never attempt a tackle and the fullbacks whose job came to an end once they had cleared the ball upfield.

Today coaches will often fit a system to their players, rather than their players to a system. Defensive combinations often consist of three or four fullbacks and a sweeper, who can be stationed either behind the fullbacks or in front as a defensive screen.

Midfielders will fall back on defense and move up on offense while the number of players operating as forwards can change from moment to moment, depending on the score, what the opposition is doing, and where the ball is.

In the final analysis it is not systems that win soccer games, it is players, and in the long run the team with the better athletes will finish on top no matter what the system used.

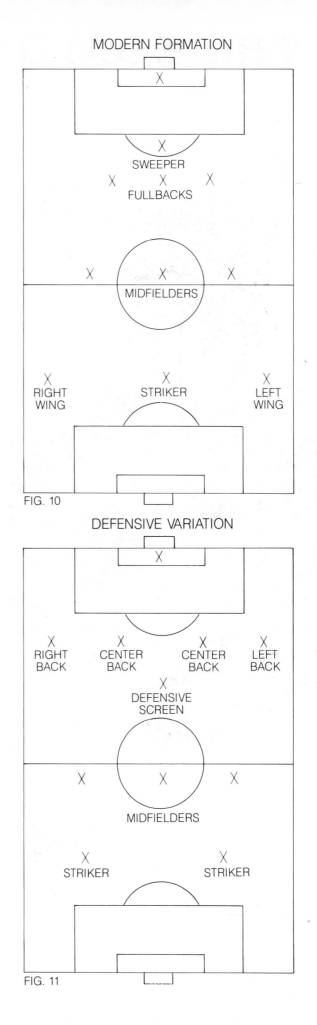

MODERN FORMATION

FIG. 10

DEFENSIVE VARIATION

FIG. 11

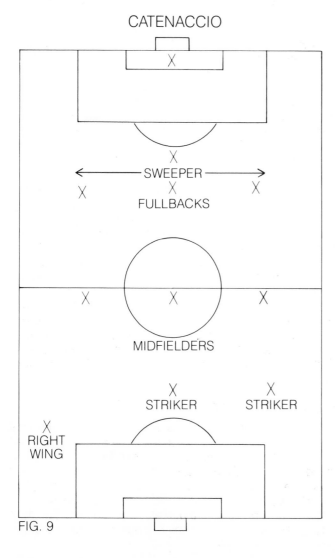

CATENACCIO

FIG. 9

3. THE WORLD CUP

West German goalkeeper Sepp Maier tries the new World Cup trophy on for size after his team became the first to win it by defeating the Netherlands 2–1 in the 1974 championship games.

There is no regular championship event in all of sports that attracts more global attention or interest than the World Cup. Baseball's World Series and football's Super Bowl are dwarfed in comparison to it. Even the Olympic Games must take second place to the intensity of public interest and nationalistic fervor generated by the World Cup. It is a competition between nations that has been compared to war and indeed, as recently as 1969, two small Central American nations, El Salvador and Honduras did resort to armed conflict to settle a dispute that had begun at one of the tournament's elimination matches.

Nations have severed soccer relations with one another because of the competition, countries have gone into states of national mourning over defeats, and dictators have pointed to victories as proof of the superiority of their totalitarian systems. It is, any way you look at it, more than just a game.

Quadrennial Competition

Staged once every four years the tournament pits nation against nation, the best soccer players of one country against the best of another until only one team, the champion, remains.

Beyond national pride there are large financial rewards for players on winning teams. Reaching the championship game in 1974 was worth at least $37,000 to each member of the squads representing West Germany and the Netherlands, and that does not include subsequent rewards harvested from product endorsements and more lucrative contracts.

The Swiss-based Fédération Internationale de Football Association (FIFA), which sponsors the cup, has devised a qualification system to select the finalists that is heavily weighted in favor of those two continental centers of soccer power, Europe and South America.

The thirty-four-member European Confederation had nine representatives among the final sixteen competing for the cup in 1978. This number included defending champion West Germany, which received an automatic invitation, Austria, France, Hungary, Italy, the Netherlands, Poland, Scotland, and Spain. Carrying the banner for the ten-nation South American Confederation were host nation Argentina, Brazil, and Peru.

The North and Central American Confederation (which includes the Caribbean) had one representative, Mexico, while Tunisia was the entrant from the thirty-four-member African Confederation. Asia, with thirty-four members, and Oceania*, with only four members, were combined and sent one team—Iran.

England Eliminated

Surviving these elimination rounds and reaching the final sixteen is no mean task. For example, Europe was divided into nine groups. One of them, Group Two, consisted of England, Finland, Italy, and Luxemburg, each of which played a two-game home and away series with the other three members of the group. For each victory a nation received two points, for a tie, one, and for a defeat, none. England and Italy dominated this group, each winning at home against the other

*Oceania consists of Australia, Fiji, New Zealand, and Papua-New Guinea.

by identical scores of 2–0, and each winning all their games against Luxemburg and Finland. But although both had amassed ten points, Italy advanced to the finals because the Italians scored more goals than the Englishmen when the former defeated Finland and Luxemburg. That made it the second time in a row that England failed to reach the final sixteen, a devastating blow for the nation that claims to have invented the game of soccer.

Great Britain, which enters four national teams, one each from England, Northern Ireland, Scotland, and Wales, was not completely shut out because Scotland, one of the surprise teams in the 1974 tournament, qualified from Europe's Group Seven over Czechoslovakia and Wales.

Solved Problem

At first the Olympic Games provided a world championship for soccer, but as more and more of the sport's best players became professionals in the early 1900's it became obvious that a different arrangement was needed, Olympic competition being open only to amateur athletes.

After decades of discussion, and an unwelcome interruption for World War I, FIFA finally agreed to stage the first World Cup in 1930. Sculptor Abel Lafluer was commissioned to create a suitable award for the winner, and the golden statuette he designed was named the Jules Rimet Trophy, in honor of FIFA's French president. It was stipulated that any nation winning the tournament three times would gain permanent possession of this art nouveau creation of winged victory bearing aloft a small cup.

Since 1950, the first post-World War II cup year, two nations, Brazil and West Germany, have dominated the competition, with one or the other appearing in every championship game prior to 1978.

Brazil reached the final game in 1950, but lost to Uruguay. Then the Brazilians came back to win in 1958, 1962, and 1970 to gain permanent possession of the Rimet Trophy, which has since been replaced by a fourteen-inch golden statuette topped by a globe. West Germany won the World Cup in 1954 and 1974 and reached the final game in 1966, when it lost, in overtime, to England, the host nation.

Five nations bid to host the first World Cup, but in the end it was decided to stage the competition in Uruguay, winner of the two previous Olympic tournaments. No teams from Great Britain competed for the first cup, because the British football associations had withdrawn from FIFA following a dispute concerning the practice of paying "amateur athletes" for time away from their regular jobs so that they could compete in the Olympics. Not until 1950 would a team from Great Britain compete for the World Cup.

The First Tournament

The first tournament was plagued with problems, not the least of which was the geographic location of Uruguay. Air travel was still in its infancy, and the host nation was a three-week steamship trip from Europe. Many of the European nations, not wanting to interrupt their regular league play for two months, withdrew, and only Belgium, France, Romania, and Yugoslavia made the long transatlantic journey to Montevideo. Joining them there were teams from Argentina, Brazil, Bolivia, Chile, Mexico, Peru, the United States, Paraguay, and, of course, Uruguay. Upon arrival they discovered they had come to quite a party.

The Jules Rimet Trophy, held aloft by Brazilian captain Carlos Alberto, became the South American team's permanent property after they won it for the third time in 1970 by defeating Italy 4–1. Brazil's previous titles had been won in 1958 and 1962.

1930 WORLD CUP: URUGUAY

Pool One
France 4, Mexico 1
Argentina 1, France 0
Chile 1, France 0
Chile 3, Mexico 0
Argentina 3, Chile 1
Argentina 6, Mexico 3

Pool Two
Yugoslavia 2, Brazil 1
Yugoslavia 4, Bolivia 0
Brazil 4, Bolivia 0

Pool Three
Romania 3, Peru 1
Uruguay 1, Peru 0
Uruguay 4, Romania 0

Pool Four
United States 3, Belgium 0
United States 3, Paraguay 0
Paraguay 1, Belgium 0

Semifinals
Argentina 6, United States 1
Uruguay 6, Yugoslavia 1

Championship
Uruguay 4, Argentina 2

Uruguay was celebrating its 100th anniversary as a republic and in only eight months' time constructed Montevideo's 100,000-seat Centenary Stadium to provide a suitable venue for World Cup competition. Europe's four representative teams made the transatlantic voyage together and upon arrival were greeted with a wild and warm reception that combined national pride with Latin gaiety.

But behind this boisterous welcome was a grim Uruguayan determination to win. For two celibate months Uruguay's team had been confined, under tight security, to its training camp in the Prado, Montevideo's major park. A strict curfew was imposed and when Mazzili, Uruguay's star goalie in the 1928 Olympics, was caught, shoes in hand, tiptoeing back into his quarters after hours, he was tossed off the squad.

The thirteen competing teams were divided into four pools, or miniature leagues, where they would play a round-robin elimination schedule, with each pool's winner advancing to the semifinals.

France and Mexico opened the proceedings on July 13th, and before their game was ten minutes old the French goalie was kicked in the jaw and knocked unconscious. Since no substitutions were permitted—a rule that would not change until after World War II—a defensive back had to replace him in the goal. France, despite being forced to play one man short, won easily, 4–1.

When Romania and Peru met one day later they spent almost as much time brawling and arguing as they did playing. Timid officiating by the referee, a Chilean, allowed matters to get out of hand, and both teams were forced to play short-handed after one Romanian player was carried from the field with a broken leg and the Peruvian captain tested the referee's patience one time too many and was thrown out of the game. When play finally ended, Romania was ahead 3–1 and both teams had established a pattern of violent play and poor sportsmanship that would be repeated again and again in World Cup competition.

Argentina faced France in a game that went from high drama to low comedy. The two teams were enmeshed in a scoreless game when, with only nine minutes left, Argentina was awarded a free kick. It had been agreed beforehand that referees would signal such kicks by raising an arm instead of blowing a whistle. For some reason the French forgot all about this and, while waiting for a whistle to blow, watched the ball booted into their net.

Minutes later, France's Marcel Langiller penetrated Argentina's defense and raced downfield with only the goalie standing between him and a tied ballgame. He was about to take his shot when, suddenly, the referee blew his whistle. The game, he said, was over. Weeping tears of joy the Argentines danced off the field, surrounded by hundreds of their fans. The French, meanwhile, chased the referee, screaming that there were still six minutes left in the game. Trapped, he looked at his watch and, his face crimson with embarrassment, cried, "I erred in good faith."

Play resumed, but France had lost its momentum and the score remained unchanged. When the game ended, this time officially, a group of Uruguayans, feeling sorry for the losers, carried several French players off the field on their shoulders. Argentina interpreted this act of affection as an insult and threatened to pull out of the World Cup altogether, claiming it

Argentina's Guillermo Stabile (arm upraised) scores to tie game at one all in the 1930 championship match against Uruguay.

was a disgrace to see South Americans encouraging Europeans at the expense of their neighbors.

Of course, the Argentines forgot about all thoughts of Latin American brotherhood in a game against Chile that saw both teams kick each other almost as often as they kicked the ball. Argentina won, but only after police were called in to break up a small riot involving both teams and their supporters.

Uruguay, cheered on by the hometown fans, shut out both Peru and Romania to advance, while Yugoslavia scored surprising victories over Brazil and Bolivia to qualify for a semifinal match against the Uruguayans.

The United States sent a team of sixteen players, eleven of whom were native-born and five of whom were former Scottish and English professionals, refugees from low-paying jobs in their native leagues. Surprising their opponents with a combination of speed and stamina, the Americans scored back-to-back victories over Belgium and Paraguay by identical scores of 3–0. Bert Patenaude scored all three goals against Paraguay, the World Cup's first "hat trick."

Visions of a United States championship were quickly shattered in the semifinal match with Argentina. Also destroyed were any illusions the U.S. team had concerning sportsmanship. Barely ten minutes had elapsed before Ralph Tracy, a centerhalf from St. Louis, was carried off with a broken leg, leaving the Americans short-handed for the remaining eighty minutes of play. Then an Argentine kicked U.S. forward Andy Auld in the face, forcing him to play the rest of the game with a cloth stuffed in his mouth to staunch the bleeding. Minutes later the referee stood silently by when U.S. goalie Jimmy Douglas was racked up during a corner-kick collision. Although the score was only 1–0 in Argentina's favor at halftime, the South Americans scored five times in the second half. Patenaude got the U.S.A.'s only goal in the game's waning moments.

There is a story about this game, perhaps apocryphal, that is worth retelling. It seems the American trainer had grown frazzled treating his team's walking wounded throughout the game. Finally, when the referee who had ignored all sorts of Argentine atrocities called a foul of dubious validity against

Jules Rimet (left) presents the trophy that bears his name to Dr. Paul Jude, Uruguayan Football Association president.

the U.S., the trainer raced onto the field to voice a protest. He carried his medicine case with him and, to emphasize a point, slammed it to the ground. Out popped a broken bottle of chloroform. As its fumes drifted upward his shouts were reduced to yawns until, like a somnambulist, he was slowly led off the field.

All things considered, the Americans had done fairly well. After Uruguay defeated Yugoslavia 6–1 in the other semifinal, the U.S. was awarded third place, because in three games it had scored seven goals while surrendering only six, one fewer than the Yugoslavs, who had also scored seven.

Now the stage was set for the first World Cup championship game; it would be between Uruguay and Argentina, two old and bitter rivals.

1930 Championship Game

Boats filled with thousands of people chanting "Argentina sí, Uruguay no!" formed a nautical conga line across the Rio de la Plata as they sailed into Montevideo hours before game time. A brigade of soldiers, standing with fixed bayonets, surrounded Centenary Stadium. For security reasons, only 90,000 spectators, well below capacity, were admitted.

Controversy raged before the kickoff as each side insisted on using soccer balls of native origin. Referee John Langenus, a Belgian, settled the issue by tossing a coin. An Argentine ball would be used in the first half, one of Uruguayan make in the second. That matter taken care of, play began. Uruguay scored first, but Argentina followed with a pair of goals and led by one at halftime.

Ten minutes into the second half Uruguay scored, then, ten minutes later, scored again. A player named Castro, called "the One-Armed" because he had indeed lost part of an arm, sealed the victory with a goal in the game's waning moments, and as the crowd sang Uruguay's national anthem the golden Jules Rimet Trophy was presented by Monsieur Rimet himself to the winner.

There was dancing in the streets of Montevideo the next day, which had been declared a national holiday. Meanwhile, in Buenos Aires, a mob stoned the Uruguayan consulate and police, trying to restore order, fired upon the crowd. Argentina's Football Federation, charging "brutality," broke off relations with its Uruguayan counterpart, and all thoughts of sports fostering international goodwill were once again relegated to the realm of mythology.

An Argentine defender (foreground) fails in his attempt to kick the ball off the goal line as Uruguay gets its final goal and a 4–2 victory in the 1930 championship.

1934 WORLD CUP: ITALY

First Round
Italy 7, United States 1
Czechoslovakia 2, Romania 1
Germany 5, Belgium 2
Austria 3, France 2*
Spain 3, Brazil 1
Switzerland 3, Holland 2
Sweden 3, Argentina 2
Hungary 4, Egypt 2

Second Round
Germany 2, Sweden 1
Austria 2, Hungary 1
Czechoslovakia 3, Switzerland 2
Italy 1, Spain 1*
Italy 1, Spain 0**

Semifinals
Czechoslovakia 3, Germany 1
Italy 1, Austria 0

Third Place
Germany 3, Austria 2

Championship
Italy 2, Czechoslovakia 1*

*Overtime
**Rematch

Although there were many outstanding athletes taking part, no player dominated the second World Cup. That role was reserved for Benito Mussolini, who left his stamp on every aspect of the competition and whose stern visage seemed to glare down from every available wall and lamppost. "The ultimate purpose of the tournament," said an Italian press release, "was to show that Fascist sport partakes of great quality, all stemming from one unique inspiration, the Duce."

Eight meetings of the organizing committee were required before it was decided to award Italy the right to stage the 1934 World Cup. The decision was made only after the Italians promised to construct several suitable stadiums throughout the country, the tournament having become too large to be held in a single city. Thirty-two nations, as compared to thirteen in 1930, were represented, requiring a series of elimination matches to narrow the field down to a manageable group of sixteen. Uruguay, still angry about the failure of so many European teams to participate in the 1930 tournament, decided to boycott the affair. Argentina, the other finalist in 1930, was furious because four of its finest players, who were of Italian ancestry, had joined Italy's national team.

Members of the Italian national team raise their right arms in the Fascist salute prior to the 1934 championship match against Czechoslovakia.

To demonstrate their displeasure the Argentines sent a squad composed almost entirely of reserves. Italy's excuse for poaching the four was that under Fascist law anyone, anywhere, born of Italian parents was an Italian.

Following the example set by Uruguay four years earlier, Italy's team was quartered under militarylike conditions near Lake Maggiore where, said coach Vittorio Pozzo, "they lived only for the events awaiting them, eager to win." One of his better players, Antonio Ghirelli, had a less complimentary view of the situation, calling the setup "a state of pure infantilism."

Instead of having the teams divided into pools, the tournament was played on an elimination basis—one loss and a team was out. The United States, with much the same squad that had played in Uruguay, had the misfortune of drawing Italy for its first-round foe in Rome. "The Duce," according to an Italian history of the proceedings, "conceded to every one of the matches played in Rome the privilege of his presence which, more than any other factor, galvanized the two teams on the field."

If anyone was in fact galvanized that afternoon it was the Italians, who coasted to an easy 7–1 victory. Their strongest opponent for the title was expected to be Austria, a squad

With the score tied 1–1 at the end of regulation time, Italian team manager Vittorio Pozzo and some of his players wait tensely for the thirty-minute overtime period to begin in the championship game with Czechoslovakia.

coached by one of soccer's great strategists, Hugo Meisl, and dubbed the *Wunderteam* after going unbeaten in eighteen international matches from 1930 to 1932. The Austrians recorded a difficult overtime win, 3–2, against France in their first match and then faced Hungary. The two nations had formed the Austro-Hungarian Empire until 1918, but there was no sense of brotherhood on the field that day. "It was a brawl," said Meisl afterwards, "not an exhibition of football." Whatever it was, Austria won it 2–1.

Germany, cheered on by thousands of fans waving Nazi flags, swept to the semifinals with wins over Belgium and Sweden. Czechoslovakia, passing with deadly accuracy, defeated Romania 3–2, and then scored a thrilling, 3–2 comeback victory over Switzerland.

Italy had the most difficult time of any of the four teams to reach the semifinals. Its obstacle was Spain, a team led by the great Ricardo Zamora, regarded as the finest goalie of his time. The two teams met in Fiesole (just north of Florence) and Zamora, battered again and again by Italian forwards who inflicted a variety of injuries by crashing into him, was magnificent. After ninety minutes of regulation time the score was knotted at one apiece, Italy's lone tally coming after a free kick was blocked by Zamora. The ball bounced to Italy's Gianini Ferrari, who booted in an easy goal. The thirty-minute overtime was a viciously played affair, but neither team was able to score. A rematch was staged the following day and Spain, forced to play without Zamora, who sat on the sidelines nursing his injuries, bowed 1–0.

Italy advanced to meet Austria on a rain-soaked field in Milan. Mud hindered Austria's smooth passing attack, which relied heavily upon deception and finesse rather than power and intimidation. Nevertheless, Austria gave a good account of itself, allowing but a single goal, scored by Guaita, one of Italy's Argentines.

In the other semifinal match, Czechoslovakia faced Germany. It was a well-played, fast-paced affair minus the violence and rough tactics so prevalent elsewhere. Scoring two late goals, the Czechs won 3–1 to set up a championship meeting with Italy.

1934 Championship Game

The Czechs repaired to a training camp in Frascati, where each day's mail brought cases of sausages, hams, and good-luck charms from supporters back home. All very nice, but nothing compared to the frenzied cheers Italian fans showered on their favorites when the two teams met in Rome. To be sure, buses and trains carrying thousands of people from Prague gave Czechoslovakia a sizable rooting section, but its shouts were constantly drowned out by thunderous roars of *"Forza Italia."*

After a scoreless first half, Czechoslovakia drew first blood, scoring with only twenty minutes left. Eight minutes later Italy tied, and there was no more scoring in regulation time.

With Il Duce watching, Italy played the thirty-minute overtime period like a team that had to win, and perhaps it did. Again it was Guaita, the Argentine, who supplied the crucial play, hitting an open teammate with a beautiful pass that led to the game-winning goal. Fireworks filled the sky and Mussolini, always on center stage, proclaimed another victory for "Fascist Sport."

1938 WORLD CUP: FRANCE

First Round

Switzerland 1, Germany 1*
Switzerland 4, Germany 2**
Cuba 3, Romania 3
Cuba 2, Romania 1**
Hungary 6, Dutch East Indies 0
France 3, Belgium 1
Czechoslovakia 3, Holland 0*
Brazil 6, Poland 5*
Italy 2, Norway 1*

Second Round

Sweden 8, Cuba 0
Hungary 2, Switzerland 0
Italy 3, France 1
Brazil 1, Czechoslovakia 1*
Brazil 2, Czechoslovakia 1**

Semifinals

Italy 2, Brazil 1
Hungary 5, Sweden 1

Third Place

Brazil 4, Sweden 2

Championship

Italy 4, Hungary 2

*Overtime
**Rematch

Stormclouds of war rolling inexorably across the European continent cast dark shadows over the 1938 World Cup. Originally thirty-six nations had agreed to participate, but when the tournament actually began only fifteen were still entered. France had been selected to host the competition and Uruguay, angered because the World Cup was being staged in Europe again, stayed home again. Argentina agreed to come but then, at the last moment, changed its mind, an act that provoked riots in the streets of Buenos Aires and left Brazil as South America's lone representative.

Several European nations had very valid and serious reasons for not sending teams. Spain was embroiled in a bitter and bloody civil war and Austria was a recent victim of Anschluss. With the annexation of Austria by Germany, many of the former's finest soccer players were absorbed into the German squad, where four of them became starters.

Once again there was a one-game elimination format, with Sweden receiving a bye into the second round. Of the seven first-round games, only two were decided in regulation time; Hungary's easy, 6–0 triumph over the Dutch East Indies (Asia's first World Cup participant), and France's 3–1 win over neighboring Belgium

Switzerland and Germany met in Paris and played to a one-goal tie. Five days later there was a rematch and Switzerland, down 2–0 at halftime, rallied to win 4–2. In Marseilles, Italy and Norway were tied at one apiece after ninety minutes, but a brilliant overtime goal by Italy's center forward, Silvio Piola,

Giuseppe Meazza (left), star center forward of the Italian team, shakes hands with Hungarian team captain Sarosi prior to the start of the 1938 championship match.

Vittorio Pozzo (holding the Jules Rimet Trophy) and his squad pose for a team portrait after having won their second straight World Cup title.

allowed the defending champions to advance with a 2–1 decision. In Le Havre, Holland surprised Czechoslovakia by allowing no goals in regulation time. But the Dutch failed to score themselves and fell before an avalanche of Czech goals in overtime to bow 3–0. In the wildest opening-round match, Brazil edged Poland 6–5 in overtime. Leonidas, "the Black Diamond," scored four times for Brazil, while blond-haired Ernest Willimowski recorded four goals for Poland.

Cuba, which entered as a replacement after Mexico dropped out, played Romania to a 3–3 draw at Toulouse. Before the rematch Cuba's goalie, Benito Carvajales, called a press conference and, shades of Muhammad Ali, predicted victory. "We shall win the replay," he announced, "no question about it. The Romanians have no more secrets for us. We will score twice, they will score once. *Adiós, caballeros.*" Final score: Cuba 2, Romania 1.

When Brazil and Czechoslovakia met for a second-round match in Bordeaux, they played one of those games that erupts now and again as a blemish on the face of international soccer. Before it ended only seventeen of the twenty-two players who started (remember, this was before substitutions were allowed) remained on the field. Two Czechs were in the hospital, one with a broken leg, the other a broken arm, and a third had been sent off for rough play. Two Brazilians were banished for the same reason. The game ended in a 1–1 tie. Brazil started nine new players in the rematch, Czechoslovakia six, and the changes seemed to have calmed both sides. Brazil, with goals by Leonidas and Roberto, won 2–1.

When France and Italy met in Paris, the French wore their customary sky-blue jerseys, while Italy dressed its players entirely in Fascist black. Paced by Piola's two second-half goals, Italy won 3–1. Sweden met, and demolished, Cuba 8–0. After the rout was completed, Cuba's talkative goalie, Carvajales, was uncharacteristically silent. Hungary, led by Dr. George Sarosi at center forward, had an easy time defeating Switzerland 2–0. Sarosi was an unusual and talented man. In addition to his prowess on the soccer field he was an outstanding competitive swimmer, fencer, and tennis player, and a scholar of some note in his native land.

Brazil faced Italy in one semifinal and surprised everyone by benching two of its stars, Tim and Leonidas, with the explanation that they were being rested for the championship game. Such optimism was not rewarded, for Italy won 2–1. The turning point came when Brazilian fullback Domingas Da Guia, a player noted for his self-control under pressure, lost his temper as Piola dribbled past him again and again. Finally Piola went by him one time too many and Da Guia lashed out his leg, sending the lithe Italian striker tumbling head over heels in the penalty area. A penalty kick followed, providing the decisive goal, and Italy had reached the final game again.

It was an unfortunate moment for Da Guia—whose son Ademir would be a member of Brazil's 1965 national team—a player Italy's coach Vittorio Pozzo called "one of the greatest defenders one is ever likely to meet."

In the other semifinal, Sweden scored after only thirty-five seconds of play and then collapsed as Hungary replied with five goals and earned the right to challenge defending champion Italy for the title.

1938 Championship Game

The championship match, played in Paris, was expected to be a contest between two outstanding center forwards, Italy's Piola and Hungary's Sarosi. Although both stars shone, the game was in actuality a test of two differing styles of play. Hungary favored a basically conservative attack, based upon precise passing and subtle strategies, while Italy relied upon a more flamboyant, all-out offense. Here, as would be the case in future title games, flamboyance carried the day.

After the two teams traded early goals, Piola put Italy out in front and before the half ended one of his teammates, Colaussi, provided what would prove to be the decisive tally. Hungary pulled within one in the second half when Sarosi scored from a goalmouth melee, but with ten minutes left Piola swept in for his second goal to put the game out of reach at 4–2 and give Italy its second straight World Cup.

As Vittorio Pozzo accepted the trophy for Italy, he gave the Fascist salute, a gesture greeted by a chorus of jeers from the thousands of Parisians in attendance. Their cries heralded hard times to come, for within a year the world was at war.

Not for another twelve years would the World Cup be staged. Italy owned the Jules Rimet Trophy until 1950, but keeping possession was not all that simple, for when Germany occupied Rome the Nazis launched an all-out search for the golden statuette. Fortunately, the Italians had expected such an eventuality and had hidden the trophy in the vault of a bank in neutral Switzerland, where it remained until the competition finally resumed.

Italy's Foni begins a scissors kick in the 1938 title game against Hungary.

1950 WORLD CUP: BRAZIL

Pool One
Brazil 4, Mexico 0
Yugoslavia 3, Switzerland 0
Yugoslavia 4, Mexico 1
Brazil 2, Switzerland 2
Brazil 2, Yugoslavia 0
Switzerland 2, Mexico 1

Pool Two
Spain 3, United States 1
England 2, Chile 0
United States 1, England 0
Spain 2, Chile 0
Spain 1, England 0
Chile 5, United States 2

Pool Three
Sweden 3, Italy 2
Sweden 2, Paraguay 2
Italy 2, Paraguay 0

Pool Four
Uruguay 8, Bolivia 0

Final Pool*
Uruguay 2, Spain 2
Brazil 7, Sweden 1
Uruguay 3, Sweden 2
Brazil 6, Spain 1
Sweden 3, Spain 1
Uruguay 2, Brazil 1

*Round-robin

n the British Crown Colony of Hong Kong an Associated Press editor answered his telephone. "Is it true, is it true?" asked an anxious voice.

Since war was raging in Korea, the editor could think of only one thing that would produce such anxiety. "No, no," he said reassuringly, "the United States and Russia have not declared war."

"That's not what I mean," shouted his caller. "Is it true the United States beat England in the World Cup?" Hearing an answer of yes, the caller could only mutter, "Why those cheeky Americans."

Back home in England the reaction was even more intense. "It marks the lowest point ever for British Sport," said a front-page story in the *Daily Express,* while a headline in the *Daily Mail* called it "The Biggest Soccer Upset Of All Time."

Who would have thought it possible for England, mighty England, historic birthplace of soccer, a nation that did not even deign to compete in the first three World Cup tournaments, to lose to a team from the United States, where the sport's popularity rested mainly with various ethnic leagues and a scattering of college teams. But it happened; on a bumpy field in Belo Horizonte, a team from America had beaten the British. England's great forward Stanley Matthews was not in his nation's lineup for this match. Instead he watched the game, in agony, from the stands. Here is his recollection of what happened that afternoon.

In the beginning we laughed and decided to allow the Americans some time to get organized. But after they scored that goal and we couldn't get a clean shot on goal, I became so frustrated and angry that I kept digging my nails into my palms, and after the game was over and we had lost 1–0, I looked at my hands and blood was flowing from them.

Of course, not all the excitement at the 1950 World Cup was provided by this one dramatic upset. The tournament was held in Brazil, and only thirteen nations showed up. Cold war politics kept all the iron curtain nations (Czechoslovakia, Hungary, the Soviet Union, Romania, etc.) at home, while France, claiming there was too much travel involved, also

This London Daily Mirror headline expresses the shock felt by British sports fans after a bunch of American "amateurs" upset England.

Uruguayan goalkeeper Maspoli makes a diving save on a shot by Brazil's Ademir Menezes (center) during the 1950 championship game.

1950 Championship Game

In Rio de Janeiro, the morning of July 17, 1950 dawned bright and clear. On the summit of Mount Corcovado, 2,310 feet above sea level, a gigantic figure of Christ, its arms upraised, gazed down upon a city gone mad with the expectation of victory. Rio seemed gripped by a fever. There had nearly been a riot, one day earlier, when tickets for the championship game went on sale. In order to prevent bloodshed, police had to be called in to take control of the distribution process. Once the 200,000 tickets had been sold, Copacabana Beach became an open marketplace as scalpers strolled back and forth demanding, and receiving, fifteen times the printed price of their wares.

Everyone, with one notable exception, was confident of victory. Brazil's coach, Flavio Costa, had said: "The Uruguayan team has always disturbed the slumbers of Brazilian footballers. I'm afraid my players will take the field on Sunday as though they already had the championship shield sewn on their jerseys. It isn't an exhibition game. It is a match like any other, only harder than the others."

An hour before gametime the blue bowl of Maracana Stadium was filled to its brim. Brazil took the field first, elegant in all-white uniforms, followed by the Uruguayans, in pale blue shirts and pitch-black shorts.

As expected, Brazil began quickly, going on the attack while Uruguay played a more conservative, defensive game. As minute after minute faded into history no goals were scored and the massive crowd, waiting for an explosion that never came, began to get restless. After forty-five minutes of play neither team had scored.

Then, two minutes into the second half, an ear-shattering roar vibrated in the air after Ademir and Zizinho cleverly combined to draw Uruguay's defenders off to the left, allowing another forward, Friaca, to streak down the right side, take a pass, and break loose to score and send the partisan crowd into a frenzy. Now was the time for Uruguay to fold, to roll over and play dead for the new champions; but, of course, they did no such thing. The Uruguayans had been playing Brazil on even terms for half a century, and there was no reason for them to stop now.

Abandoning its defensive posture, Uruguay went on the attack and seized control of the game's flow for the next twenty minutes. Then, midway through the second half, Juan Schiaffino, a tall, slender, almost fragile-looking forward, took a pass from teammate Alcide Ghiggia and scored.

An unreal silence hung over Maracana Stadium now as Brazil began to play for a tie that would, after all, assure it of the title. Uruguay refused to cooperate and played to win. With eleven minutes left Ghiggia eluded the man guarding him and scored. Brazil played out the contest as if in a trance. Quietly the huge crowd slowly filed out, the few Uruguayans in the throng celebrating silently, lest they be torn limb from limb.

The following morning a mass funeral was staged in Rio because, said one local newspaper, "soccer had died." Meanwhile, back in Uruguay, three people had succumbed to heart attacks while listening to the match and five more died during the wild postgame celebration in the streets of Montevideo. Of the four World Cup tournaments played, Uruguay, a nation of fewer than three million people, had won two. One more victory and the Uruguayans would gain permanent possession of the Jules Rimet Trophy. They would get their chance four years later in Switzerland.

declined an invitation. The most insulting no-show was Argentina, who snubbed its neighbor's tournament because of a squabble with Brazil's Football Federation.

The pool system, first used in 1930 and then abandoned, was reinstated, an unfortunate move that lent an air of farce to the proceedings. The manner in which the miniature leagues were established left Pool Four with only two teams, allowing Uruguay to win that round-robin competition by crushing a weak Bolivian team 8–1. The winner of each pool advanced into a final pool, where the champion would also be selected by a round-robin competition.

Near Rio de Janeiro's Maracana River, Brazil constructed the immense Maracana Stadium with a seating capacity of 200,000, and on opening day delighted the hometown crowd by defeating Mexico 4–0. Switzerland played the host team to a two-goal draw, but then the Brazilians defeated Yugoslavia 2–0 to advance into the final pool.

The United States, assigned to Pool Two, was coached by Bill Jeffrey. A Scot who had emigrated to America in the 1920's, he eventually became the soccer coach at Penn State University, where his teams recorded thirteen undefeated seasons. He prepared his squad well and in their first match the Americans led Spain 1–0 for much of the game, following a goal by John Souza. Then the powerful Spaniards spoiled American dreams of an upset by banging in three goals in the last ten minutes. After scoring their historic upset over England, on a goal by Joe Gaetjens, the Americans were eliminated by Chile 5–2, while Spain went on to dominate Pool Two with victories over England and Chile.

In Pool Three, Sweden defeated Italy and tied Paraguay, teams that each lost one game, to advance into the finals.

Brazil opened play in the final pool like a whirlwind, breezing past Sweden 7–1 and Spain 6–1. The dazzling Brazilian attack featured Ademir, who scored four goals against Sweden, and Zizinho, a masterful dribbler.

Uruguay had a much more difficult time, being held to a 2–2 draw by Spain and having to struggle from behind to defeat Sweden 3–2. The final pool was arranged so that each win was worth two points, each tie one point. Two victories gave Brazil four points, while Uruguay had three. When the two teams met, Brazil needed only a tie to win its first World Cup.

1954 WORLD CUP: SWITZERLAND

Pool One
Yugoslavia 1, France 0
Brazil 5, Mexico 0
France 3, Mexico 2
Brazil 1, Yugoslavia 1*

Pool Two
Hungary 9, South Korea 0
West Germany 4, Turkey 1
Hungary 8, West Germany 3
Turkey 7, South Korea 0
West Germany 7, Turkey 2**

Pool Three
Austria 1, Scotland 0
Uruguay 2, Czechoslovakia 0
Austria 5, Czechoslovakia 0
Uruguay 7, Scotland 0

Pool Four
England 4, Belgium 4
England 2, Switzerland 0
Switzerland 2, Italy 1
Italy 4, Belgium 1
Switzerland 4, Italy 1**

Quarterfinals
West Germany 2, Yugoslavia 0
Hungary 4, Brazil 2
Austria 7, Switzerland 5
Uruguay 4, England 2

Semifinals
West Germany 6, Austria 1
Hungary 4, Uruguay 2*

Third Place
Austria 3, Uruguay 1

Championship
West Germany 3, Hungary 2

*Overtime
**Playoff for second place in pool

The 1954 World Cup is famous, perhaps infamous is a more suitable adjective, for the "Battle of Berne." Here is how a correspondent for the *London Times* described soccer's darkest hour:

In one of the bitterest, fiercest, and tensest matches probably ever fought—and that is the correct word—Hungary reached the semifinal for the World Cup with a victory by four goals to two over Brazil. Here were two of the greatest sides in the world finally destroying their own superb artistry by the barefaced and attempted annihilation of each other by unethical tactics. Never in my life have I seen such cruel tackling, the cutting down of opponents as if with a scythe, followed by threatening attitudes and sly jabs, when officialdom was engaged elsewhere.

Trouble began when the game, played from start to finish in rain and mud, was only three minutes old. Nandor Hidegkuti scored for Hungary and had his shorts ripped off by angry Brazilian defenders—a provocative gesture to say the least. As tackling grew more and more ruthless, both teams seemed to spend as much time brawling as they did playing soccer. English referee Arthur Ellis banished Hungary's Josef Bozsik and Brazil's Nilton Santos, who had stood toe-to-toe exchanging blows, but that gesture served to inflame rather than soothe already frayed tempers.

The final whistle failed to quell the fighting, which continued in the dressing room. Brazilian officials claimed the postgame fracas began when one of the Hungarian team members slammed a bottle into the face of João Pinheiro. Hungary laid the blame on a Brazilian player who clasped a Hungarian in an apparently friendly handshake and then clipped him with a left to the jaw. No matter who started the melee, it required a platoon of Swiss police, who also suffered a variety of injuries, to pry the two warring factions apart.

It was one of many sour notes sounded in the tournament involving sixteen teams, none of whom seemed satisfied with the revised, and rather complicated, format. Once again teams would be divided into pools of four nations each, but this time the squads would be seeded, with the two top-seeded teams in each pool not scheduled to meet in opening-round play. Each team would in fact play only two games, with the top two teams advancing to the quarterfinals. Such an arrangement made it possible for two nations that played in an opening round to meet again in the championship game.

As luck would have it, that is exactly what happened. Hungary, the pretournament favorite, scored an easy 8–3 victory over West Germany. It was a strategic defeat for the

England's Nat Lofthouse (with ball) moves to avoid a challenge from Uruguay's Andrade during a quarter-final match won by Uruguay 4–2.

Swiss gendarmes provide an escort for victorious West German players after they had surprised Hungary, 3–2, to win the 1954 World Cup.

Germans, who fielded a squad composed almost entirely of reserves for that match. The Germans knew they would be able to handle their other pool opponent, Turkey, and they did, twice, their second victory coming in a playoff game with the Turks for second place in the pool and a spot in the quarterfinals.

Minutes after its quarterfinal with West Germany had begun, Yugoslav center Ivan Horvat put his team in a hole by kicking a hard pass backwards, right past his startled goal-keeper's outstretched arms. Although Yugoslavia dominated play throughout, West Germany allowed no goals, got a late score from forward Helmut Rahn, and won 2–0.

Austria and Switzerland staged a shootout in Lausanne, scoring an incredible total of twelve goals, with Austria coming out on top 7–5. Defending champion Uruguay, led by the brilliant center halfback José Santamaria, advanced by eliminating England 4–2.

In the semifinals, West Germany had no trouble brushing past Austria 6–1, while Hungary, survivor of the "Battle of Berne," became the first team ever to defeat Uruguay in World Cup competition, winning 4–2 in overtime, when Sandor Kocsis headed in a pair of goals. Now the championship game would be a rematch of West Germany and Hungary.

Maspoli of Uruguay moves to snatch the ball away from the feet of an English forward.

1954 Championship Game

It was generally agreed that Hungary had the world's finest team in the early 1950's. In 1953 the Hungarians made a trip to London's Wembley Stadium to face England, which had never lost at home to a team from outside the British Isles. That afternoon the myth of English invincibility on its native turf was shattered forever, as the Hungarians outpassed, outdribbled, outshot, and totally outplayed their hosts to record an astonishing 6–3 victory.

Six months later an English team, hungry for revenge, traveled to Budapest. This time there was no question as to which was the superior team. Hungary, scoring almost at will, routed England 7–1, playing a game based on speed combined with imagination. There was, naturally, one other vital ingredient. Just as Brazil would be in the sixties, Hungary was blessed with a group of marvelously talented athletes, including such brilliant players as Josef Boszik, Nandor Hidegkuti, Sandor Kocsis, and Ferenc Puskas.

Not unexpectedly, the Hungarians were heavily favored before their title game with the West Germans. But as so often happens in sports, especially on the championship level, the team that is best on paper is often not the best on a given day against a particular opponent.

Tens of thousands of Germans poured across the Swiss border and into Berne, where the game would be played. Only 65,000 tickets were available, and as demand rose while supply diminished the pasteboards, normally priced at thirty-six francs ($8.35), were selling, at a brisk rate, for 500 francs ($116). In open spaces outside the packed stadium radio and television booths were erected. For a franc (twenty-three cents), a fan could listen to a broadcast of the game; for two francs, he could watch it on TV.

Puskas, who had missed most of Hungary's World Cup games because of a leg injury, returned for the final and scored after only six minutes of play. Despite this early display of brilliance Puskas, still hobbling from the effects of his injury

and out of shape, proved in the long run to be more of a hindrance than a help to Hungary's title hopes. Nevertheless, Hungary controlled the early moments, scored a second goal, and appeared headed for victory.

Then it began to rain, and just as the weather changed, so did the game. Fritz Walter, Germany's thirty-four-year-old captain and inside left forward, sent a pass across Hungary's goalmouth to teammate Max Morlock, who booted the ball past goalie Gyula Grosics. Six minutes later Helmut Rahn drove home a corner kick and the score was tied.

With both goalies performing yeomanlike tasks, neither team was able to score again, although both came close. Then, with only six minutes left to play, Germany's Rahn knocked in what proved to be the decisive goal. Hungary tried to rally, and appeared to have succeeded when Puskas, who had not been a factor for much of the second half, took a beautiful pass and scored. But no, said the linesman, Puskas was offside and the goal was disallowed. Time ran out and Germany owned the World Cup.

It was a remarkable achievement for the West Germans, who had only recently been readmitted to FIFA. There was general rejoicing from Bonn to Berlin, and East Germany, a bitter cold-war antagonist, broadcast congratulations. Back in Hungary, 15,000 demonstrators took to the streets of Budapest to give vent to their frustrations by protesting the loss. They blamed the government, accused the team management of "selling out to the Germans," and broke windows at the state-run football organization.

Hungary might have been a factor at the 1958 World Cup competition had not other events intervened. When the 1956 Hungarian Revolution exploded many of the nation's soccer stars, including Puskas and Kocsis, were on tour with their club team, Honved. They took the opportunity to defect and signed professional contracts in the West. The great Hungarian team was no more but, offstage, Brazil was waiting to step into the spotlight.

1958 WORLD CUP: SWEDEN

Pool One
West Germany 3, Argentina 1
N. Ireland 1, Czechoslovakia 0
West Germany 2, Czechoslovakia 2
Argentina 3, N. Ireland 1
West Germany 2, N. Ireland 2
Czechoslovakia 6, Argentina 1

Pool Two
France 7, Paraguay 3
Yugoslavia 1, Scotland 1
Yugoslavia 3, France 2
Paraguay 3, Scotland 2
France 2, Scotland 1
Yugoslavia 3, Paraguay 3

Pool Three
Sweden 3, Mexico 0
Hungary 1, Wales 1
Wales 1, Mexico 1
Sweden 2, Hungary 1
Sweden 0, Wales 0
Hungary 4, Mexico 0
Wales 2, Hungary 1*

Pool Four
England 2, U.S.S.R. 2
Brazil 3, Austria 0
England 0, Brazil 0
U.S.S.R. 2, Austria 0
Brazil 2, U.S.S.R. 0
England 2, Austria 2
U.S.S.R. 1, England 0*

Quarterfinals
France 4, N. Ireland 0
West Germany 1, Yugoslavia 0
Sweden 2, U.S.S.R. 0
Brazil 1, Wales 0

Semifinals
Brazil 5, France 2
Sweden 3, West Germany 1

Third Place
France 6, West Germany 3

Championship
Brazil 5, Sweden 2
*Rematch

This was the year soccer fans learned all about Brazilian nicknames. Because of complicated proper names capable of transforming a public-address-system announcer's tongue into a corkscrew, many of Brazil's players either adopted, or were simply given, new, easier-to-pronounce handles. Thus a man called Monoel Francisco dos Santos became Garrincha, or "Little Bird," and joined a team filled with players known as Didi, Vava, Zito, Zagalo, and, oh yes, some seventeen-year-old kid, rumored to be sensational, called Pelé.

In point of fact, Pelé really was just a rumor to most of the sixteen teams gathered in Sweden to prepare for this World Cup. Many had heard of him, but only a few had actually seen him play. Besides, he had injured a knee in practice and it proved serious enough to keep him sidelined for Brazil's first two games. At the time there seemed little chance of this youngster breaking into Brazil's starting lineup, which was filled with enough talented and experienced players to make the Brazilians a pretournament favorite.

Once again the teams were divided into four pools, only this time, unlike 1954, each nation would play a complete round-robin schedule. Once again, the first two teams in each pool would advance to the quarterfinals.

Argentina made its first World Cup appearance since 1934 and, all things considered, may have come back too soon. This following report from the *New York Times* illustrates one of the many problems Argentina had:

> Police had to be called to disperse a mob of excited girls trying to force their way into Argentina's training camp. The Argentine manager, Guillermo Stabile, scoffed at charges from Swedish parents that his players had been fraternizing. "Nonsense," he said, "the behavior of my players has been absolutely correct." But a source close to the team said that players' wives back home were unsettled and threatening to fly to Sweden.

In 1957, Argentina had won the South American championship with an attack featuring three forwards known as *El Trio de la Muerte,* the trio of death. Unfortunately, at least for Argentina, all three—Humberto Maschio, Valentin Angelillo, and Omar Sivori—had signed lucrative contracts with Italian

Garrincha (above) passes the ball across Sweden's goalmouth to teammate Vava (20), who knocked in Brazil's first goal during its 5–2 victory in the 1958 championship match. Northern Ireland's goalkeeper Harry Gregg (near right) failed to stop this shot by West Germany's Uwe Seeler in a match that ended in a 2–2 tie. Sweden's Kurt Hamrin (far right) receives a pass over the outstretched leg of Brazil's Nilton Santos during the title game.

clubs and now played for Italy's national team. Missing these three stars, Argentina fell before West Germany 3–1 and was crushed by Czechoslovakia 6–1. When they finally returned home, the feckless Argentines were showered with garbage at the Buenos Aires airport.

For the first time all four of Great Britain's national teams—England, Scotland, Wales, and Northern Ireland—were among the final sixteen, the Irish having advanced after winning their zone with a playoff victory over Italy. Both England and Northern Ireland fielded teams tragically weakened; for a few months earlier an airplane carrying the Manchester United team had crashed in Munich. Three members of England's national squad and two from Northern Ireland had died.

The Soviet Union was competing for the first time and had on its team Lev Yachin, regarded as the finest goalkeeper of his time. Yachin wore an all black uniform, claiming the color served as a magnet for the ball and drew it to him. Missing was the U.S.S.R.'s outstanding forward Edouard Streltsov, who just before the World Cup had been sent to a labor camp.

In Pool Four, Brazil opened with a somewhat sluggish win over Austria, and then played a scoreless tie with England. Obviously something had to be done to spark the Brazilian offense, so the team's manager, Vicente Feola, made some wholesale changes in his starting lineup. He inserted Garrincha, a brilliant young forward; Zito, a clever midfielder; and a seventeen-year-old who had created quite a stir during his rookie season with Santos of the São Paulo League. The kid's name was, of course, Pelé.

The Soviet Union was the first team to face this rejuvenated Brazilian eleven, which demonstrated its new-found vigor in the opening two minutes of play. Twice they cut through the rugged Soviet defense only to have shots bounce off a post. One minute later, they found the range on a shot by Vava, the first of his two goals and the only ones scored that afternoon as Brazil coasted to an easy victory.

A few days later, Pelé scored his first World Cup goal in a quarterfinal game against Wales. Catching a high pass on his chest, he let it drop to his right foot, lifted it over a defender's head and, before the ball hit the ground, blasted it past the Welsh goalkeeper.

In terms of quantity, the great scorer of this tournament was not Pelé, but a Frenchman named Juste Fontaine who scored an amazing thirteen times—and, with some able assistance from Raymond Kopa, led his team to a semifinal showdown against Brazil. In the other semifinal, West Germany was paired off against Sweden, who surprised everyone, including its own fans, by eliminating the Soviet Union 2–0 in the quarterfinals.

Sweden, who even its supporters didn't consider a serious contender until the semifinals, defeated West Germany 3–1 before a wildly cheering crowd in Gothenburg. In Stockholm, Brazil and France squared off, with Fontaine being the first player in the tournament to penetrate the Brazilian defense and score a goal. It wasn't enough though—Pelé got three and Brazil, with a 5–2 victory, moved on to face Sweden for the championship.

1958 Championship Game

The normal hurly-burly of Rio de Janeiro street life had been silenced, and to the south, in the industrial and business center of São Paulo, the wheels of commerce ground to a temporary halt as Brazilians from all walks of life crowded around radios to listen to the broadcast from Stockholm's Rasunda Stadium, where 58,000 people, including the Swedish king Gustaf Adolf, had gathered for the big game.

Both teams fenced for a while and then a Swedish cheer of "Heja Sverige" split the air when, after seven minutes of play, Nils Liedholm scored for the host team. George Raynor, an Englishman who served as Sweden's coach, had predicted Brazil would panic if his team scored first. He was whistling in the wind. Vava scored twice, and at the half Brazil led 2–1.

Early in the second half Pelé crushed Swedish hopes with an incredible goal. Getting a pass in Sweden's penalty area, he juggled the ball on his thigh, flicked it over the head of a defender, caught it on his thigh again, repeated this performance against another baffled defender, and smashed the ball into Sweden's net.

Brazil now had complete control of the game. Zagalo put his team up by three, Agne Simonsson brought Sweden to within two, and then Pelé headed in another goal to put the contest out of reach. After it was over, Pelé, at seventeen the tournament's youngest player, wept openly on the shoulder of his teammate Didi—but back in Brazil there were no tears.

Victory had erased all memories of past World Cup defeats, especially the traumatic loss to Uruguay in 1950. Earlier failures had been interpreted as weaknesses of national character and victory was regarded as a symbol of national vindication.

Automobiles and trucks decorated with Brazilian flags careened through city streets with their horns blaring. Samba lines snaked through Cinelandia, Rio's Times Square area, to the beat of carnival drums and sang "Brazil's hour has arrived at last; there are no Russians, English, Swedes, or French," while overhead, rockets filled the sky.

Brazil had introduced a new kind of soccer. Daring and freewheeling, yet at the same time intelligent and controlled. Coaches around the world wondered how they could derail this juggernaut in 1962.

1962 WORLD CUP: CHILE

Group One
Uruguay 2, Colombia 1
U.S.S.R. 2, Yugoslavia 0
Yugoslavia 3, Uruguay 1
U.S.S.R. 2, Uruguay 1
Yugoslavia 5, Colombia 0
U.S.S.R. 4, Colombia 4

Group Two
Chile 3, Switzerland 1
West Germany 0, Italy 0
Chile 2, Italy 0
West Germany 2, Switzerland 1
West Germany 2, Chile 0
Italy 3, Switzerland 0

Group Three
Brazil 2, Mexico 0
Czechoslovakia 1, Spain 0
Brazil 0, Czechoslovakia 0
Spain 1, Mexico 0
Brazil 2, Spain 1
Mexico 3, Czechoslovakia 1

Group Four
Argentina 1, Bulgaria 0
Hungary 2, England 1
England 3, Argentina 1
Hungary 6, Bulgaria 1
Argentina 0, Hungary 0
England 0, Bulgaria 0

Quarterfinals
Yugoslavia 1, West Germany 0
Brazil 3, England 1
Chile 2, U.S.S.R. 1
Czechoslovakia 1, Hungary 0

Semifinals
Brazil 4, Chile 2
Czechoslovakia 3, Yugoslavia 1

Third Place
Chile 1, Yugoslavia 0

Championship
Brazil 3, Czechoslovakia 1

Chile's selection as host for this World Cup was in part an act of charity. Still recuperating from a devastating earthquake, its shaken economy would receive a much-needed boost from the tournament. In addition Chile, not a major soccer power, would have its morale lifted because a host nation receives an automatic berth among the tournament's final sixteen teams. Chile, as events were to prove, was to make the most of this opportunity.

Brazil, with a squad virtually unchanged since 1958, was, of course, favored to win again. Assigned to Group Three—no longer would these miniature leagues be called "pools"—Brazil opened with an uninspired 2–0 victory over Mexico. Pelé scored an absolutely brilliant goal in this match, dribbling around and past five bewildered Mexicans before firing a bullet past a baffled goalkeeper. Unfortunately, it was to be Pelé's last goal in this tournament. A few days later against Czechoslovakia, a dreary game ending in a scoreless tie, Pelé, often guarded by as many as four Czechs, suffered a serious muscle pull and was forced to attend Brazil's remaining games in this tournament as a spectator.

In Group Two, Chile pleased its fans by dispatching Switzerland 3–1, and then faced Italy in another one of those brawls that keep reappearing in World Cup competition. An article written by an Italian journalist served to stoke the fire. He had visited Chile and returned home to write in a disparaging manner about the nation and to question the morals of some of its women, which, to the Chileans, was tantamount to a declaration of war.

With the journalist safely at home it was left to Italy's soccer team to receive Chile's wrath, from both players and fans alike. Before the game even began Chilean players were spitting in the faces of their Italian counterparts, while spectators shouted obscenities and made a variety of provocative gestures. The Italians, with Latin temperaments of their own, replied in kind. Referee Ken Aston, an Englishman, tried everything to maintain order, but an official has only two eyes and cannot keep constant track of twenty-two men intent on wreaking havoc. What Aston did see after only eight minutes of play was enough for him to banish Giorgio Ferrini, Italy's inside left, for fighting and then, only moments later, Italian halfback Mario David, who was detected kicking Chileans when he should have been kicking the ball.

As luck would have it, Aston did not see the game's most flagrant foul, although it did occur in full view of several hundred million television viewers watching on a world-wide hookup. It was a left hook thrown by Chile's Lionel Sanchez that broke the nose of Humberto Maschio, even further weakening Italy's already thinned ranks. Oh yes, Chile won the game 2–0.

The Soviet Union dominated Group One as Lev Yachin, a virtual octopus in the goalmouth, shut out Yugoslavia and let Uruguay score but once. Then, mysteriously, Colombia, who was to score only one other goal in the tournament, scored four times against Yachin in a contest that ended in a 4–4 tie. An embarrassment to be sure, but not serious enough to keep the Soviets out of a place in the quarterfinals.

Hungary, although held to a scoreless tie by Argentina, beat England and Bulgaria to finish first in Group Four. Argentina and England finished with identical records, but the latter advanced, having won 3–1 when the two teams met.

Chile's Leonel Sanchez (right) leaps high to block a shot, while teammate Eladio Rojas (6) rushes to recover the ball during the host team's 3–1 victory over Switzerland.

Chilean goalkeeper Escuti (right) dives in vain as the ball enters the net for Switzerland's lone goal in the opening match. With Pelé sidelined by an injury, Garrincha (above, left) emerged as his team's leader to guide Brazil to its second straight World Cup title.

The English had sent some fine young players to Chile, men like Bobby Moore and Bobby Charlton who would one day lead them to a world title. But that day still lay in the future, and for the present England was not yet ready to cope with the likes of Brazil. No longer playing under Pelé's shadow, Garrincha had come into his own as a team leader. Against England he scored twice as his team won 3–1 and advanced to the semifinals.

Only five-foot-six, Garrincha had been born with a right leg two inches shorter than his left, which, to compensate, bowed outward. "He wobbles so much," said England's Jimmy Graves, "that even when he comes at you to shake hands you don't know which way he's going." Despite what might have been a handicap he was extremely fast and, as the father of seven daughters, liked to joke that, "I can outrun everyone but the stork."

As Chile prepared to meet the U.S.S.R., hardly anyone in Santiago gave the hometown favorites much of a chance. One newspaper, *El Mercurio,* editorialized that: "Football is not very logical, maybe a miracle will happen against the Russians." Maybe what happened wasn't a miracle, but to be sure it was an upset; Leonel Sanchez and Eladio Rojas each scored against Yachin and Chile won 2–1.

Could it happen? Could Chile actually win the World Cup? Brazil was to provide an answer to that question in the semifinals, and its answer was an emphatic no! Two goals by Garrincha, two by Vava, and Brazil was in the championship game again.

Czechoslovakia, with a 3–1 victory over Yugoslavia, would provide the opposition. With the brilliant Wilhelm Schroiff in their goalmouth, the Czechs had already held Brazil to a scoreless tie—and that was when the Brazilians had a healthy Pelé. His absence might prove to be the crucial difference when the two teams met again.

1962 Championship Game

Nobody was more concerned about playing in the final without Pelé than Brazil's coach, Aymore Moreira. "Yes Garrincha is a great player," he admitted, "but we still miss Pelé. No one else is like him in the world. Garrincha plays only three notes; do, re, mi. He plays them well, but Pelé plays the whole scale; do, re, mi, fa, sol, la, ti, do. And he plays each note better than anyone else."

Garrincha, as things turned out, was not to be a decisive factor as close-guarding Czech defenders kept him under control most of the afternoon. These tactics were effective only up to a point, for this was a great Brazilian team and if one star faltered there was always another to take his place. This time it was Amarildo who rose to the occasion. Surprisingly, Czechoslovakia scored first as Josef Masopust got loose and fired one past Gilmar, the Brazilian goalie who would not let another ball by him that afternoon.

Schroiff, who had been so brilliant the first time he had faced Brazil, did not fare so well this day. Amarildo was the first to best him, with a left-footed kick from thirty yards out, making the score 1–1 at halftime.

Twenty-four minutes into the second half, Amarildo lofted a soft, arching pass across the Czech goalmouth. Schroiff tried to grab it, missed, and Zito headed in Brazil's go-ahead goal. A few minutes later, after Schroiff knocked away a long shot, Vava pounced on it, scored, and Brazil had its second World Cup. One more and the Brazilians would gain permanent possession of the Jules Rimet Trophy.

1966 WORLD CUP: ENGLAND

Group One
England 0, Uruguay 0
France 1, Mexico 0
Uruguay 2, France 1
England 2, Mexico 0
Uruguay 0, Mexico 0
England 2, France 0

Group Two
West Germany 5, Switzerland 0
Argentina 2, Spain 1
Spain 2, Switzerland 1
Argentina 0, West Germany 0
Argentina 2, Switzerland 0
West Germany 2, Spain 1

Group Three
Brazil 2, Bulgaria 0
Portugal 3, Hungary 1
Hungary 3, Brazil 1
Portugal 3, Bulgaria 0
Portugal 3, Brazil 1
Hungary 3, Bulgaria 1

Group Four
U.S.S.R. 3, North Korea 0
Italy 2, Chile 0
Chile 1, North Korea 1
U.S.S.R. 1, Italy 0
North Korea 1, Italy 0
U.S.S.R. 2, Chile 1

Quarterfinals
England 1, Argentina 0
West Germany 4, Uruguay 0
Portugal 5, North Korea 3
U.S.S.R. 2, Hungary 1

Semifinals
West Germany 2, U.S.S.R. 1
England 2, Portugal 1

Third Place
Portugal 2, U.S.S.R. 1

Championship
England 4, West Germany 2*
*Overtime

Like an uncontrollable virus spreading from nation to nation, defensive tactics infected soccer with a conservative style of play that transformed what might have been a sensational World Cup into a rather dreary affair with only a few sparkling moments.

Almost every team participating in the 1966 tournament kept six or seven men (not counting goal-keepers) back on defense, waiting for an opponent to make a mistake and then dashing back upfield in soccer's equivalent of basketball's fast break. On paper this was a sound strategy, but in actual competition with both teams playing careful, defensive soccer few mistakes were made—and as a consequence few goals were scored.

It was a style of play developed and perfected by the Swiss and Italians, so perhaps it was poetic justice when both teams were hoisted with their own petards. In Group Two Switzerland, not expected to accomplish much anyway, scored only one goal in three games against 4–3–3, 5–2–3, and in some instances 6–2–2 alignments. West Germany and Argentina, who played to a scoreless tie, dominated this group and advanced to the quarterfinals.

On-field violence marred the 1966 tournament. Here Pelé lies injured after having been cruelly fouled by a Bulgarian who seemed intent on crippling the great forward. A few days later, Pelé was so badly hurt in a game against Portugal he was forced to withdraw from the competition.

In Group Four were the Italians, perfectors of the *catenaccio* defense, which featured a *libero,* or sweeper, who was stationed in front of the goalie and whose job it was to seal any holes opened among the four fullbacks deployed in front of him. This strategy worked against Chile, then backfired against the Soviets, who were a bit more rugged on defense. Against North Korea, the surprise team of this tournament, it spelled disaster in the form of a 1–0 defeat.

Russia and North Korea advanced in this group, while Italy returned home to banner headlines of *Vergogna, Vergogna* (Shame, Shame) and denunciations in the Italian parliament where there were serious calls for an investigation of the coach and players who had "humiliated their nation."

The tournament's three most offensive-minded teams—Brazil, Hungary, and Portugal—were all assigned to Group Three along with a stolid, conservative Bulgarian team. Brazil beat Bulgaria in its first match, but Pelé sustained such a fearful pounding, while the referee did almost nothing to help him, that he was unable to take the field a few days later when his team lost to Hungary 3–1. He returned against Portugal only to have a pair of vicious fouls put him out of the competition again, as Brazil lost 3–1.

"I am not sad at defeat," he said afterwards, "only that I have not been allowed to play soccer. Ideal soccer has become impossible. This is terrible for the game and for the spectators who want a show. Only by allowing the other team to attack can you do so yourself. But the present negative trend chokes all this and there are only two ways to beat it: by playing the same way or by having good referees. We just happened to be unfortunate with our referees this time."

North Korea's Pak Doo Ik (left) duels Russia's Khurtsilava for the ball in a World Cup match won by the Russians 3–0.

West Germany's Uwe Seeler climbs over an Argentine to head the ball
to a teammate during game that ended in a scoreless tie.

England, under the management of Alf Ramsey, a player on its 1950 World Cup team, went through three games in Group One without surrendering a single goal. As a matter of fact, in the six games played by this group a total of only seven goals were scored as England and Uruguay advanced.

With Gordon Banks in the goalmouth, England kept its unscored-upon record intact against Argentina in the quarterfinals. This was not a pretty game; the Argentines deliberately and systematically fouled their opponents throughout. Late in the first half, the game was delayed for eleven minutes when Antonio Rattin, Argentina's captain, was ordered off the field by the referee and refused to leave. After much argument, and not a few hysterics, he finally departed and England, now playing with a one-man advantage, won 1–0 on a goal scored by Geoff Hurst with only thirteen minutes left in the game.

The North Koreans were both the surprise and mystery team of the tournament. No one knew very much about them, so rumor and fantasy surrounded their every move. It was said each team member was an officer in North Korea's armed forces, assigned to a special training camp where for years they had been drilled in the strategies, techniques, and nuances of soccer. Stamina, speed, and military precision were their onfield trademarks, and in forward Pak Doo Ik they had a striker of world-class quality.

For the first twenty minutes of their quarterfinal match against powerful Portugal, the Koreans played flawlessly and fired three goals past José Pereira, Portugal's bewildered goalkeeper. In fact, the Koreans were so good it appeared as if they had suddenly uncovered a formula for playing perfect soccer. Nothing, it seemed, could stop these muscular visitors from the Orient. Then, almost as quickly as it had been conjured, the illusion was destroyed. It was Eusebio, Portugal's Mozambique-born "Black Panther," who restored a sense of reality to the match by scoring twice before the first half came to a conclusion, and then adding two more goals in the second half to pace a remarkable Portuguese rally that resulted in a 5–3 come-from-behind victory and a place in the semifinal round.

As for the North Koreans, they vanished from the world soccer scene as quickly as they had appeared, and have not since been a factor in World Cup competition.

The Soviet Union, with Lev Yachin as its goalie, withstood Hungary's furious attacks to win 2–1, while West Germany simply overpowered Uruguay 4–0 to set up the other semifinal match. This was a game plagued with fouls and penalties, with the Germans winning 2–1 on goals by Helmut Haller and eighteen-year-old Franz Beckenbauer.

One day later, England and Portugal played a crowd-pleasing match before 100,000 demonstrative spectators in Wembley Stadium. Bobby Charlton scored twice for England, and although Eusebio became the first player in this competition to kick a ball past Gordon Banks, once wasn't enough, as England won 2–1 and a showdown with West Germany for the title was on.

No, this isn't Pelé's chorus line—it's just a photo of the great Brazilian forward (third from right) leading his team in a training exercise during the 1966 World Cup tournament.

Hungary's Meszoly (left) and Brazil's Bellini both try to get their heads in front of the ball. Bellini won this contest, but Hungary won the game 3–1.

1966 Championship Game

They still come every summer. Not as many as once did, back in the late sixties and early seventies—just a few really, but enough to be noticed. They are German tourists visiting London who trek out to the northwestern reaches of the city, thirteen stops from Piccadilly Circus on the underground's Bakerloo Line, all the way to Wembley Stadium so they can see for themselves the exact spot where "it" happened. Usually they ask to meet with the head groundskeeper who, over the years, has become accustomed to these visits. He cheerfully escorts them across the wide green field, straight to the spot where England scored its go-ahead goal in the 1966 World Cup title game against West Germany, a ball many Germans still believe never actually crossed the goal line.

The story of this championship game reaches its climax with that goal, but it really begins three years earlier, in 1963 to be exact, when England's Football Association named Alf Ramsey as manager of its national team. Ramsey, usually the most reticent of men, surprised everyone in attendance when his appointment was announced by stating categorical-

ly that England, which in previous tries had never advanced past the quarterfinals, would win the World Cup in 1966.

There was much criticism, both in print and in the pubs, of the players Ramsey selected to help make his uncharacteristically rash prediction come true. Eschewing self-centered, albeit talented, athletes in favor of hard-working team players, he chose a group of men that could be molded to his kind of game, which demanded a combination of dedication, stamina, and unselfishness.

No choice for the starting eleven was more controversial than that of Manchester United's Nobby Stiles, picked to fill a midfield position. "Stiles," recalls Ken Jones, one of England's leading sports journalists, "represented the physical democracy of soccer. Weighing less than 145 pounds, standing barely five-foot-five, missing four front teeth, he looked less like a professional athlete than any man I've ever seen on a playing field." Fortunately, looks mattered little to Ramsey; it was what Stiles had inside that counted.

As the tournament progressed it became more and more apparent that Ramsey was right and his critics wrong. Stiles provided the spark that was necessary to ignite an often workmanlike team. He was the sort of holler guy who could wake up a dozing defense or give a sudden boost to a sagging offense. In short, he provided the extra ingredient that transformed a merely good squad into a championship team.

Not that he didn't have some very talented accomplices in this endeavor. Guarding England's goal was Gordon Banks, one of the world's best at that position, and providing leadership in the defensive area was blond Bobby Moore, who always managed to remain icily calm and competent no matter how harried the going got. To assist him, Moore had three able fullbacks in Jackie Charlton, Ray Wilson, and George Cohen.

Geoff Hurst scores his third goal as England wins the 1966 World Cup with a 4–2 extra-time victory over West Germany.

In midfield with Stiles, Ramsey placed Alan Ball, a red-haired twenty-one-year-old whose ability to ignore fatigue and run all day would prove to be a decisive factor in the final game. As a third midfielder, Ramsey chose balding Bobby Charlton (Jackie's brother), England's most potent offensive weapon in the 1962 World Cup. Operating from the forward positions were Martin Peters, Roger Hunt, and Geoff Hurst, who would establish a new scoring record in the final.

Over 100,000 people, including Queen Elizabeth, filled Wembley's huge stands for the big event. Dressed in bright red jerseys—prompting a highly partisan crowd to sing "Oh when the reds, go marching in," to the tune of "When the Saints Go Marching In"—England entered the game as an odds-on (at 1–2) betting favorite.

Those who had invested a few pounds on the hometown boys must have been a little disappointed in the early going, as England fell behind after only thirteen minutes when Helmut Haller slipped a loose ball past Banks, only the second tally England's goalkeeper had allowed in six games.

The six thousand German fans tucked off in a corner were able to savor their lead for only six minutes. Then Geoff Hurst neatly bounced a free kick by Bobby Charlton off his head and into Germany's net. Neither team scored again until, with only thirteen minutes left in the second half, Hurst's shot from close in was blocked into the waiting foot of Martin Peters, who smashed it home.

It appeared England could not now be stopped. The Englishmen controlled play until the final minute, when West Germany was awarded a free kick on a questionable call by the Swiss referee. Jackie Charlton was accused of interfering with Siggi Held. England thought it was just the other way around, that Held had fouled Charlton, but the official's decision stood and on the ensuing free kick by Luther Emerich, Held got the ball and passed to Wolfgang Weber who, with only thirty seconds left, scored to tie the match and send it into a thirty-minute extra time period, the first in a World Cup title game since 1934.

Now it was time for the indefatigable Alan Ball to come into his element. Racing tirelessly up and downfield he seemed never to stop, and after ten minutes he literally ran away from a weary German defender, sent the ball across the penalty area to a waiting Hurst, and then watched his teammate kick the most controversial goal in World Cup history.

Hurst's right foot lashed out when the ball came to him, sending it on a line drive to the crossbar of Germany's goal cage. The ball hit the crossbar's underside and bounced straight down. Englishmen jumped for joy while Germans screamed in protest. The Swiss referee consulted a Soviet linesman, Tofik Bakhramov, who was positioned near the goal cage. Both agreed the ball had fallen inside the goal line. Now all England had to do was hold on for twenty more minutes.

Even Queen Elizabeth was caught up by the tension, asking her escorts again and again: "How much longer to go?" Minutes sped by as England grew stronger, taking complete control. With only seconds left, Hurst, who had already scored once with his head and once with his right foot, raced through West Germany's demoralized defense to score with his left foot, becoming the only player ever to score three goals in a World Cup title game.

As time ran out the BBC's play-by-play announcer threw British reserve to the wind and, employing a peculiarly English idiom, began to shout, "England have won it! England have won it!" While down on the field below Nobby Stiles, smiling his gap-toothed grin, danced a little jig and hugged a triumphant Alf Ramsey.

1970 WORLD CUP: MEXICO

Group One
Mexico 0, U.S.S.R. 0
Belgium 3, El Salvador 0
U.S.S.R. 4, Belgium 1
Mexico 4, El Salvador 0
U.S.S.R. 2, El Salvador 0
Mexico 1, Belgium 0

Group Two
Uruguay 2, Israel 0
Italy 1, Sweden 0
Uruguay 0, Italy 0
Sweden 1, Israel 1
Sweden 1, Uruguay 0
Italy 0, Israel 0

Group Three
England 1, Romania 0
Brazil 4, Czechoslovakia 1
Romania 2, Czechoslovakia 1
Brazil 1, England 0
England 1, Czechoslovakia 0
Brazil 3, Romania 2

Group Four
Peru 3, Bulgaria 2
West Germany 2, Morocco 1
Peru 3, Morocco 0
West Germany 5, Bulgaria 2
West Germany 3, Peru 1
Morocco 1, Bulgaria 1

Quarterfinals
West Germany 3, England 2*
Brazil 4, Peru 2
Italy 4, Mexico 1
Uruguay 1, U.S.S.R. 0*

Semifinals
Italy 4, West Germany 3*
Brazil 3, Uruguay 1

Third Place
West Germany 1, Uruguay 0

Championship
Brazil 4, Italy 1

*Overtime

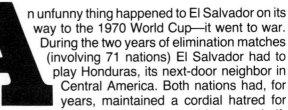

An unfunny thing happened to El Salvador on its way to the 1970 World Cup—it went to war. During the two years of elimination matches (involving 71 nations) El Salvador had to play Honduras, its next-door neighbor in Central America. Both nations had, for years, maintained a cordial hatred for each other—a hatred that was exacerbated by some half-million Salvadorans living in Honduras and competing for jobs in a dormant economy.

Each nation won at home in rough games followed by riots, which developed into border skirmishes that led to all-out war, complete with tanks and planes. Although it was jokingly referred to as "the soccer war," there was nothing funny about the results. After four days of fighting, 2,000 people had been killed and several villages laid waste. Only swift intervention by the Organization of American States brought the bloodshed to an end.

After the ceasefire had taken effect, a playoff game was staged in Mexico. El Salvador won and then defeated Haiti to advance into the final sixteen.

With that kind of prologue it was hard to predict what to expect at this World Cup. One potential trouble point emerged when Morocco qualified from Africa and announced its refusal to play Israel, the Asian-zone victor. To head off this

Some 100,000 packed Mexico City's Aztec Stadium for the opening ceremonies of the 1970 World Cup. Host team Mexico played Russia to a scoreless tie in the match that followed these festivities.

problem, the organizers assigned Israel to Group Two and Morocco to Group Four. Now the only place these comparatively weak teams could meet would be in the semifinals, a remote possibility no one wanted to contemplate.

A few nations approached the tournament as if it were a holy crusade. Mexico's President Gustavo Dìaz Ordaz told his national team: "I don't believe in the old saying about competition for the sake of competition. I want you to compete to win. To play, as they say, until death to win."

Well, FIFA's leadership decided, it was one thing if some players decided to play themselves to death, but they certainly weren't going to be allowed to try and kill each other anymore. To eliminate such incidents as the near crippling of Pelé in 1966, strict instructions were given to all tournament referees to crack down on unnecessary roughness. A new system of warning players with colored cards—one yellow, the other red—was instituted. The yellow card was a caution: it meant stop fouling. If a player failed to heed this advice, he was shown a red card. This meant get off the field, you've been ejected. It was simple and it transcended the language barrier that often separated officials and players in international matches.

Another rule change permitted substitutions, only two per game, for the first time in World Cup play. This may have been a recognition of two problems worrying the competitors, heat

and height. To accomodate European television, the games would begin at noon under a broiling sun. Then there was Mexico City's altitude. Nearly 8,000 feet above sea level, even athletes in peak condition found the city's rarified atmosphere grueling. Finally there was that venerable Mexican institution known as Montezuma's Revenge.

To avoid this malady, England's defending champions brought with them tons of frozen and canned food from home. An act that seemed prudent to the British was interpreted as an insult to Mexican cuisine by local journalists. A bit of diplomacy on the part of England's coach, Sir Alf Ramsey (knighted after 1966's triumph), might have cooled tempers. Instead, his inbred disdain for public relations and his cavalier treatment of the press only made matters worse. The night before England's game with Brazil, in Guadalajara, hundreds of people marched around the English team's hotel blowing horns and banging drums to keep the British delegation awake. The following afternoon 70,000 fans showed up for the game. Five thousand Englishmen cheered for their team. Everyone else rooted for Brazil.

Hostile fans and lack of sleep failed to weaken England's defense, impenetrable for fifty-nine minutes against the strongest attacking trio in all of soccer: Jairzinho, Tostao, and Pelé. Brazil had come close to scoring after only ten minutes of play when English goalie Gordon Banks made a sensation-

Pelé and Roberto Rivelino (leaping) combined to baffle Uruguay's defense, as Brazil won this quarterfinal match 3–1.

The joy of victory is expressed by Tostao (left), Pelé, and Jairzinho as Brazil wins its third World Cup title with a 4–1 victory over Italy.

al acrobatic save of a Pelé header. It was typical of Banks's performance. He made just one mistake that day, but one was enough for Brazil.

Pelé engineered Brazil's lone goal by artfully dribbling past several English defenders and then, at precisely the right moment, passing off to Jairzinho. Banks came out of his goalmouth to cut down the shooting angle, giving Jairzinho just enough space to rocket the ball through. England failed to score, and that was that.

Jairzinho's goal was the only one Banks surrendered in Group Three competition. The English only scored two themselves, but shutouts of Czechoslovakia and Romania sent them on to the quarterfinals along with Brazil, which had scored eight goals while giving up only three.

Mexico and the Soviet Union opened Group One competition in Mexico City's 112,000-seat Aztec Stadium by playing a scoreless tie noteworthy only for the number of fouls called. The referee stopped play repeatedly and flashed his yellow card five times. It made for a dull game, but served notice that referees would not tolerate rough play in this World Cup.

Mexico brought unexpected joy to its fans, much as Chile had done for its supporters in 1962, by registering shutout victories over El Salvador and Belgium, to advance to the quarterfinals. The Soviet Union defeated the same two teams and also advanced.

The four teams in Group Two, playing in Pueblo, managed to score a paltry total of six goals in six games. Uruguay got both its goals while defeating Israel 2–0. It was a costly victory as the Uruguayans lost the services of their best player, Pedro Rocha, who was injured and unable to return.

Israel engineered a pair of surprises, first tying Sweden and then, the real shocker, playing to a scoreless draw with Italy. Both Italy and Uruguay advanced, the latter because it had surrendered one fewer goal than Sweden, although both had identical records of one win, one loss, and one tie.

The Moroccans provided some excitement in Group Four by leading West Germany by a goal for fifty-six minutes. Then Ewu Seeler, playing in his fourth World Cup, scored the tying goal, and Gerd Müller followed with the winning tally. The Germans displayed more offense than any other team in the opening rounds, scoring ten goals in three games and advancing along with Peru. The Peruvians, who had eliminated Argentina en route to Mexico, were crowd favorites. They began with the sympathy of the spectators (Peru had recently suffered a devastating earthquake) and then quickly earned their affection with a wide-open style of play. Coached by Didi, a former member of Brazil's national team, Peru defeated Bulgaria 3–2 and Morocco 3–0, and advanced despite a 3–1 loss to West Germany.

Chants of "Me-he-co, Me-he-co" filled Aztec Stadium when Mexico met Italy in their quarterfinal match. Beginning at a peak and then heading straight up, the decibel level reached ear-shattering proportions when, after only twelve minutes, Mexico scored. Italy managed to tie though, and at halftime the score was 1–1. Then Giovanni Rivera scored once, Luigi Riva scored twice and, as the chants of "Me-he-co" faded away, Italy won 4–1.

Seventy fouls were called when the Soviet Union played Uruguay, a match forced into overtime before, with only one minute left, Uruguay got the game's only goal.

Peru played well against Brazil, getting goals from Gallardo and Cubillas, but two goals by Tostao and one each by Rivelino and Jairzinho gave the game to Brazil.

England remembered not to eat any Mexican food but forgot about not drinking the water. Montezuma struck, and he struck with a vengeance, forcing English goalie Gordon Banks to the sidelines when England played West Germany. An hour before gametime Peter Bonetti was told that he would replace Banks, who had allowed only one goal in three games.

Throughout the first half, England seemed not to miss

Two Italians guard Pelé (right), while his teammate Jairzinho moves toward the ball in final game of the 1970 World Cup.

Banks at all, beating German goalie Sepp Maier twice for a 2–0 halftime lead. Germany seemed a beaten team when its coach, Helmut Schoen, made a tactical move—switching Franz Beckenbauer from fullback to halfback—that seemed to rejuvenate his team. In an attacking position, Beckenbauer quickly displayed his effectiveness on offense by beating Bonetti for an easy goal. Then, with eight minutes left, Uwe Seeler tied the game when, with his back to the goal, he headed the ball past Bonetti.

Now, shades of 1966, the game went into overtime. West Germany had all the momentum, having come back from being two goals down, and dominated these extra minutes, winning the game on Gerd Müller's goal.

Italy and West Germany played a semifinal match that began as a cautious defensive game and ended in a wild display of offensive fireworks. Italy scored after seven minutes and then reverted to time-consuming, ball-control tactics, showing little interest in scoring more, seemingly content to protect its slender lead.

West Germany, led by Beckenbauer's total control of the midfield area, launched an all-out assault on Italy's goal in the second half, but failed to score. With time running out, Beckenbauer was brutally fouled. He fell to the turf writhing in agony. The German team doctor came running out and, while the referee kept close track of the number of minutes ticking away, bound Beckenbauer's right arm across his chest so that he could continue to play.

West Germany had failed to score after ninety minutes, but still had a chance to get a goal in the added injury time. Karl-Heinz Schnellinger capitalized on this last opportunity, scored, and the game went into extra time.

The Germans began this thirty-minute period by going on the attack. Müller intercepted a pass near Italy's goal and put West Germany ahead for the first time that afternoon. But not for long. Tarcisio Burgnich and Riva each scored, and Italy was on top again 3–2. Germany came roaring right back, and minutes later Müller headed in a pass from Seeler. Now it was Italy's turn to rally, and it did, as Rivera scored the game-winning goal to put Italy in the championship match.

Brazil and Uruguay played to decide who would be Italy's opponent. Uruguay had never been an easy team for Brazil (e.g., 1950), and would not be this time. It was like old times when Uruguay scored first and maintained its lead for most of the first half until Clodoaldo scored the equalizer minutes before halftime.

In the second half, Brazil's speed and overall talent proved too much for the Uruguayans to handle. Tostao spotted Jairzinho racing down the right side unattended, fed him a quick pass that was caught in full stride and then fired into the goal. Pelé displayed his brilliance by breaking loose and charging Uruguay's goal, drawing the goalie out of position and then passing to Rivelino, who blasted the ball into an unguarded net. Brazil was in the final game for the fourth time since World War II.

Brazil's captain, Carlos Alberto, executes a perfect sliding tackle against Italy's Alessandro Mazzola.

England's Bobby Charlton (left) leaps past West Germany's Karl Schnellinger in a game that brought together the two 1966 finalists. This time it was the Germans who won in extra time, 3–2.

1970 Championship Game

Italy had won the World Cup in 1934 and 1938. Brazil had won in 1958 and 1962. No matter which nation won this match, FIFA would have to commission a new symbol of international soccer supremacy, for the first three-time winner would gain permanent possession of that rather ugly, foot-high golden statuette called the Jules Rimet Trophy.

After Mexico had been eliminated, the Aztec Stadium crowd, in a display of Latin American solidarity, adopted Brazil as its favorite against Italy, replacing the chant of "Me-he-co, Me-he-co" with a new cry that went, "Bra-sil, Bra-sil," lending further inspiration to a team already thought to be the more talented of the two.

If anything could stop the speedy, high-powered Brazilian attack it would be the elements and, as luck would have it, rain drenched the field right up until gametime. With a field slightly muddy and slippery, both teams played cautiously at the beginning. Then, as the clouds drifted away and the turf began to dry, Brazil shifted gears and went on the attack. Its first goal began with a throw-in by Tostao. He tossed the ball to Rivelino, who lifted a floating pass to Pelé, who, although guarded closely by three defenders in front of Italy's goalmouth, leaped high into the air and headed the ball past the groping fingers of Enrico Albertosi, Italy's goalie.

Just when it looked as if Brazil were going to run away with the game, a silly error gave Italy new life. It happened when Clodoaldo carelessly passed the ball behind him deep in Brazilian territory and Italy's Roberto Boninsegna, running at full tilt, intercepted. Felix, Brazil's goalkeeper, came out to stop him, but the blue-shirted Italian swerved, got by, and scored easily.

That was the only bit of offensive flash Italy would ignite this day. Most of their attacking strategy seemed based on trying to get the ball to Luigi ("Gigi") Riva—who back home was the highest-paid player in the history of Italian soccer. "You could kill Riva," said one disgruntled Italian, "and everyone would still pass to him." Brazil was not oblivious to this attitude. They stopped Riva, and Italy did not score again.

Brazil, with its galaxy of stars, had no such problems. They were a team of great individual athletes who managed to mesh together perfectly, accommodating one another's strengths and weaknesses. The overall superiority of this unit became apparent in the second half when, with the score tied at one apiece, Brazil simply took charge of the game.

Gerson, a short, balding midfielder, put Brazil in control with his passing and playmaking. He even got Brazil's go-ahead goal on a play that began with his passing to Everaldo, who put the ball ahead to Jairzinho, who passed back to Gerson, who scored.

Brazil's third goal was also instigated by Gerson, who spotted Pelé relatively unattended near the Italian goalmouth. Pelé again leaped high to take the pass, but instead of heading it toward the goal he sent the ball to Jairzinho, who scored with ease.

Brazil's final goal was a gift to team captain Carlos Alberto, primarily a defensive player who seldom scored. Another series of precise passes had given Pelé the ball near Italy's goal. He had an easy shot but seemed to sense Alberto charging downfield behind him. With perfect timing, Pelé sent the ball out to Alberto who blasted it past Albertosi to make the score Brazil 4, Italy 1.

No sooner had the final whistle blown than all of Brazil erupted into an orgy of celebration. When they returned home to a hero's reception, each player was awarded a $20,000 bonus at a luncheon in Brasilia's Palace of the Dawn.

Some 6,350 miles away, Italians accepted the fact that a better team had won and celebrated Italy's second-place finish. "Bravos, Thanks All The Same," read a banner headline on Rome's *Il Messaggero*. And an estimated 15,000 fans greeted the team's return at Rome's Fiumicino Airport with cheers of *"Grazie! Grazie!"* It was a far better reception than the Italian team would receive four years hence, when it returned home from the 1974 World Cup.

1974 WORLD CUP: WEST GERMANY

Group One
West Germany 1, Chile 0
East Germany 2, Australia 0
West Germany 3, Australia 0
East Germany 1, Chile 1
East Germany 1, West Germany 0
Chile 0, Australia 0

Group Two
Brazil 0, Yugoslavia 0
Scotland 2, Zaïre 0
Brazil 0, Scotland 0
Yugoslavia 9, Zaïre 0
Scotland 1, Yugoslavia 1
Brazil 3, Zaïre 0

Group Three
Netherlands 2, Uruguay 0
Sweden 0, Bulgaria 0
Netherlands 0, Sweden 0
Bulgaria 1, Uruguay 1
Netherlands 4, Bulgaria 1
Sweden 3, Uruguay 0

Group Four
Italy 3, Haiti 1
Poland 3, Argentina 2
Argentina 1, Italy 1
Poland 7, Haiti 0
Argentina 4, Haiti 1
Poland 2, Italy 1

Second Round

Group A
Brazil 1, East Germany 0
Netherlands 4, Argentina 0
Netherlands 2, East Germany 0
Brazil 2, Argentina 1
Netherlands 2, Brazil 0
Argentina 1, East Germany 1

Group B
Poland 1, Sweden 0
West Germany 2, Yugoslavia 0
Poland 2, Yugoslavia 1
West Germany 4, Sweden 2
Sweden 2, Yugoslavia 1
West Germany 1, Poland 0

Third Place
Poland 1, Brazil 0

Championship
West Germany 2, Netherlands 1

Scotland's Denis Law (right) lost this battle, but his team won the game, defeating Zaïre 2–0.

For 1974, the World Cup had a new trophy that was a fourteen-inch-high creation of solid eighteen-carat gold, several new teams, and a host of new problems involving politics and money—especially money.

Host West Germany and defending champion Brazil were given automatic berths among the final sixteen. That left 126 prospective tenants competing for a mere fourteen vacancies. Many found fault with the selection system. In some of the zones established by FIFA, traditional soccer powers battled amongst themselves for advancement. In others, the inexperienced triumphed over the inept. This arrangement allowed three weak squads, Australia, Haiti, and Zaïre (derisively referred to as "mattress teams") to reach the final rounds while many stronger units were eliminated in much tougher divisions.

International politics lifted one team into the finals when the Soviet Union refused to play the second match of its home and home-elimination series with Chile. Before the first game, a scoreless tie played in Moscow, Chile's Marxist government was toppled and President Salvador Allende killed. When Santiago's National Stadium, which had been used as a detention camp for alleged enemies of Chile's new ruling junta, was selected as the location for game two, the U.S.S.R. insisted the match be relocated to a neutral site. Negotiations broke down and FIFA issued an ultimatum to the Russians: play or forfeit. They forfeited.

Holland's Johann Neeskens writhes in agony after being kicked by Uruguay's Pablo Forlan. Luckily he recovered quickly and helped lead his team to a 2–0 victory.

That political hot potato disposed of, a new factor had to be dealt with—demands by players to share the wealth. When England won the World Cup in 1966, each member of its triumphant team received a bonus of $5,000. By 1974, any winning player offered a sum that small would have been insulted.

The Netherlands had not reached the World Cup finals since 1938. Now they had qualified but their team, a pretournament betting favorite, would not board its plane for West Germany until a suitable financial agreement was arranged. Final terms gave each player a down payment of $24,000, plus 70 per cent of the earnings realized by the Dutch Football Association from gate receipts and other revenues.

This was not an isolated incident. West Germany's players were promised $37,000 each if they won the title, while the Italians were guaranteed a cool $50,000 per man if they brought back the new trophy. Even small nations got into the big-money act. Haiti had no realistic chance of winning the tournament, but if the Haitians did manage to at least tie one game, President Jean Claude ("Baby Doc") Duvalier would give his players $200,000 to divide amongst themselves and, if they should actually pull off a major upset and win, the ante would be raised to $300,000.

The tournament would last twenty-four days, during which thirty-eight games would be played at nine different locations throughout West Germany. With bitter memories of the massacre of eleven Israeli athletes during the Munich Olym-pics two years earlier still fresh in German minds, strict security measures were enforced at every game.

The sixteen finalists were divided into four groups. Each team would play three matches, gaining two points for a win, one for a tie. The first and second-place finishers in each group would then advance into one of two quarterfinal groups and play another three-game round-robin schedule. The winners of these divisions would then meet for the title.

This was supposed to be the tournament of "total football," a new style of play that had taken Europe by storm. Simply stated this meant a team would commit everyone except its goalie to the offense when it went on the attack; it was a wide-open, fan-pleasing game that produced lots of goals. At least, that is what was supposed to happen. When actual play began, almost everyone reverted to the cautious, conservative style of play that had been the hallmark of recent World Cup action.

West Germany was one of the teams that seemed to forget all about its pretournament advocacy of total football. The West Germans wanted to win, not just for the money, but also, as the host team, out of a sense of national pride. *Kein Wein, kein Weib, wenig Gesang* ("no wine, no women, little song") was the team motto. They may well have added "no flair" after their showing in the opening game against Chile as they fumbled and muddled their way to a sloppy 1–0 victory before a hostile crowd of Berliners who taunted their countrymen with shouts of *"Bayerisches Schwein"* ("Bavarian pig").

These insults were prompted in part by the West Germans' poor performance and in part by the fact that there were six Bavarians on the starting team and no Berliners.

East Germany, playing in its first World Cup, was the surprise team in Group One, and actually won the division, defeating West Germany 1–0 in the process, although both teams advanced because of the point system.

"Win or die!" was the farewell message Zaïre President Mobutu Sese Seko gave his team before they departed for Germany. He also gave each player a new Volkswagen and sent them off with their own witch doctor and an ample supply of monkey meat for strength. Not surprisingly, monkey meat and magic were no substitutes for skill. The Africans were completely outclassed by their Group Two opponents, surrendering fourteen goals while scoring none themselves. They weren't killed after returning home, but President Mobuto did take back all their new cars.

The other three teams in this group—Brazil, Scotland and Yugoslavia—finished with identical records of one victory and two ties. On the basis of goals scored Yugoslavia, with a total of ten (nine of them scored against Zaïre), was awarded first place. Brazil, which had permitted no goals, was given second place over Scotland, a team that had allowed one in a 1–1 tie with Yugoslavia.

The Netherlands, led by Johann Cruyff—who had recently been part of a $2.2 million transfer deal that sent him from Ajax-Amsterdam to Barcelona*—was the class team of Group Three. The Dutch beat Uruguay 2–0 on a pair of goals scored by Johnny Rep in a rough-and-tumble opening game. Uruguay's Montero Castillo was suspended from the tournament for kicking Dutchmen, but Cruyff, a major target for violent tackles, was contemptuous of attempts to intimidate

*Ajax was paid $1.2 million, while Cruyff received a $1 million bonus for signing with Barcelona.

It looks as if Brazil's Jairzinho has scored here as he slips the ball past Yugoslav goalie Vladislav Bozicevic. But the ball rolled by the goalcage and the game ended in a scoreless tie.

him, saying, "I'm too fast for these old men. When they stuck out their legs I just stepped over them."

Only Sweden managed to put a damper on Holland's total-football offense, playing the Dutchmen to a scoreless tie and advancing to the next round with another 0–0 tie against Bulgaria and a 3–0 victory over Uruguay.

Poland, which had eliminated England in the preliminaries, was the unexpected power in Group Three. In their first game the Poles ripped through a normally tough Argentine defense for two goals before the match was eight minutes old. Argentina, led by the talented Carlos Babington, rallied, but Poland scored once more to win 3–2.

Italian goalie Dino Zoff had not permitted a goal in eleven consecutive international games until Haiti's Emmanuel Sanon penetrated Italy's defense to give his team a 1–0 lead over the *azzurri* (so-called because of their royal-blue jerseys) after only five minutes of play. Following a brief celebration (the

Haitians would divide $300,000 if they won), Haiti succumbed to Italy's overpowering attack and lost 3–1.

It was, in retrospect, the *azzurri's* best performance. They were tied by Argentina and then defeated 2–1 by Poland. Upon returning home the Italians tried to sneak out of Milan's airport in cars flanked by two busloads of armed carabinieri, but nothing could protect them from a stone-throwing mob shrieking, *"Buffoni! Buffoni!"*

Poland, undefeated and untied, advanced along with Argentina, which was promoted because it had scored more goals than Italy.

Playing without Pelé, who after taking part in four World Cups had retired from international competition, Brazil was a pale shadow of the powerful offensive unit that had been so dominant in 1970. Operating from a sterile, 4-4-2 formation with four players back, four in midfield, and only two in an attacking position, the Brazilians did not generate much

West German captain Franz Beckenbauer gets a pass by the flying form of Holland's Van Hanegem in the 1974 World Cup championship game.

offense. A goal by Rivelino lifted them past East Germany 1–0, and a few days later they managed to squeak past Argentina, 2–1. But against the total football concept of the Netherlands (ten men up on offense, ten men back on defense), the Brazilians were simply outclassed. Frustrated by a failure to score, they resorted to a deliberate policy of violence, a tactic that had so often been employed against Brazil when it had the world's most potent attacking unit. Annoyed, but not intimidated, the Dutch shook off a series of fouls and, with goals by Johann Neeskens and Cruyff, advanced to the championship game with a 2–0 victory.

West Germany won its first two games in the other playoff group, turning back Yugoslavia 2–0, and then winning a seesaw battle with Sweden 4–2. The two teams had traded goals and the lead until, with twelve minutes left, a goal by Rainer Bonhof put the Germans ahead for keeps.

Poland, a team that combined speed with stamina, continued to play impressively with victories over Sweden and Yugoslavia and moved to Frankfurt for a showdown match with West Germany. Hours before gametime it began to pour, and despite a valiant effort by the Frankfurt fire brigade to drain the field, parts of it were still under water when play began. Although the muddy pitch hampered their fast-paced attack, Poland carried the game to Germany and might have taken a quick lead had not Grzegorz Lato slipped twice as he bore down unopposed on goalie Sepp Maier.

Seven minutes into the second half the West Germans were awarded a penalty kick. Uli Hoeness sent a rocket toward the goalmouth and watched helplessly as Polish goalie Jan Tomaszewski plucked it out of the air. Instead of demoralizing them, that save seemed to inspire the Germans, who remained on the attack. Only fourteen minutes were left when Bonhof spotted Gerd Müller unguarded near the Polish goal. Müller, who had been nicknamed "Der Bomber" for his shooting ability, sent a low shot that flew across the mud and into a corner of the Polish goal. For the third time in six World Cup tournaments since 1954 West Germany was in the championship game.

Johann Neeskens converts the first penalty kick ever awarded in a World Cup championship game.

A happy group of West Germans surround Gerd Müller after he scored the winning goal in their 2–1 victory over the Netherlands. From the left, Jurgen Grabowski, Franz Beckenbauer, Müller, Wolfgang Overath, and Paul Breitner.

1974 Championship Game

On July 6th, Poland captured third place by defeating Brazil 1–0 on a goal by Grzegorz Lato, his seventh of the tournament. One day later, 80,000 fans and 2,200 working journalists filtered through a screen of 3,000 security men to fill Munich's Olympic Stadium for the championship game.

Six members of West Germany's team were also members of Bayern Munich and were playing on their club's home field before a highly partisan crowd, an atmosphere that should have given them an early edge. Instead, Germany found itself one goal behind before any of its players even had an opportunity to touch the ball.

The Dutch kicked off and passed the ball amongst themselves, kicking it back and forth fifteen times before Johann Cruyff took it and sped toward Germany's goal. He was two feet inside the penalty area when, in an act of sheer desperation, Uli Hoeness tripped him from behind.

For the first time ever, a penalty kick was awarded in a World Cup championship contest. From the white penalty spot located just twelve yards from Germany's goal Johann Neeskins hammered a shot straight at Sepp Maier who, guessing incorrectly, had dived to his right.

After only eighty seconds the Dutch led 1–0, but history was against them, for in six of the previous nine title matches the losing team had scored first.

The shock of falling behind so quickly seemed to galvanize Germany while causing Holland's orange-shirted players to, perhaps unconsciously, relax. While the Dutch seemed to wander, the Germans regrouped and attacked. Twenty min-

utes passed and suddenly the scales were balanced when English referee Jack Taylor ruled that Wim Jansen had tripped Bernd Holzenbein in Holland's penalty area. Now Paul Breitner would get an unobstructed shot, which he quickly converted, beating Dutch goalie Jon Jongbloed.

Neither team managed another goal until two minutes before halftime when Holland committed a fatal error, leaving Gerd Müller unmarked near their penalty area. Rainer Bonhof spotted him before the Dutch did and fired a pass to Der Bomber who quickly hooked it past Jongbloed. It was Müller's fourth goal of this tournament and his fourteenth in World Cup competition, a new scoring record.

Sepp Maier must have felt he was a shooting-gallery target throughout the second half as the entire Dutch team went on the attack, bombarding him with shot after shot from all angles. But Maier and his teammates—especially Franz Beckenbauer, Berti Vogts, Wolfgang Overath, Breitner, and Bonhof—caught, kicked, or headed away every Dutch attempt to tie the game. The Dutch attack was so overwhelming that West Germany managed but one shot on goal in the last forty-five minutes of play.

No matter, West Germany had all the goals it would need and soon, their white shirts gray with sweat, the German players were circling the field in a victory lap, led by team captain Franz Beckenbauer, who trotted along holding up the new World Cup trophy. It would belong to West Germany until 1978, when sixteen teams gathered in Argentina and began the process of selecting a champion all over again.

1978 WORLD CUP: ARGENTINA

First Round

Group One
Italy 2, France 1
Argentina 2, Hungary 1
Italy 3, Hungary 1
Argentina 2, France 1
France 3, Hungary 1
Italy 1, Argentina 0

Group Two
West Germany 0, Poland 0
Tunisia 3, Mexico 1
Poland 1, Tunisia 0
West Germany 6, Mexico 0
Poland 3, Mexico 1
West Germany 0, Tunisia 0

Group Three
Austria 2, Spain 1
Brazil 1, Sweden 1
Brazil 0, Spain 0
Austria 1, Sweden 0
Spain 1, Sweden 0
Brazil 1, Austria 0

Group Four
Peru 3, Scotland 1
Netherlands 3, Iran 0
Scotland 1, Iran 1
Netherlands 0, Peru 0
Peru 4, Iran 1
Scotland 3, Netherlands 2

Second Round

Group A
Italy 0, West Germany 0
Netherlands 5, Austria 1
Italy 1, Austria 0
Netherlands 2, West Germany 2
Austria 3, West Germany 2
Netherlands 2, Italy 1

Group B
Brazil 3, Peru 0
Argentina 2, Poland 0
Poland 1, Peru 0
Brazil 0, Argentina 0
Brazil 3, Poland 1
Argentina 6, Peru 0

Third Place
Brazil 2, Italy 1

Championship
Argentina 3, Netherlands 1*
* Overtime

Recognizing its value as a means of boosting national morale while at the same time providing their regime with a valuable tool for international propaganda, Argentina's hard-nosed military rulers put on a happy face for *El Mundial '78*. Explained junta member Admiral Emilio Massera, "The tournament is a magnificent window for the world to see that Argentina is a country that only aspires to live in peace and security."

The impoverished Argentine treasury was tapped for $700 million so that three new stadiums could be constructed and three old ones refurbished. The money also paid for the nation's first color-television broadcasting system, a sophisticated international telecommunications network, and the complete renovation of Buenos Aires' Ezeiza Airport.

Argentinians were bombarded with tv commercials urging them to welcome foreigners, and even the nation's security police received special lessons in etiquette. Sidearms, they were admonished, were to be holstered, not brandished as had been the custom.

Although spoilsports such as Amnesty International tried to organize a boycott of the tournament—by pointing out that 15,000 persons had disappeared since the junta seized control in 1976—the games began as scheduled with only a couple of important absentees: West Germany's Franz Beckenbauer and Holland's Johann Cruyff, the major stars of the 1974 World Cup.

Beckenbauer's new club, the NASL's Cosmos, refused to release him for the tournament, while Cruyff announced his retirement from the Dutch national team for "personal" reasons that included an often-expressed fear of being kidnapped by political terrorists.

Matches were to be played in five different cities: Córdoba and Rosario in the north, Mendoza in the west, the seaside resort of Mar del Plata in the south and, of course, in the great capital city of Buenos Aires. Play began on June 1st and ran through the 25th. It was late autumn in Argentina, and the weather was brisk and cool in the north and damp and chilly in the south.

The sixteen finalists were assigned by lot to one of four groups, where each would play a three-game, round-robin schedule. Victories were worth two points, ties one. The two leaders in each group would win promotion to the second round of the tournament.

France, making its first appearance in the World Cup finals since 1966, was unlucky in the lottery, drawing an assignment to Group One—which proved to be the strongest of the first-round leagues with such powerful teams as Argentina, Italy, and Hungary.

Luck seemed to be against France from the very beginning. Before he left for the tournament, two men tried to kidnap French coach Michel Hidalgo (Cruyff's fears may not have been so farfetched after all), but the physically fit team leader managed to fight off his would-be captors and escape.

Then Hidalgo had to put down a revolt among his athletes, who threatened not to play their opening match against Italy unless one of the team's sponsors, Adidas, upped their promotional pay. When their demands were refused the players, in a fit of pique, painted over the Adidas three-stripe trademark on their shoes.

Once on the field, France performed well and needed a mere thirty seconds to score against Italy on a header by Bernard Lacombe. Although in the end the Italians proved too strong for France—as did Argentina two days later—the French played a crowd-pleasing, wide-open brand of soccer and had three outstanding performers in midfielder Michel Platini, forward Didier Six, and defender Marius Tresor, a native of Martinique who served as team captain.

Had France been in another group it might have gone farther, but as it was, the French were eliminated—along with winless Hungary—while Italy and Argentina advanced.

In Group Two, Tunisia became the first African team ever to win a match in the finals when it defeated Mexico 3–1. The Tunisians fielded a young team coached by Omar Sharif look-alike Majid Chetali. Getting outstanding performances from Temime Lahzami, Ali Kaabi, Moktar Dhouib, Tarak Dhiab, and Raouf Ben Aziza, the Tunisians threw a scare into Poland before losing 1–0 and played defending champion West Germany to a scoreless tie. Poland finished first in this group while West Germany, which did not surrender a single goal in its three games, came in second. Tunisia was eliminated along with a Mexican squad that lost all three of its matches.

Pretournament favorite Brazil was assigned to Group Three and made the odds-makers look misguided in the early going. First came a 1–1 tie with Sweden, and then a scoreless tie with Spain. Brazilian fans who had made the trip south reacted by carrying the burning effigy of coach Claudio Coutinho through the streets of Mar del Plata, while Pelé, covering the games for Venezuelan television, groaned: "Brazil, my beloved Brazil, has given me cause to weep. I hate to sit in the press box. I want to play myself. I feel so impotent . . ."

Brazil did manage to finish in a tie with Austria for first place in this group, but only after defeating the Austrians 1–0 while team captain and midfield star Roberto Rivelino watched from the sidelines, immobilized by an ankle injury. Winless Sweden and Spain, whose lone victory came over Sweden, were both eliminated.

Scotland provided Group Four with two surprisingly inept performances, a breath of scandal, and some comic relief. First the Scots were upset 3–1 by Peru and then received a severe blow to their morale when a routine drug test revealed that left-winger Willie Johnston had used fencafamine, an amphetamine that is one of 460 drugs proscribed by FIFA. Johnston flew home in disgrace, barred for life from Scotland's national team.

After lightly regarded Iran played Scotland to a 1–1 tie, the *Scottish Daily Express* put everything in perspective by heading the game story with four-inch letters that proclaimed, "End Of The World." After that same match, fourteen Scottish fans were detained by police in Córdoba for spitting, making obscene gestures, and shouting threats—at members of their own team.

Peru advanced from this group along with the Netherlands, but not before Scotland saved some face by defeating the Dutchmen 3–2. In that match, Scottish midfield leader Archie Gemmill, a balding, stocky, thirty-one-year-old, scored two

Austria's Robert Sara (left) and Bruno Pezzey battle West Germany's Rolf Ruessmann for the ball. The Austrians won the ball and the second-round match 3–2.

goals. His second was a thing of beauty that saw Gemmill weave like an eel through three close-marking defenders and then chip the ball past Dutch goalkeeper Jan Jongbloed.

Round two began with Italy, West Germany, the Netherlands, and Austria in Group A, and Brazil, Argentina, Peru, and Poland in Group B. After completing a round-robin schedule, the winner of each group would play for the championship and the runners-up would meet for third place.

A dense fog engulfed Buenos Aires' River Plate Stadium when Italy met West Germany, and the weather seemed perfectly suited to the negative defensive strategy conceived by Helmut Schoen, in his fifteenth and final year as coach of the German team.

Missing the field generalship of Beckenbauer and the goal-scoring talent of Gerd Müller—who at thirty-four had retired from international play—Schoen had his troops concentrate on keeping the opposition from scoring, rather than trying to score themselves. The plan half worked. Goalkeeper Sepp Maier established a new World Cup record by playing 476 consecutive minutes (dating back to the 1974 title match) without surrendering a goal. On the other hand, Maier's teammates were shut out three times and six of their ten goals came against Mexico, the only team West Germany managed to defeat.

For Italy it had not, by any standards, been a very good year. In May, former Prime Minister Aldo Moro was murdered by terrorists who had kidnapped him nearly two months earlier. Then the republic's president resigned amidst charges of corruption, and finally, as if to add a note of the ridiculous, thieves broke into the headquarters of the Italian Football League in Milan and stole $8,000 worth of silver trophies.

But like a ray of sunlight piercing thick clouds, the Italian team did manage to bring some cheer into the lives of their depressed fellow citizens. Under the guidance of coach Enrico Bearzot, the *azzurri* abandoned the sterile defensive tactics that had served them so poorly in 1974 and adopted a new attacking style that sent swarms of blue shirts pouring into the enemy's penalty area.

With a superb front line of Franco Causio, Paolo Rossi, and Roberto Bettega leading the way, Italy won all three of its first-round games; it was the only team to do so, and completely outplayed West Germany in a match that ended in a scoreless tie.

Although Austria lost to Italy 1–0, the Austrians did better than expected. Their best moment came when, sparked by the goal-scoring ability of forwards Wilhelm Kreuz and Johann Krankl, they upset West Germany 3–2 in a match that had the folks back home in Vienna cheering over their mid-morning *kaffee mit schlag.*

Unfortunately for the Austrians, they had to play Holland on the day its potent Dutch whirl offense began spinning away to perfection. Forewards, midfielders, and defenders all attacked and peppered Austria's goal with shots from all directions. The result was a 5–1 victory for the Netherlands.

Finally, there was a showdown match between Holland and Italy to decide who would represent Group A in the championship game. For forty-five minutes, Italy was indisputably the better team. Veteran Dino Zoff, at thirty-six still one of the world's best at his position, was a stone wall in goal. Defenders Claudio Gentile and Gaetano Scirea let few attackers get near Zoff, and fair-haired Romeo Benetti was responsible for Italy's complete domination of the midfield area.

Despite its clear superiority, Italy managed to score only once and that was when Holland's Erny Brandts got involved in a struggle for the ball with Bettega and accidentally kicked it into his own goal.

Brandts redeemed himself six minutes into the second half when he scored from twenty-five yards out. After that, it was all Holland. The Van De Kerkhof twins, Willie and Rene, Johann Neeskens, and Arie Haan seized control of midfield, slamming the door on each offensive thrust before the Italians could generate any momentum.

It was Haan who scored his team's winning goal—a thirty-five-yard cannonball that ricocheted wildly off the left post making Zoff's diving attempt for a save a gallant but futile gesture—giving Holland, runners-up in 1974, another shot at the World Cup title.

Peru's success was the tournament's biggest surprise. It had one of the competition's most exciting players in midfielder Teofilo Cubillas, who scored five goals in his team's first three games, an outstanding leader in defender Hector Chumpitaz, and a marvelous goalkeeper in Ramon Quiroga. Unfortunately, it was only a matter of time before the Peruvian bubble burst, and that time came in the second round when Peru lost all three of its matches.

Poland had one of the oldest teams in the World Cup and,

as had been expected, the Poles simply ran out of steam in the second round, edging Peru 1–0 for their only victory.

Brazil finally got its act together against Peru, winning 3–0 when José Dircue, a dynamo in midfield, scored twice and Zico converted a penalty shot.

Argentine coach Cesar Luis Menotti worked hard to mold a group of flamboyant individuals into one hard-working, disciplined unit and, to the surprise of many in his own country, he succeeded. Argentina swept past its first two opponents, stumbled against Italy, and then recovered to defeat Poland 2–0.

This led to a face-to-face confrontation with Brazil in the port city of Rosario before 41,000 hysterical spectators in a stadium known as the "Devil's kettle" because of the close proximity of fans to field. In could have been a classic match, instead it was a nasty display of fury and spite. Hungarian referee Karoly Palotai flashed his yellow card four times, and one particularly crunching tackle sent Argentina's midfield ace Osvaldo Ardiles hobbling off with an injured leg seconds before a scoreless first half ended.

Without Ardiles to guide it, Argentina's offense floundered. Brazil, meanwhile, was having troubles of its own, and the game ended with neither team able to score. As a result, there was the unattractive possibility of the Group B winner being selected on the basis of goal differential. When Brazil beat Poland 3–1 on the afternoon of June 21st, it meant Argentina would have to defeat Peru by more than four goals that evening in order to advance. The Argentines proved up to their task and, with forwards Mario Kempes and Leopoldo Luque scoring two goals each, routed the Peruvians 6–0. Thus, for the seventh time in eleven tournaments the host team reached the championship match of the World Cup.

Meanwhile, Brazil defeated Italy 2–1 for third-place honors and finished with a record of four wins and three ties—the only team in the tournament not to lose a single match.

1978 Championship Game

No European team had ever won the World Cup on Latin American soil, and the Dutch players must have felt terribly lonely in their attempt at becoming the first to do so. More than 78,000 people had been packed into River Plate Stadium. A few thousand were quietly neutral, a few hundred hardy souls waved Dutch colors, and everyone else screamed their lungs out, chanting, "Ar-gen-*teen*-ah, Ar-gen-*teen*-ah," over and over again.

Still, if any team could silence this mob it was Holland. The Dutch entered the match with fourteen goals (Argentina had an equal number), five of them scored by forward Rob Rensenbrink.

Against Scotland, Rensenbrink had made a bit of history by converting a penalty kick for the one-thousandth goal scored in the World Cup. The first had been booted across by Bart McGhee of the United States in a game with Belgium forty-eight years earlier.

In addition to Rensenbrink, the Netherlands had seven veterans of the 1974 championship game in its starting lineup, and there was little chance they would be intimidated by this crowd no matter how loud it roared.

The match got off to a sour start when right from the beginning Italian referee Sergio Gonella adopted for himself the role of spectator rather than law enforcer. Both sides were guilty of a series of flagrant, and sometimes violent, fouls that went largely unpunished and disrupted the game's tempo.

Argentine coach Menotti, dapper in an elegant navy-blue

double-breasted suit, appeared outwardly serene, his inner tension exposed only by the forty cigarettes he managed to smoke during the course of the match. He had intended to limit his team to players from Argentine clubs but had made an exception in the case of Mario Kempes, who had knocked in twenty-seven goals for Valencia to lead the Spanish League in scoring.

It proved a wise move. All afternoon Kempes, his dark mane of hair flapping about, plagued the Dutch defense. With thirty-eight minutes elapsed, he took a pass from Luque, spun around one defender and sent a low kick past Jongbloed for the first half's only goal. Neither team scored again until, with only nine minutes left in regulation time, Holland's Dirk Nanninga leaped high over a group of players to head in the equalizer.

Then, with only a minute left, Rensenbrink got off a clean shot that Argentine goalie Ubaldo Fillol, brilliant throughout the tournament, had no chance of stopping. The crowd gasped as the ball slammed into the left post and then bounced harmlessly away, allowing the match to go into a thirty-minute overtime period.

In overtime, the tackling became vicious as Holland's defense toughened and Argentina continued to press forward, finally breaking through after fourteen minutes. Again it was Kempes to the rescue, as he beat a pair of Dutchmen to the ball and scored the go-ahead goal.

Right-winger Daniel Bertoni sealed the verdict with only six minutes remaining after he took a pass from Kempes and scored on a low, grass-grazing shot through a tangle of Dutchmen.

Argentina, runners-up at the first World Cup in 1930, had won the eleventh one, and the nation set off on an orgy of celebration that lasted for days while the losers began to think about the next tournament four years hence in Spain.

Argentina's Mario Kempes celebrates his first goal in the championship match with the Netherlands. Kempes was the tournament's leading goal scorer with a total of six.

4. BRITISH SOCCER

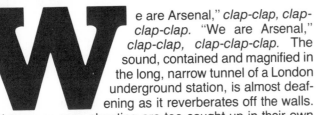

We are Arsenal," *clap-clap, clap-clap-clap.* "We are Arsenal," *clap-clap, clap-clap-clap.* The sound, contained and magnified in the long, narrow tunnel of a London underground station, is almost deafening as it reverberates off the walls. But the young men chanting are too caught up in their own emotions to notice that other, less committed travelers are cringing away, silently praying that this eardrum-shattering group, all of whom are dressed rather drably save for the bright red-and-white mufflers wound round their necks, will climb into a different car once the train finally arrives.

When the train at last does pull in, the noisemakers swarm into a car where they are greeted with much commotion by a boisterous band of compatriots, all similarly dressed, some with red-and-white scarves, others with knit hats striped with the identical bright colors. It is Saturday afternoon in England, and all over the nation groups like this one are getting ready for the day's chief activity, a league football match. This group

happens to be part of the 35,000 people who will fill Old Highbury, which since 1913 has been the home to one of England's oldest and most successful football clubs, Arsenal.

As the train reaches the Arsenal station the chants change to songs, many with obscene lyrics directed at the lifestyle and personal habits of Tommy Docherty, manager of this afternoon's opponent, Derby County. Leaving the underground station, the revelers join a thick stream of fans clogging the streets and pouring into Arsenal Stadium. It is now nearly 3:00 p.m., just a few minutes before kickoff time, and many in the crowd have just left nearby pubs where they have been fortifying themselves against the damp chill of a London November afternoon.

Standing Room Only

More than half of the 35,000 spectators will remain on their feet throughout today's match, paying 70 pence (about $1.40) for some space in the stands (called terraces in England) behind each goal line. Throughout the contest they will periodically and spontaneously—without the aid of cheer-

Alan Ball blasts a goal in for Arsenal during a 1972 game against Norwich at Old Highbury.

The famous Liverpool Kop—12,000 of the world's most demonstrative sports fans.

leaders—burst into chants or songs, and whenever anything extraordinary happens on the field the loudest roar, either of approval or despair, will come billowing forth from the terraces like a tidal wave of noise rolling across the pitch.

There are also seats in Arsenal Stadium, located in the covered stands along both touchlines and priced to sell at from one to three pounds (between two and six dollars), but the real backbone that supports English football can be found in the noisy and boisterous terraces. In England, soccer is a sport that draws most of its fans and players from those who labor for a living, rather than from those with a profession or a university education.*

It has been said this great sports division of the classes occurred in 1863, when the newly codified rules of soccer outlawed much of the rough play and physical contact that had been an integral part of the sport as it was practiced on the playing fields of Eton and Harrow. Many of the public school old boys who had helped develop the game preferred the more rugged tactics that had been ruled out and in protest

*Phil Woosnam, currently commissioner of the North American Soccer League, played in the First Division during the late fifties and early sixties following his graduation from the University of North Wales. During his playing days he was such a novelty that English sportswriters would refer to him as "the footballing B.A." In recent years there have been several college graduates playing in the football league, but they are still a definite minority.

withdrew to adopt the bone-crunching sport of rugby, which soon became the more popular game among young gentlemen fortunate enough to be born into England's upper classes. The advance of professionalism further widened the breach in the late nineteenth century, and by the time the twentieth century arrived, soccer in England was dominated by professional athletes drawn from the nation's factories, shops, and mines.

Unlike Our System

The great distinction between English soccer and professional sports in the United States is that American teams have traditionally used the country's colleges to develop football and basketball players for the professional leagues, and American baseball teams seldom sign an athlete who has not yet completed high school. In England the opposite is true. Soccer is considered a trade like any other, and most of the nation's players become attached to professional clubs before their sixteenth birthday. In fact, many first join a club as "associated schoolboys" when they are only thirteen.

Each member of the English League is permitted to sign a maximum of forty associated schoolboys who usually spend two evenings a week at the club's practice grounds receiving special coaching and training. Once a boy signs with a club, he becomes club property until team officials decide they no

How the League Is Organized

England's Football League consists of ninety-two clubs, which are divided into four divisions. The twenty-two strongest clubs are grouped in Division One, the next best twenty-two in Division Two. Divisions Three and Four consist of twenty-four clubs each. The regular league season is a long one, beginning in August and running through the winter until May. Clubs play every member of their division twice each season on a home and away basis. Teams receive two points for a victory and one for a tie. The championship of each division is awarded to the team accumulating the most points. F.A. Cup and League Cup games do not count in the standings.

At the conclusion of each season the league is reorganized. The three weakest teams in Division One, those amassing the fewest points, are relegated to Division Two, while the three best teams in that group are promoted to First Division. A similar exchange takes place betweeen Divisions Two and Three. Divisions Three and Four exchange four teams. Teams finishing on the bottom of Division Four must apply for reelection to the Football League, a process that is more than just a formality. In 1976–77, Workington finished dead last in Division Four and was replaced by Wimbledon, a semipro club that had won three consecutive Southern League championships. Listed at right are the Football League clubs as they were divided for the 1977–78 season.

First Division	Second Division
Arsenal	Blackburn Rovers
Aston Villa	Blackpool
Birmingham City	Bolton Wanderers
Bristol City	Brighton & Hove Albion
Chelsea	Bristol Rovers
Coventry City	Burnley
Derby County	Cardiff City
Everton	Charlton Athletic
Ipswich Town	Crystal Palace
Leeds United	Fulham
Leicester City	Hull City
Liverpool	Luton Town
Manchester City	Mansfield Town
Manchester United	Millwall
Middlesbrough	Notts County
Newcastle United	Oldham Athletic
Norwich City	Orient
Nottingham Forest	Sheffield United
Queen's Park Rangers	Southampton
West Bromwich Albion	Stoke City
West Ham United	Sunderland
Wolverhampton Wanderers	Tottenham Hotspur

longer want him. If the youngster is an exceptional athlete the club may offer his parents a large, and according to league rules illegal, bonus to get the boy's name on a contract. This is one of the few opportunities an English footballer—grossly underpaid by American professional sports standards—will be given to receive a great deal of money in one lump sum, sometimes as much as $25,000.

Scouting for Players

Only about one out of every ten associated schoolboys proves good enough to be offered an apprentice's contract when he reaches age sixteen (school is compulsory in England until that age). To help fill out their ranks, successful clubs maintain a network of fulltime and parttime scouts, who scour the countryside searching for promising young athletes. If a scout discovers a boy good enough to be offered an apprentice's contract, he will usually receive a bonus of about 50 pounds when the boy signs, another 75 pounds if he proves good enough to be offered a full professional contract, and an additional 150 pounds if he starts ten games for the club's first team. There are further bonuses if the player becomes a member of his country's national team.

It was such a scout who in 1961 spotted fifteen-year-old Johnny Hollins playing for a local team in Guildford and one year later signed him as an apprentice for London's Chelsea club. Hollins served a three-year apprenticeship with Chelsea, receiving seven pounds a week his first year and a one-pound raise each succeeding year.

Starting at the Bottom

As an apprentice Hollins would arrive at the Chelsea training grounds an hour before the professionals and with the other apprentices lay out shoes, warm-up suits, and towels. These housekeeping chores were followed by a two-hour practice session with the club and then a meal. Afterwards Hollins and the other apprentices had to clean and sweep the locker room before their workday was completed.

Hollins and other junior members of the Chelsea club would play under game conditions each week in the South-East Counties League. Reserve members of the club played in the Football Combination League, while the best fifteen members of the fifty-player organization participated in the Football League's First Division.

After completing his three-year apprenticeship, Hollins signed a regular professional contract and became a full member of the Chelsea club. Until 1961, salaries for soccer players were low even by English standards. The maximum salary a player could receive was twenty pounds a week, but a threatened player's strike shattered that ceiling and allowed salaries to double, and in some cases triple, overnight. Still, even today there are probably not more than twenty players in the ninety-two-club English League who earn a regular salary that exceeds $500 a week. Of course, this sum is paid weekly throughout the year, even in the short, two-month summer offseason, and it is supplemented with a bonus formula based on a team's won-lost record.

Third Division	Fourth Division
Bradford City	Aldershot
Bury	Barnsley
Cambridge United	AFC Bournemouth
Carlisle United	Brentford
Chester	Crewe Alexandra
Chesterfield	Darlington
Colchester United	Doncaster Rovers
Exeter City	Grimsby Town
Gillingham	Halifax Town
Hereford United	Hartlepool United
Lincoln City	Huddersfield Town
Oxford United	Newport County
Peterborough United	Northampton Town
Plymouth Argyle	Reading
Portsmouth	Rochdale
Port Vale	Scunthorpe United
Preston North End	Southend United
Rotherham United	Southport
Sheffield Wednesday	Stockport County
Shrewsbury Town	Swansea City
Swindon Town	Torquay United
Tranmere Rovers	Watford
Wrexham	Wimbledon
Walsall	York City

Johnny Hollins, who began his professional career as a sixteen-year-old apprentice with Chelsea, is shown here in action for Queen's Park Rangers against Birmingham City.

Laurie Cunningham became the first black to play for England when he started this international match against Scotland for players under twenty-three years of age.

Money for Points

For example, a First Division club member receives a bonus of thirty pounds every time his team earns a point (two for a victory, one for a tie). If his team is among the division's top ten, this bonus rises to fifty pounds a point and can go as high as one hundred pounds a point for each starter on a first-place team. If a player is good enough to be capped for England's national team, he receives 250 pounds each time he wears his nation's colors in an international match.

A player can also receive additional compensation if he is transferred from one club to another. After a successful ten-year career playing midfield for Chelsea—a time span that included one appearance for England against Spain in 1967—Johnny Hollins was transferred to another London club, Queens Park Rangers. A transfer is simply the sale of a player. The club making the sale receives 90 per cent of the transfer fee, while the player gets a 5 per cent share. The remaining 5 per cent goes into a players' pension fund. In recent years, English transfer fees have gone as high as $600,000 for top players.

A final word about players' salaries. Although they may seem small when compared with the huge sums some American baseball and basketball players receive, they must be viewed in the context of the English tax system, in which personal income tax rates may reach the 80 per cent bracket. An enormous salary means little to an English player when he knows that past a certain amount the government will take eight of every ten pounds he earns. Some of the nation's best athletes have gotten around this problem the same way English movie stars have; they have simply left the country. That is exactly what Kevin Keegan, England's player of the year in 1976, did in 1977 when he left Liverpool to sign a contract with SV Hamburg of the West German Bundesliga.*

Profits Are Limited

Lest there be any misunderstanding, it should be emphasized that nobody gets rich directly from soccer in Great Britain. Profits to club shareholders from the game are strictly limited by the Football Association to 7.5 per cent a year, hardly a princely return for a large investment. Only about a dozen clubs actually exceed this margin, and those that do must pour their profits back into the club to improve facilities and buy better players.

With the profit motive taken away club directors, who receive no remuneration whatsoever for their efforts, tend to

*In order to acquire Keegan, SV Hamburg had to pay Liverpool $920,000, a record transfer fee for West Germany. Keegan signed a three-year contract for $165,000 a year.

Organization of the Scottish League

The thirty-eight clubs that comprise the Scottish League are divided into three divisions. Premier Division clubs each play a thirty-six game schedule, meeting every other member of the division four times during the course of a season. The top two teams in the First and Second divisions are promoted each year, while the bottom two in the Premier and First divisions are demoted. Queen's Park of Glasgow, a Second Division team, is currently the only all-amateur club in senior British soccer. The club was founded in 1867 and its home field, Hampden Park, also serves as the official ground for Scotland's national team. In 1937, 149,547 people filled Hampden Park to watch Scotland defeat England 3–1.

For the 1977–78 season, the Scottish League was organized as follows:

Premier Division	First Division
Aberdeen	Airdrieonians
Ayr United	Alloa
Celtic	Arbroath
Clydebank	Dumbarton
Dundee United	Dundee
Hibernian	East Fife
Motherwell	Hamilton Academical
Partick Thistle	Heart of Midlothian
Rangers	Kilmarnock
St. Mirren	Montrose
	Morton
	Queen of the South
	St. Johnstone
	Stirling Albion

Second Division	
Albion Rovers	Falkirk
Berwick Rangers	Forfar Athletic
Brechin City	Meadowbank Thistle
Clyde	Queen's Park
Cowdenbeath	Raith Rovers
East Stirling	Stenhousemuir
	Stranraer

Goalkeeper Pat Jennings makes a save for Arsenal in 1977 game against Bristol City.

Dennis Tueart (right) tries an overhead scissors kick while playing for Manchester City. In 1978, Tueart joined the Cosmos for a transfer fee of $185,000 and a "signing-on bonus" of $200,000. Below, Kevin Keegan is shown in action with SV Hamburg.

The English League Cup

This is a seven-round, single-elimination tournament open only to the members of the Football League. Begun in 1960 without any of the history and tradition of the F.A. Cup, it has attracted increased attention in recent years because the winners qualify for lucrative European competitions. The 1977 final pitted Aston Villa against Everton in a match that seemed destined never to end. The two clubs met first in Wembley Stadium and played to a scoreless tie. Four days later the replay ended, after extra time, in a 1–1 tie. Nearly a month passed before another replay could be arranged. This time Aston Villa won, in extra time, 3–2.

The tournament begins in mid-August with first-round matches between Third and Fourth Division clubs. First and Second Division teams begin play in the second round. The final is usually played during the second week of March.

Two matches were needed to decide the 1978 final between Nottingham Forest and Liverpool. The first game was still knotted at 0–0 after extra time, so a replay was staged and won 1–0 by the Nottingham club.

Past Winners

1961: Aston Villa	1970: Manchester City
1962: Norwich City	1971: Tottenham Hotspur
1963: Birmingham City	1972: Stoke City
1964: Leicester City	1973: Tottenham Hotspur
1965: Chelsea	1974: Wolverhampton
1966: West Bromwich Albion	1975: Aston Villa
1967: Queen's Park Rangers	1976: Manchester City
1968: Leeds United	1977: Aston Villa
1969: Swindon Town	1978: Nottingham Forest

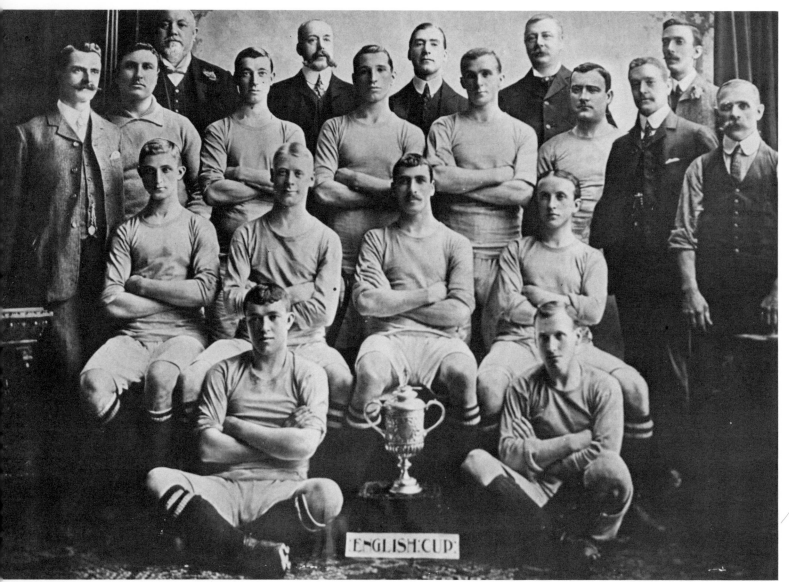

The Manchester City club of 1904.

be civic-minded individuals who perform their duties as a public service and for the prestige involved—when the club wins—with being part of a successful organization. In many instances, the club chairman will be a particular city's wealthiest businessman but, just as in American sports, business acumen does not always equate itself with the ability to build a winning team. Len Shackleton, one of England's top players in the 1950's, wrote a book upon his retirement that contained a chapter entitled: "The Average Director's Knowledge of Football." It consisted of one blank page.

Rich and Poor Clubs

Theoretically it is possible for a Fourth Division club to work its way up to First Division by putting together three consecutive winning seasons. In practice, though, such a rise from the bottom to the top is nearly impossible, and the reason is simple economics. Third and Fourth Division clubs are the financial stepchildren of English soccer. Most play in small, antiquated stadiums and must struggle each season just to meet expenses. They are helped by the fact that there is almost no live television coverage of regular league games.

Taped highlights and replays of important soccer games are televised by the British Broadcasting Company and England's commercial network. The league sells these TV rights for a lump sum, which when divided amongst the 92 clubs in 1978 came to less than $20,000 each. By contrast, in the United States each National Football League club took in approximately $5 million from the sale of television rights.

Many Third and Fourth Division clubs survive by developing outstanding players and then selling them for a large transfer fee to First and Second Division clubs—in effect functioning as farm teams for the richer clubs. In fact, many Second Division clubs survive by sending their best players to First Division teams.

Such was the case in 1977 when Orient, a Second Division team, sent Laurie Cunningham, a promising young forward and the first black to play for England's national team, to West Bromwich Albion of the First Division for a transfer fee of 110,000 pounds.

Necessity Forced Sale

"I didn't want to sell him," said then Orient manager George Petchey, "but I've been with Orient for six years and I know we can't survive without selling some of our best players."

Orient's situation is typical of many British clubs. Located in the unfashionable far eastern reaches of London, the club's home ground is Leyton Stadium, an impressive name for a facility that holds 34,000 but can only seat 3,400. The highest league position Orient has ever attained was a twenty-second-place (last) finish in the First Division in 1963.

Since then, Orient has competed in the Second Division with one brief, three-season visit to the Third. Any season in which the club can balance its books is considered a success, but often the best players must be sold to richer clubs just to make ends meet. It is a realistic view of the way soccer in England works, a view expressed in the words of manager Petchey that would seem to banish any thoughts of a low-ranking team rising to the top of the league.

The Pros Take Over

In 1876, James Lang left his native Glasgow and traveled south to make soccer history by agreeing to join the Yorkshire club Sheffield Wednesday and play in exchange for a salary. Until then soccer had been a stictly amateur affair—and in fact, remained so on paper until 1885, when professionalism was officially legalized.

Aston Villa plays Newcastle United for the 1905 F.A. Cup.

Betting on Soccer

Unlike American pro football officials who cringe in horror every time the word "gambling" is mentioned, the men who run British soccer enjoy a cozy and profitable relationship with the men who promote Britain's football pools. Every week about twelve million people take "a flutter on the pools" by filling out a coupon with their predictions on that Saturday's games. There is no equivalent of the "point spread" so popular in American football betting. All choices are recorded simply as home win, away win, or tie. Six or seven times a year the tax-free individual winnings on these pools will exceed one million dollars, and more often than not the big winner will be someone whose only interest in soccer comes from playing the pools.

In return for its cooperation in supplying the official schedules, the Football League receives about $1.5 million a year from the pool operators. This relationship is so open and above board that the Moores family, operators of one of England's largest soccer betting pools, Littlewoods, have been allowed to maintain a long and successful relationship with Everton, a Liverpool club that may well be the richest in all of English soccer. In 1978 John Moores, the head of Littlewoods, served as vice chairman of the Everton club.

Soccer pools are a popular form of gambling throughout the world. In 1977, Spanish immigrant laborer Manuel Zamora won a record $1.5 million in the West German soccer lottery. Zamora said he was not a fan and had never even seen a game during his two years in Germany. Previous to that win, the record high had been $1.2 million, won by a blind woman in São Paulo, Brazil, in 1975.

Harry Hampton (fourth from right) scored both goals as
Aston Villa defeated Newcastle United 2–0 to win the 1905
F.A. Cup.

Soccer In Northern Ireland

The high point for Northern Ireland in international play came in 1958, when the Irish qualified for the World Cup finals with a team led by midfielder Danny Blanchflower. Like most great Irish players Blanchflower went south to play in the English League, where he captained Tottenham Hotspur to its "double" in 1961. Fifteen years later Blanchflower returned home to be named manager of the national team.

Since 1966 only four teams have won the championship of the twelve-team Irish League, which was formed in 1891. The four are Glentoran, with five titles; Linfield, with four; Crusaders, with two; and Coleraine, with one.

The aftermath of a free-for-all at a Rangers-Celtic game in
1969. The match was for the Scottish F.A. Cup.

Bentley scores for England while Scotland's goalkeeper Cowan looks on helplessly during a 1950 match at Hampden Park. England won the game 1–0.

The change came after a decade of under-the-table payments that had shifted the balance of soccer power away from southern England and to the industrialized north where talented athletes poured out of the mines and factories and across the border from Scotland to play the game for a living. The great club of the 1890's was, indisputably, Birmingham's Aston Villa. The "Villans" won five league championships and two F.A. Cups between 1894 and 1899. In 1890 the Scottish League was organized, and three years later it, too, accepted professionalism as a fact of life.

Scotland's Bitter Rivals

Two Glasgow clubs, Celtic and Rangers, have dominated Scottish soccer for nearly a century and have conducted one of the bitterest rivalries in all of sports, a rivalry that has often erupted into fan violence that has resulted in injury, and sometimes death, for hundreds of supporters on both sides.

The main bone of contention between the two has nothing to do with sports, but instead stems from religious differences. Over the years Celtic has remained a predominantly Catholic club, while the Rangers have been exclusively Protestant. In 1976, the Rangers announced a dramatic change in club policy. Hoping it would curb fan violence at Celtic games, the Rangers announced that in the future they would sign players irrespective of religion and would discourage the singing of sectarian songs at Rangers-Celtic games. Whether this will make any difference still remains to be seen.

Between them Celtic and Rangers have, as of 1977, won the Scottish League championship a combined total of sixty-four times (thirty-four titles for the Rangers, and thirty for Celtic) and the Scottish F.A. Cup forty-six times (Celtic has won twenty-five times and the Rangers, twenty-one). No other club in Scotland has come close to the unique record established by these two teams. One reason is that today, just as in the past, many of the best players in Scotland travel south to play in the English League where, in general, salaries

and playing conditions have always been better. The same situation also holds true for many of the top players from Wales and Ireland.

One real indication of the quality of Scottish soccer is Scotland's record in international play against England. Between 1872 and 1977, the two nations met ninety-five times, with Scotland winning thirty-eight of the matches while England took thirty-five and twenty-two ended in a tie. It should also be noted that while Scotland qualified for the World Cup finals in both 1974 and 1978, England failed to reach the final sixteen on both occasions.

The Wee Blue Devils

Many experts still consider Scotland's 1928 team its best national squad ever. Nicknamed the "Wembley Wizards," they demolished England 5–1 behind the inspired play of four outstanding forwards; Alex Jackson, Hughie Gallacher, Alex James, and Alan Morton. None of the last three stood more than five-feet-six inches, and together they were known as the "Wee Blue Devils."

Wales also had its greatest teams in the 1920's. A squad captained by Fred Keenor won the annual series between England, Scotland, Wales, and Northern Ireland four times from 1924 to 1934. During this time span, in 1927 to be exact, Cardiff City became the only club ever to take the F.A. Cup out of England. They did it by defeating mighty Arsenal 1–0 when goalkeeper Dan Lewis, himself a Welshman, fumbled a shot into his net.

The Rise of Arsenal

England suffered her first defeat at the hands of a foreign (meaning overseas) team in 1929, losing to Spain 4–3 in Madrid. Two years later Spain visited England, but unfortunately the great Spanish goalkeeper Ricardo Zamora had one of his worst days ever and the Spaniards were easily defeated 7–1.

Spain's legendary goalkeeper Ricardo Zamora (right) shakes hands with England's Blenkinsop before 1931 match at Old Highbury. Zamora had the worst game of his career and England won 7–1.

Soccer in Wales

With a team led by center forward John Charles, who played first for Leeds United and later for Juventus of the Italian League, the Welsh national team reached the finals of the 1958 World Cup. They did well, reaching the quarterfinal round before being eliminated by Brazil, the eventual champions, 1–0.

Many of the best Welsh club teams compete in the English League, including the two that have dominated the Welsh Cup competition—Wrexham, which has won the F.A. Cup twenty times and Cardiff City, winners nineteen times.

There is a thirty-six team Welsh League, which is divided into two divisions. In 1977 the Premier Division title was won by Llanelli, while Caerau won the First Division championship.

Seven members of England's team that day were also starters for Arsenal, a club that had begun life in 1886 as an amateur squad for workers in the Woolwich Royal Arsenal. Even today, the club emblem is a cannon mounted on wagon wheels. Arsenal won the league championship four times in the 1930's, finished second once, and third once. The team included goalkeeper Frank Moss, fullbacks Eddie Hapgood and George Male, Ted Drake—a player who once scored seven times in a match against Aston Villa—at center forward, and, as its midfield leader one of the Wee Blue Devils, Alex James.

In 1938, just prior to World War II, England visited Germany for a match. The game was played in Berlin and England's players were forced to give the Nazi salute to the crowd of 110,000. Infuriated by what they had been made to do, the Englishmen then proceeded to play brilliantly and, led by

Stanley Matthews on the right wing and Cliff Bastin on the left, scored an easy 6–3 victory over the Germans.

Big Blue Dynamo

World War II brought with it a six-year suspension of league play that began after the 1938–39 season and was not lifted until 1946. The highlight of this first postwar season was a visit by a team from the Soviet Union, Moscow Dynamo. A sports columnist for the *Sunday Express* watched the visitors work out and wrote, "They are not nearly good enough to play our class professional team. . . . They have a fairly good idea of passing, but nearly all their work is done standing still, and they are so slow that you can almost hear them think."

Despite this poor advance notice, an overflow crowd packed itself into Stamford Bridge Stadium to watch the Russians play Chelsea. Clad in blue shirts and baggy blue

Bobby Charlton in action for Manchester United.

shorts, the Russians demonstrated that they could indeed think while running as they dazzled their opponents with short, precise passes and played Chelsea to a 3–3 draw.

Next, Dynamo traveled to Wales for a match with Cardiff City, then a Third Division club. With their speedy and talented forwards Kartsev, Bobrov, and Archangelski scoring almost at will, the Soviets recorded ten goals and coasted to an almost ridiculously easy victory. "The Russians," said Cardiff City's bewildered manager Cyril Spiers, "are the finest team I have ever seen. They are a match for any side in Britain. They are a machine, not an ordinary football team."

English pride had been stung and for the next match the Football Association allowed Dynamo's scheduled opponent, Arsenal, to borrow several top players from other British teams. This match, played in a pea-soup-thick fog that shrouded Old Highbury, was a rough-and-tumble affair that

the Soviets, who supplied the referee, won 4–3. After it was over, there were hard feelings on both sides. The Russians complained about the brutality of some English players, the English about the partiality of the referee who, they claimed, never blew his whistle when an Arsenal player was fouled but, said one, "if there was the slightest suspicion of a foul on a Dynamo player, he would sound a veritable *obbligato*."

An Orwellian View

Before flying home, the Russians visited Glasgow and played the Rangers to a 2–2 tie and ended their four-game tour without suffering a single defeat. For the British, who had considered themselves the supreme world power in soccer, the visit was a shocking experience.

For weeks afterwards sportswriters analyzed what had happened, but perhaps the most interesting comment was

The ball sails past Gil Merrick, England's goalkeeper, as Hungary adds another goal during its historic 6–3 victory at Wembley in 1953.

made by George Orwell who, in the weekly *Tribune,* wrote: "Now that the brief visit of the Dynamo team has come to an end, it is possible to say publicly what many people were saying privately before the Dynamos ever arrived. That is, that sport is an unfailing cause of ill will, and that if such a visit as this had any effect at all on Anglo-Soviet relations, it could only be to make them worse than before."

The success Dynamo had against British teams should have been a signal that the British Isles' mythical dominance of soccer had come to an end, but nobody seemed to pay any attention to the reality of the situation. Even the United States' 1–0 upset victory over England in the 1950 World Cup—the first World Cup a team from Great Britain had ever entered—was glossed over as a ridiculous mistake as the British continued to delude themselves about their natural superiority in a sport they claimed to have invented and perfected.

A Rude Awakening

The English approach to soccer favored stamina over skill. It was thought that the ability to control the ball was a natural attribute that could not be taught. The proper way to train for soccer, or so thought the English, was to run seemingly endless laps in an effort to increase lung power and leg strength, two attributes necessary to carry a player through the wet, muddy fields of the long British winter.

Coaching, tactics, and strategy, concepts that met with great acceptance elsewhere, were ideas that had little appeal to the powers controlling English soccer. In the end, it took one great shock to awaken England to the new realities of world soccer, and it fell to an outstanding team of Hungarian soccer players to administer that shock.

To set the stage for this pivotal event in soccer history it must be noted that in forty-five years of international competition no foreign team had ever defeated England on its native soil. Then, in the early 1950's, reports started to drift across the Channel that Hungary had put together a superteam, a group of outstanding players who were blended together by a brilliant coach.

Finally a game was scheduled and on a bleak, cold November afternoon in 1953 the two national teams met in Wembley Stadium while 100,000 people filled the stands and millions sat by their radios listening to the play by play. What they saw and heard was Hungary quickly penetrate England's defense and, after only ninety seconds, take the lead when center forward Nandor Hidegkuti fired the ball past goalkeeper Gil Merrick.

Although they fought on bravely, England was never really in the contest after those opening moments. Hidegkuti scored two more goals, Ferenc Puskas tallied twice, and Josef Boszik added one as the Hungarians, coached by Gusztav

Sebes, completely outplayed the English and rolled to an easy 6–3 victory.

Six months later the two teams met again, this time in Budapest. Playing at home the Hungarians were, if anything, better, coasting to a 7–1 win that traumatized English soccer and gave a much-needed jolt to the whole concept of coaching in England.

Busby's Tragic Babes

The great club team of the mid-1950's was the young Manchester United squad managed by Matt Busby and nicknamed "Busby's Babes." They won the league championship in 1956 and 1957 and seemed destined to become one of the greatest club teams of all time.

Then, on a stormy winter night in 1958, while returning home from a successful European Cup game in Belgrade, United's plane crashed after a refueling stop in Munich. Eight players died and two had their playing careers ended by injuries. One of the survivors of this tragic accident was a young forward named Bobby Charlton, who went on to become England's most popular soccer player in the 1960's.

In 1962, Liverpool won promotion from the Second Division and for the next six seasons clubs from Lancashire ruled the league. Everton, also located in Liverpool, won the championship in 1963, followed in successive years by Liverpool, Manchester United, Liverpool again, United again, and then Manchester City. Finally Yorkshire's Leeds United, with Billy Bremner and Johnny Giles in midfield and Peter Lorimer and Allan Clarke up front, broke this Lancashire streak and won the title in 1969.

A Change in the Rules

For more than a century the apostles of the stiff-upper-lip attitude toward adversity had fought gallantly against any change in the rules that would permit substitutions. It was felt that if fate intervened and injured one player, his remaining teammates should continue to fight on against the odds without further assistance.

Then, in 1965, a mild revolution occurred. The Football Association voted to allow each team one substitution during the course of a game. What could a team do if one of its players were injured after a substitution had already been made? Well, in that case they could carry on against the odds with a stiff upper lip. The very idea of unlimited substitution, as practiced in American football, is abhorrent to the British sports mentality.

Celtic Rules Scotland

While England was celebrating its 1966 World Cup victory, Glasgow Celtic began its unprecedented run of Scottish League and Cup championships. Under the managerial guidance of Jock Stein, "The Bhoys" won nine consecutive league titles and five successive Scottish F.A. Cups.

The highlight of this championship streak occurred in 1967, when Celtic also won the European Cup with a 2–1 victory over Inter-Milan. Celtic gained international admiration by playing an exciting brand of soccer that favored attack over defense, an exact reversal of the type of game popular in Europe during the 1960's.

In 1968, ten years after the Munich air disaster, Manchester United won the European Cup in dramatic fashion against Benfica of Lisbon. The two teams had played to a spine-chilling 1–1 tie before a packed house in Wembley Stadium when, only minutes before regulation time expired, United's goalkeeper Alex Stepney forced the match into overtime by making a sensational save of a shot by Benfica's Eusebio.

In the thirty-minute extra time period, George Best took a pass from Brian Kidd and then eluded two tacklers and the

A reunion of the Manchester United team that won the 1968 European Cup. Back row, left to right: Heno, Sadler, Stepney, Crenand, Brennan, Kidd, Burns, and Matt Busby. Front row, Charlton, Stiles, Law, Dunne, and Best.

goalkeeper to put United ahead. Minutes later Kidd helped celebrate his nineteenth birthday by scoring himself. Finally Bobby Charlton, a survivor of the 1958 crash, put the game safely out of reach with his second goal of the afternoon.

Arsenal's Double

During the 1970–71 season Arsenal became only the fourth club in history to win both the league championship and the F.A. Cup in the same season.* In order to win the league title, Arsenal had to earn twenty-seven points out of a possible thirty in its last fifteen games to edge Leeds by a single point.

Liverpool won the championship in 1973, finished second the next two seasons, and then won the title in 1976 and again in 1977, when they also won the European Cup by defeating West Germany's Borussia Möenchengladbach 3–1. In 1978 Nottingham Forest, which had just been promoted to the First Division at the start of the season, won the league championship.

After England won the World Cup in 1966, the team's manager was knighted by the queen, but even this royal endorsement was not enough to save Sir Alf Ramsey's job after England failed to qualify for the 1974 World Cup finals.

Ramsey's replacement was Don Revie, who had just completed a dozen successful seasons as the manager of Leeds United. Revie's tenure as head of the national team began with hope and optimism but ended in a wave of

*The only other clubs to accomplish this feat were: Preston North End, 1888–89; Aston Villa, 1895–96; and Tottenham Hotspur, 1960–61.

Former Liverpool manager Bill Shankly, who joined the club in the late 1950's and guided it to the top of the league, leads the Kop in a cheer.

criticism and recrimination when England failed to qualify for the 1978 Cup finals.

Just a few months before England was officially eliminated, Revie announced his resignation and signed a four-year contract for a reported $450,000 (tax-free) to coach the United Arab Emirates, an association of oil-rich states in the Persian Gulf. In December of 1977, the Football Association named Ron Greenwood, who had spent nearly fifteen years as manager of West Ham United, England's new mentor.

A Game for Hard Men

During the 1970's English soccer tended to be a hard-tackling, long-passing, physical game that often seemed to place more emphasis on strength and endurance than on skill and ability. The so-called "hard man" became a favorite of many managers who spoke euphemistically of a player's ability to "get stuck in," when in reality they were referring to the kind of brutal play and cynical fouling that have marred English soccer for the past decade, often destroying the quality of play and provoking fan violence.

A positive note has been struck by the expressed intention on the part of league officials to crack down on rough tactics through the increased employment of player suspensions. In the meantime, the English League remains one of the most competitive in the world and the F.A. Cup ranks as one of the premier attractions in all of sports.

Brian Talbot (left) of Ipswich Town is tackled by West Ham United's Keith Coleman.

Everton forward Bob Latchford (left) gets "stuck in" against a defender.

Charlton's Jim Giles (left) jumps to foil Sunderland's Ian Porterfield in 1975 match.

5. THE F.A. CUP

In 1870, Charles W. Alcock, an outstanding player and secretary of the Football Association, had a great idea. He suggested that the association sponsor an open competition to annually decide a national champion. The winner would receive a silver chalice purchased for twenty quid and christened the F.A. Cup.

More than one hundred years and three cups later, the competition remains the oldest continuous championship tournament in all of sports. It is open to every soccer club in England, be it professional, semiprofessional, or amateur. Each year several hundred clubs enter the tournament that begins in October and ends eight months later on a Saturday afternoon in May before 100,000 cheering spectators in London's Wembley Stadium.

The original F.A. Cup. In 1894 it was won by Notts County.

The preliminary and qualifying rounds are played by non-Football League teams. Those that survive advance to the first round of this single-elimination tournament where they begin to compete with clubs from the League's Third and Fourth divisions.

Things really begin to get serious in the third round when clubs from the league's First and Second divisions begin to compete. By round eight the field is narrowed down to just two teams that play to decide who will gain one year's possession of the most coveted prize in English soccer.

Somebody Swiped the Cup

Although there have been many startling upsets in cup play, with amateur teams advancing into the late rounds with victories over First and Second Division clubs, the last time an all-amateur team actually won the cup was in 1882, when the Old Etonians, led by the Hon. Arthur Kinnard—later Lord Kinnard, the high commissioner for the Church of Scotland—defeated Black Pool Olympic 2–1.

One year later Olympic, with two professionals among its eleven, won by the identical score. In 1895, Aston Villa won the cup, which has a one-quart capacity, and put it on display in the shop window of William Shillcock, a Birmingham craftsman who made soccer balls and boots.

On the evening of September 11, 1895, some blackguard broke Shillcock's shop window and stole the cup. A hue and cry was raised, but the thief got away and the cup's whereabouts remained a mystery for sixty years. Then, in February

In 1895, Aston Villa won the cup and put it on display in the window of this Birmingham shop. But someone broke the window and stole the cup.

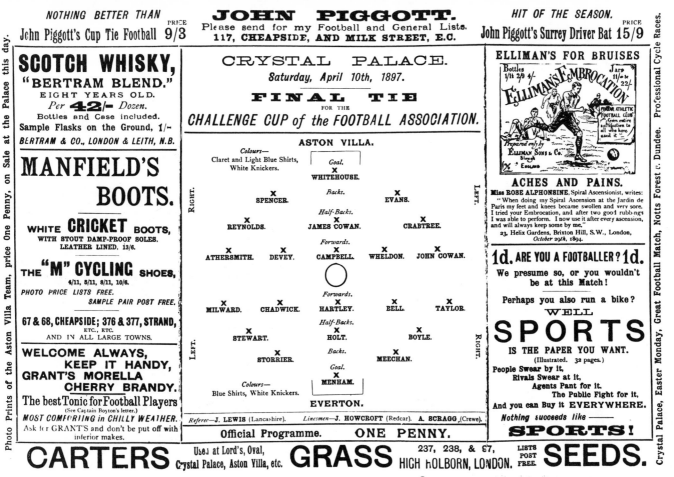

One–penny program for the 1897 F.A. Cup final between Aston Villa and Everton.

Despite this offer of a ten–pound reward, the cup was never returned.

of 1958, Harry Burge, an eighty-three-year-old resident of a Birmingham welfare hostel, confessed to the crime.

Burge, who in his lifetime had served a series of prison terms that totaled up to forty-six years, told how he and two confederates stole the cup, melted it down, and then used the silver to forge counterfeit half crowns.

Burge's confession came much too late to help Aston Villa, which was fined twenty-five pounds, the money going to purchase a new cup. In 1911, this trophy was presented to Lord Kinnard, who had played in a record nine cup finals, for his services to the game. A third cup was commissioned and this is the trophy that is still in use today.

Wembley Overflows

The first F.A. Cup final was played in 1872 at Kennington Oval, where 2,000 polite spectators watched the Wanderers defeat the Royal Engineers 1–0. In 1895 the final was moved to Crystal Palace, and by 1901 there were over 100,000 people on hand to watch Tottenham Hotspur defeat Sheffield United 3–1. At the time, the Spurs were members of the Southern League and they remain the only nonleague club to win the cup since the Football League was formed in 1888.

In 1923, recently opened Wembley Stadium was expected to be filled to its 127,000 capacity for the cup final, but hours before the game was to begin over 200,000 people had forced their way in and at kickoff time the field was covered with a sea of humanity. *The Daily Mirror* reported:

Official records will claim that the first contest to be staged at the Empire Stadium, Wembley, was the final for the Football Association Challenge Cup between West Ham United and Bolton

A newspaper account of the first F.A. Cup final ever played at Wembley Stadium. The date was April 29, 1923.

Wanderers. *The many thousands who journeyed to Wembley on Saturday will, however, long retain the memory of an earlier struggle in which the opposing elements were police and public, the ultimate victory resting with the Force, whose efforts eventually produced order from utter chaos.*

The great hero of the day was a lone policeman on a white horse who used his conspicuous mount to push the crowd back to the touchlines, where they remained throughout the match. Bolton won 2–0, the first of its three cup victories in the 1920's.

Bad Luck for Arsenal

In one of the most controversial cup finals of all time, Newcastle United defeated Arsenal 2–1 in 1932. After the game, photographs clearly showed that United had scored its winning goal off a pass that had been kicked into play from behind the goal line.

One year later Arsenal, the defending league champion, was knocked out of the cup competition 2–0 by Walsall of the Third Division in what many experts consider the greatest cup upset of all time. Three years later, Arsenal did come back to win the 1936 F.A. Cup by defeating Sheffield United 1–0.

The 1938 cup final between Preston North End and Huddersfield Town was scoreless at the end of regular time and remained that way through the first twenty-nine minutes of the thirty-minute extra time period. Then, with one minute left, the referee whistled a foul in front of Huddersfield's goal and

Preston's George Mutch booted in the penalty shot to give his team a victory.

After a six-year layoff, Derby County won the first postwar cup by defeating Charlton Athletic 4–1 in 1946. One year later, Charlton received another chance and this time cashed in on the opportunity and beat Burnley 1–0.

Matthews Wins a Medal

Newcastle United won the cup in 1951 and 1952 and again in 1955, but the big cup story of the early 1950's occurred in 1953 when Stanley Matthews and Blackpool faced the Bolton Wanderers.

Stooped, balding, bowlegged, and thirty-eight years old, Matthews had appeared with Blackpool in the cup final twice before, but both times his side had gone down to defeat—first in 1948 to Manchesterr united by a score of 4–2, and then in 1951 to Newcastle United when the score was 2–0.

Now Matthews, arguably the most popular player in English soccer history, was getting what many thought was his last chance to earn a cup-winner's medal. World War II had robbed him of six years of his playing career, but not of his ability as the sport's premier dribbler. He had an uncanny knack for controlling the ball that could bewilder defenders and literally leave them spinning helplessly as he raced downfield.

In the first half of the 1953 cup final it was not Matthews who was the star; instead that role was filled by Blackpool's Nat Lofthouse, who scored twice to give the Wanderers a 2–1 lead, with Blackpool's lone goal coming off the foot of Stan Mortensen.

Cartoonist Frank Gillett's impressions of the 1902 F.A. Cup
final between Sheffield United and Southampton.

Ten Against the Odds

Things seemed to be turning in Blackpool's favor when Bell, Bolton's left halfback, pulled up with a leg injury shortly after the second half began. This being the era before substitution, the Wanderers had to continue with ten fit men and a badly limping Bell. Then, ten minutes later, the impossible happened. Bell, barely able to walk by now, had positioned himself near Blackpool's goal and when a high-crossing pass came his way he headed it in to give Bolton a 3–1 lead. Now the real drama was about to begin.

While Bolton's fans with their north of England accents cheered their favorites with cries of "Coom on the ten men!" Matthews suddenly took charge of the game. Zigging and zagging toward Bolton's goal, faking out one defender here and side-stepping a tackle there, he ran nearly the length of the field to set up Mortensen with a perfect pass. The other Stan converted to make the score 2–3 with time fast running out. Again and again Bolton's white-shirted, short-handed defenders—another player, Ralph Banks, was now hampered by a leg cramp—repelled Blackpool, which, throughout the closing minutes, seemed always to be on the attack.

Then, just when it seemed they might hold onto their slender lead, a Wanderers foul gave Mortensen, one of the hardest dead-ball kickers in soccer, a direct free kick from only twenty yards out. Taking full advantage of this extraordinary opportunity, Mortensen drilled the ball into Bolton's net to tie the match at three apiece.

Injury time added the few extra minutes that were all Blackpool and Matthews now needed. All eyes were on his slight figure, easy to spot with his balding head and bright tangerine jersey. With an amazing delicacy he guided the ball

Stanley Matthews makes the winning pass as Blackpool defeats Bolton to win the 1953 F.A. Cup.

through the now demoralized Bolton defense. Nearing the Wanderers' goal he drew one last defender out of position and let go a perfect pass to his left winger Perry, alone in the middle, who kicked in the winning goal. At last Stanley Matthews owned an F.A. Cup-Winner's Medal.

Former POW Stars

Bert Trautmann, began World War II as a private in the German army and ended it in an English prisoner-of-war camp. He liked his keepers so much that he remained in England after the war and eventually became the goalkeeper for Manchester City. With fifteen minutes left in the 1956 cup final against Birmingham City, Trautmann hurt his neck in a goalmouth collision but refused to leave the game. Later, after his team had won the game 3–1, the injury was diagnosed as a cracked vertebra. Trautmann had played on with what amounted to a broken neck.

It was generally believed an impossible assignment for a club to win both the league championship and the F.A. Cup in the same season. Many had come close but all had failed since Aston Villa last turned the trick in 1896. Then Tottenham Hotspur, a north London club headquartered at White Hart Lane, copped both prizes in 1961. Led by Danny Blanch-flower, who went on to become manager of the Northern Ireland national team, Tottenham defeated Leicester City 2–0 in the final. In all, the Spurs have reached the cup final five times and won on every occasion.

Everton staged one of the greatest comebacks in cup history against Sheffield Wednesday in the 1966 cup final. Down by two goals, the Toffeemen stormed back with three of their own and proudly carried the F.A. Cup back to Liverpool. Two years later, they were back in Wembley again, this time to face Birmingham's West Bromwich Albion. Neither team managed a goal in regulation time and the match was decided in extra time when Albion's Jeff Astle gave his team the victory by scoring the game's only goal.

Chelsea Wins the Cup

Chelsea is a London neighborhood famous for its fashionable King's Road shops and boutiques, its resident artists, and the Royal Army Hospital, home of the blue-uniformed retired soldiers known as Chelsea pensioners. It is also home to a soccer club that for the first sixty-five years of its existence never won the F.A. Cup.

Chelsea can count among its fans many stars of the British stage and screen. One of them, Richard Attenborough,* is on the club's board of directors. When he was asked, in early 1970, about the most exciting moment in his career, he said, "It hasn't come yet. It will come when Chelsea wins the cup."

In 1967 the Blues came close, but lost in the final to Tottenham Hotspur. When they got another chance three years later they made good on it, but it wasn't easy. As a matter of fact, it required four hours of playing time, 180 minutes more than the scheduled 90 when Chelsea took the field against Leeds in the 1970 cup final.

The first match, before the usual sellout crowd at Wembley, ended in a 2–2 tie after regulation and extra time so a replay had to be staged at Old Trafford in Manchester. At the end of regulation time, the score was knotted 1–1, and once again the two weary teams went into extra time. Chelsea's Eddie Webb headed in the lone goal of this overtime period, and the London club finally had the cup victory its fans had waited for so long.

*Attenborough is not the only show-business celebrity closely associated with a league team. Rock star Elton John serves as chairman of the board for Watford, a Fourth Division club during the 1977–78 season.

West Bromwich Albion goalkeeper Jim Sanders (foreground) turns his back on the action and prays as a teammate attempts a penalty shot that tied the score in the 1954 cup final against Preston North End. After his team won the game 3–2 Sanders explained his actions. "I was praying and touching the goalpost for good luck . . . I just daren't look . . . then I heard the crowd roar and I thought, 'That's it.'"

Some Giant Killers

Hereford United of the Southern League earned itself a place in F.A. Cup history during the 1972 competition when it knocked New Castle United of the First Division out of the tournament. The two clubs had tied 2–2 in their first meeting, but Hereford, a semipro at the time, won the replay 2–1. Although later eliminated by West Ham United, Hereford had shown so well that the following season it was elected to the Football League, and by 1976 had risen to the Second Division before sliding back to the Third in 1977–78.

Arsenal won both the league championship and the cup in 1971, but the Gunners had their hopes for back-to-back cup wins dashed by Leeds United, 1–0, in 1972. One year later, it was Leeds that was in position to record two cup wins in a row.

Leeds's opponent was Sunderland, which was trying to become the first Second Division club to win the cup since West Bromwich Albion had done so forty-two years earlier in 1931. On paper it looked like Sunderland didn't have a prayer. Leeds fielded a starting eleven of current or soon-to-be full internationals,* and was generally regarded as one of the best clubs in all of Europe. Sunderland, on the other hand, had begun the season near the bottom of its division and only a late-season rally had lifted it to near the top.

Thirty-one minutes into the first half of this seeming mismatch Sunderland's Ian Porterfield scored and after that the underdogs held on for dear life. Leeds came close several times, but never closer than it did twenty minutes into the second half when Sunderland goalkeeper Jim Montgomery made a magnificent, some thought miraculous, save.

The play began when Leeds's Trevor Cherry sent a well-placed header to the right post. Montgomery went flying across the goalmouth to knock it away, but it went directly to the feet of Leeds's Peter Lorimer, who quickly fired a shot to the far post. Montgomery sprang from the ground and leaped

*For England, Scotland, Wales, or Northern Ireland.

Manchester City goalkeeper Bert Trautmann makes a save in the 1955 cup final against Newcastle United, which eventually won the match 3–1.

An injured Bert Trautmann is led off the field after his Manchester City team defeated Birmingham City 3–1 to win the cup in 1956.

Frank Gray of Leeds United holds his head in anguish after diverting the ball into the path of Manchester United's Jimmy Greenhoff (on ground), who promptly kicked it into the Leeds net. Action took place in the 1977 semifinal round. Manchester won the match, and then went on to defeat Liverpool for the cup.

back toward the ball and managed to bang it up to the underside of the bar. The B.B.C. announcer cried goal, but the ball had bounced down in front of the goal line. Sunderland regained control, hung on to its slender lead, and won.

Fulham of the Second Division reached the cup final in 1975, but lost to West Ham United 2–0. In 1976, Southampton of the Second Division emulated Sunderland's feat by upsetting heavily favored Manchester United 1–0.

One year later, it was United's chance to play the spoiler's role. Liverpool came into the game with the possibility of achieving what no club had ever done before. Already league champions, Liverpool was in position to win the F.A. Cup and, four days later, the European Champions' Cup. They did win the latter, but were stopped from taking the former when, with all three goals coming within one five-minute period at the start of the second half, Manchester United won 2–1.

In 1978, Ipswich Town won its first F.A. Cup by defeating Arsenal 1–0

The F.A. Cup Today

For one day each year Wembley is the center of attraction for Great Britain. All police leaves in London are canceled, and 2,000 Bobbies are on duty in the stadium itself while others stand guard on trains carrying fans to and from the game. Scalpers demand seventy-five dollars for tickets with a ten-dollar face value, and across the English Channel the match attracts a European television audience estimated at 400 million.

While 100,000 fans pack themselves inside Wembley thousands more loiter outside, following the game's progress on portable radios and by deciphering the roars of the crowd inside. An overnight guard is mounted outside the stadium for the express purpose of keeping fans without tickets from tunneling their way in, or scaling the huge gray walls with mountaineering equipment.

The F.A. Cup competition, though more than a century old, is still very much alive and well.

Wolverhampton's Deely jumps for joy after Blackburn's McGrath (extreme right) accidentally kicked the ball into his own net during the 1960 cup final that was eventually won by the Wolves 3–0.

Manchester United's brother team of Jimmy (left) and Brian Greenhoff celebrates United's 2–1 victory over Liverpool in 1977 cup final.

F.A. Cup Winners Through the Years

1872:	The Wanderers	1904:	Manchester City	1946:	Derby County
1873:	The Wanderers	1905:	Aston Villa	1947:	Charlton Athletic
1874:	Oxford University	1906:	Everton	1948:	Manchester United
1875:	Royal Engineers	1907:	Sheffield Wednesday	1949:	Wolverhampton Wanderers
1876:	The Wanderers	1908:	Wolverhampton Wanderers	1950:	Arsenal
1877:	The Wanderers	1909:	Manchester United	1951:	Newcastle United
1878:	The Wanderers	1910:	Newcastle United	1952:	Newcastle United
1879:	Old Etonians	1911:	Bradford City	1953:	Blackpool
1880:	Clapham Rovers	1912:	Barnsley	1954:	West Bromwich Albion
1881:	Old Carthusians	1913:	Aston Villa	1955:	Newcastle United
1882:	Old Etonians	1914:	Burnley	1956:	Manchester City
1883:	Blackburn Olympic	1915:	Sheffield United	1957:	Aston Villa
1884:	Blackburn Rovers	1920:	Aston Villa	1958:	Bolton Wanderers
1885:	Blackburn Rovers	1921:	Tottenham Hotspur	1959:	Nottingham Forest
1886:	Blackburn Rovers	1922:	Huddersfield Town	1960:	Wolverhampton Wanderers
1887:	Aston Villa	1923:	Bolton Wanderers	1961:	Tottenham Hotspur
1888:	West Bromwich Albion	1924:	Newcastle United	1962:	Tottenham Hotspur
1889:	Preston North End	1925:	Sheffield United	1963:	Manchester United
1890:	Blackburn Rovers	1926:	Bolton Wanderers	1964:	West Ham United
1891:	Blackburn Rovers	1927:	Cardiff City	1965:	Liverpool
1892:	West Bromwich Albion	1928:	Blackburn Rovers	1966:	Everton
1893:	Wolverhampton Wanderers	1929:	Bolton Wanderers	1967:	Tottenham Hotspur
1894:	Notts County	1930:	Arsenal	1968:	West Bromwich Albion
1895:	Aston Villa	1931:	West Bromwich Albion	1969:	Manchester City
1896:	Sheffield Wednesday	1932:	Newcastle United	1970:	Chelsea
1897:	Aston Villa	1933:	Everton	1971:	Arsenal
1898:	Nottingham Forest	1934:	Manchester City	1972:	Leeds United
1899:	Sheffield United	1935:	Sheffield Wednesday	1973:	Sunderland
1900:	Bury	1936:	Arsenal	1974:	Liverpool
1901:	Tottenham Hotspur	1937:	Sunderland	1975:	West Ham United
1902:	Sheffield United	1938:	Preston North End	1976:	Southampton
1903:	Bury	1939:	Portsmouth	1977:	Manchester United
				1978:	Ipswich Town

Leading English Teams

ARSENAL

Field: Arsenal Stadium, Highbury, London.
Founded: 1886.
Nickname: "Gunners."
Most Goals: 127, First Division, 1930–31.
Most Points: 66, First Division, 1930–31.
Most Appearances: George Armstrong, 500, 1960–77.
Top Scorer: Cliff Bastin, 150, 1930–47.
Titles: Football League, First Division, Champions: 1930–31, 1932–33, 1934–35, 1937–38, 1947–48, 1952–53, 1970–71; Second place: 1925–26, 1931–32, 1972–73; Second Division, Second place: 1903–04; F.A. Cup Winners: 1929–30, 1935–36, 1949–50, 1970–71; Runners-up: 1926–27, 1931–32, 1951–52, 1971–72. League Cup, Runners-up: 1967–68, 1968–69. Fairs Cup: 1969–70.
Club Colors: Red shirts with white sleeves, white shorts, red and white stockings.
Alternate Uniform: Yellow shirts with blue shorts, yellow stockings.
Record Win: 12–0, vs. Loughborough Town, 1900.
Record Loss: 0–8, vs. Loughborough Town, 1896.

ASTON VILLA

Field: Villa Park, Birmingham.
Founded: 1874.
Nickname: "The Villans."
Most Goals: 128, First Division, 1930–31.
Most Points: 70, Third Division, 1971–72.
Most Appearances: Charlie Aitken, 560, 1961–76.
Top Scorer: 213, Harry Hampton, 1904–20; and Billy Walker, 1919–34.
Titles: Football League, First Division, Champions: 1893–94, 1895–96, 1898–99, 1899–1900, 1909–10; Second place: 1888–89, 1902–03, 1907–08, 1910–11, 1912–13, 1913–14, 1930–31, 1932–33. Second Division, Champions: 1937–38, 1959–60; Second place: 1974–75; Third Division, Champions: 1971–72. F.A. Cup Winners: 1887, 1895, 1897, 1905, 1913, 1920, 1957; Runners-up: 1892, 1924. League Cup, Winners: 1961, 1975, 1977.
Club Colors: Claret shirts with light blue sleeves, white shorts, blue stockings.
Alternate Uniform: White shirts with claret and light blue collar and cuffs, blue shorts, white stockings.
Record Win: 13–0, vs. Wednesbury Old Athletic, 1886.
Record Loss: 1–8, vs. Blackburn Rovers, 1888.

BIRMINGHAM CITY

Field: St. Andrews, Birmingham.
Founded: 1875.
Nickname: "Blues."
Most Goals: 103, Second Division, 1893–94 (28-game season).
Most Points: 59, Second Division, 1947–48.
Most Appearances: Gil Merrick, 486, 1946–60.
Top Scorer: Joe Bradford, 249, 1920–35.
Titles: Football League, First Division, best season, 1955-56 (6th); Second Division, Champions: 1892-93, 1920-21, 1947-48, 1954-55; Second place: 1893-94, 1900-01, 1902-03, 1971-72; F.A. Cup, Runners-up: 1931, 1956, League Cup Winners: 1963.
Club Colors: Royal blue shirts, three vertical stripes on sleeves, white shorts blue trim, white stockings with blue trim.
Alternate Uniform: Yellow shirts, three vertical blue stripes on sleeves, yellow shorts and yellow stockings with blue trim.
Record Win: 12–0, vs. Walsall Town Swifts, 1892; and Doncaster Rovers, 1903.
Record Loss: 1–9, vs. Sheffield Wednesday, 1930.

BLACKBURN ROVERS

Field: Ewood Park, Blackburn.
Founded: 1875.
Nickname: "Blue and Whites."
Most Goals: 112, Second Division, 1954–55.
Most Points: 60, Third Division, 1974–75.
Most Appearances: Ronnie Clayton, 580, 1950–69.
Top Scorer: Tommy Briggs, 140, 1952–58.
Titles: Football League, First Division Champions: 1911–12, 1913–14; Second Division Champions: 1938–39, Second Place, 1957–58; Third Division Champions: 1974–75; F.A. Cup Winners: 1884, 1885, 1886, 1890, 1891, 1928; Runners-up: 1882, 1960.
Club Colors: Blue and white shirts, white shorts, blue stockings.
Alternate Uniform: Red shirts, blue shorts, red stockings.
Record Win: 11–0, vs. Rossendale United, 1885.
Record Loss: 0–8, vs. Arsenal, 1933.

BLACKPOOL

Field: Bloomfield Rd. Ground, Blackpool.
Founded: 1887.
Nickname: "The Seasiders."
Most Goals: 98, Second Division, 1929–30.
Most Points: 58, Second Division, 1929–30, 1967–68.
Most Appearances: Jimmy Armfield, 568, 1952–71.
Top Scorer: Jimmy Hampson, 247, 1927–38.
Titles: Football League, First Division, Second Place: 1955–56; Second Division Champions: 1929–30; Second Place: 1936–37, 1969–70; F.A. Cup Winners: 1953; Runners-up: 1948, 1951.
Club Colors: Tangerine shirts, white shorts.
Alternate Uniform: White shirts, tangerine shorts.
Record Win: 10–0, vs. Lanerossi Vicenza, 1972.
Record Loss: 1–10, vs. Small Heath, 1901; and Huddersfield, 1930.

BOLTON WANDERERS

Field: Burden Park, Bolton.
Founded: 1874.
Nickname: "Trotters."
Most Goals: 96, Second Division, 1934–35.
Most Points: 61, Third Division, 1972–73.
Most Appearances: Eddie Hopkinson, 519, 1956–70.
Top Scorer: Nat Lofthouse, 255, 1946–61.
Titles: Football League, First Division, Third place: 1891–92, 1920–21, 1924–25; Second Division Champions: 1908–09; Second place, 1899–1900, 1904–05, 1910–11, 1934–35; Third Division Champions: 1972–73; F.A. Cup Winners: 1923, 1926, 1929, 1958; Runners-up: 1894, 1904, 1953.
Club Colors: White shirts, navy blue shorts.
Alternate Uniform: Red shirts, white shorts.
Record Win: 13–0, vs. Sheffield United, 1890.
Record Loss: 0–7, vs. Manchester City, 1936.

BRISTOL CITY

Field: Ashton Gate, Bristol.
Founded: 1894.
Nickname: "Robins."
Most Goals: 104, Third Division, 1926–27.
Most Points: 70, Third Division, 1954–55.
Most Appearances: John Atyeo, 597, 1951–66.
Top Scorer: John Atyeo, 315, 1951–66.
Titles: Football League, First Division, Second place: 1906–07; Second Division Champions: 1905–06; Second place: 1975–76; Third Division Champions: 1922–23, 1926–27, 1954–55; Third Division, Second place: 1964–65; F.A. Cup Runners-up: 1909.
Club Colors: Red shirts, white shorts, white stockings.
Alternate Uniform: White shirts, black shorts, black stockings.
Record Win: 11–0, vs. Chicester, 1960.
Record Loss: 0–9, vs. Coventry City, 1934.

BURNLEY

Field: Turf Moor, Burnley.
Founded: 1882.
Nickname: "Clarets."
Most Goals: 102, First Division, 1960–61.
Most Points: 62, Second Division, 1972–73.
Most Appearances: Jerry Dawson, 530, 1906–29.
Top Scorer: George Beel, 178, 1923–32.
Titles: Football League, First Division Champions: 1920–21, 1959–60; Second place: 1919–20, 1961–62; Second Division Champions: 1897–98, 1972–73; Second place: 1912–13, 1946–47; F.A. Cup Winners: 1914; Runners-up: 1947, 1962.
Club Colors: Claret shirts with sky blue "V," white shorts and stockings.
Alternate Uniform: All yellow.
Record Win: 9–0 vs. New Brighton, 1957.
Record Loss: 0–10, vs. Aston Villa, 1925; Sheffield United, 1929.

CARDIFF CITY

Field: Ninian Park, Cardiff, Wales.
Founded: 1899.
Nickname: "Bluebirds."
Most Goals: 93, Third Division, 1946–47
Most Points: 66, Third Division, 1946–47
Most Appearances: Tom Farquharson, 445, 1922–35
Top Scorer: Len Davis, 127, 1921–29
Titles: Football League, First Division, Second place: 1923–24; Second Division, Second place: 1920–21, 1951–52, 1959–60; Third Division Champions: 1946–47; F.A. Cup Winners: 1927 (only Welsh club ever to win cup); Runners-up: 1925.
Club Colors: Blue shirts and shorts with yellow and white trim.
Alternatate Uniform: All yellow.
Record Win: 9–2, vs. Thames, 1932.
Record Loss: 2–11, vs. Sheffield United, 1926.

CHARLTON ATHLETIC

Field: The Valley, Floyd Rd., Charlton, London.
Founded: 1905.
Nickname: "Haddicks" or "Valiants."
Most Goals: 107, Second Division, 1957–58.
Most Points: 61, Third Division, 1934–35.
Most Appearances: Sam Bartram, 583, 1934–56.
Top Scorer: Stuart Leary, 153, 1953–62.
Titles: Football League, First Division, Second place: 1936–37; Second Division, Second place: 1935–36; Third Division (S) Champions: 1928–29, 1934–35; F.A. Cup Winners: 1947; Runners-up: 1946.
Club Colors: Red shirts, white shorts, red stockings.
Alternate Uniform: Yellow and black.
Record Win: 8–1, vs. Middlesbrough, 1953.
Record Loss: 1–11, vs. Aston Villa, 1959.

CHELSEA

Field: Stamford Bridge, London.
Founded: 1905.
Nickname: "Blues."
Most Goals: 98, First Division, 1960–61.
Most Points: 57, Second Division, 1906–07.
Most Appearances: Peter Bonetti, 553, 1960–77.
Top Scorer: Bobby Tambling, 164, 1958–70.
Titles: Football League, First Division Champions: 1954–55; Second Division, Second place: 1906–07, 1911–12, 1929–30, 1962–63, 1976–77; F.A. Cup Winners: 1970; Runners-up: 1915, 1967; Football League Cup Winners: 1965; Runners-up: 1972; European Cup-Winners' Cup, Champions: 1971.
Club Colors: All royal blue with white stripe on shorts, white stockings.
Alternate Uniform: All yellow.
Record Win: 13–0, vs. Jeunesse Hautcharage (European Cup-Winners' Cup, 1st Rd.), 1971.
Record Loss: 1–8, vs. Wolverhampton Wanderers, 1953.

COVENTRY CITY

Field: Highfield Rd., Coventry.
Founded: 1883.
Nickname: "Sky Blues."
Most Goals: 108, Third Division (S), 1931–32.
Most Points: 60, Fourth Division, 1958–59; Third Division, 1963–64.
Most Appearances: George Curtis, 486, 1956–70.
Top Scorer: 171, Clarrie Bourton, 49, 1931–32.
Titles: Football League, Second Division Champions: 1966–67; Third Division Champions: 1963–64; Third Division (South) Champions: 1935–36; Highest League Position: First Division, Sixth place: 1969–70.
Club Colors: Sky-blue shirts and shorts with navy and white trim.
Alternate Uniform: Red shirts and shorts with navy and white trim.
Record Win: 9–0, vs. Briston City, 1934.
Record Loss: 2–10, vs. Norwich City, 1930.

CRYSTAL PALACE

Field: Selhurst Park, London.
Founded: 1905.
Nickname: "The Eagles."
Most Goals: 110, Fourth Division, 1960–61.
Most Points: 64, Fourth Division, 1960–61.
Most Appearances: Terry Long, 432, 1956–69.
Top Scorer: Peter Simpson, 54, 1930–36.
Titles: Football League, Second Division, Second place: 1968–69; Third Division (South) Champions: 1920–21; Highest League position, First Division, 18th place: 1970–71.
Club Colors: White shirts with red and blue band, white shorts and stockings.
Alternate Uniform: Royal blue and red vertically striped shirts, blue shorts.
Record Win: 9–0, vs. Barrow, 1959.
Record Loss: 4–11, vs. Manchester City, 1926.

DERBY COUNTY

Field: Baseball Ground, Shaftsbury Crescent, Derby.
Founded: 1884.
Nickname: "The Rams."
Most Goals: 111, Third Division (N), 1956–57.
Most Points: 63, Second Division, 1968–69 and 1962–63.
Most Appearances: Jack Parry, 478, 1949–66.
Top Scorer: Steve Bloomer, 291, 1892–1906 and 1910–14.
Titles: Football League, First Division Champions: 1971–72, 1974–75; Second place: 1895–96, 1929–30, 1935–36; Second Division Champions: 1911–12, 1914–15, 1968–69; Third Division (North) Champions: 1956–57; F.A. Cup Winners: 1946; Runners-up: 1898, 1899, 1903.
Club Colors: White shirts, blue shorts, white stockings.
Alternate Uniform: Light and dark blue striped shirts, light blue shorts, black stockings.
Record Win: 12–0, vs. Finn Harps (UEFA Cup, third round), 1976.
Record Loss: 2–11, vs. Everton, 1889.

EVERTON

Field: Goodison Park, Liverpool.
Founded: 1878.
Nickname: "Toffeemen" or "Blues."
Most Goals: 121, Second Division, 1930–31.
Most Points: 66, First Division, 1969–70.
Most Appearances: Ted Sager, 465, 1929–53.
Top Scorer: Dixie Dean, 349, 1925–37.
Titles: Football League, First Division Champions: 1890–91, 1914–15, 1927–28, 1931–32, 1938–39, 1962–63, 1969–70; Second Division Champions: 1930–31; F.A. Cup Winners: 1906, 1933, 1966; Runners-up: 1893, 1897, 1907, 1968.
Club Colors: Royal blue shirts with white trim, white shorts and stockings.
Alternate Uniform: Amber shirts, shorts, and stockings with blue trim.
Record Win: 11–2, vs. Derby County, 1889.
Record Loss: 4–10, vs. Tottenham Hotspur, 1958.

FULHAM

Field: Craven Cottage, London.
Founded: 1880.
Nickname: "Cottagers."
Most Goals: 111, Third Division (S), 1931–32.
Most Points: 60, Second Division, 1958–59 and Third Division, 1970–71.
Most Appearances: Johnny Haynes, 598, 1952–70.
Top Scorer: Johnny Haynes, 159, 1952–70.
Titles: Football League, Second Division Champions: 1948–49; Second place: 1958–59; Third Division (South) Champions: 1931–32; Third Division, Second place: 1970–71; F.A. Cup, Runners-up: 1975; Highest League position: First Divison, 10th place: 1959–60.
Club Colors: White shirts with black trim, black shorts, white stockings.
Alternate Uniform: Red shirts with black stripes, red shorts, black stockings.
Record Win: 10–1, vs. Ipswich Town, 1963.
Record Loss: 0–9, vs. Wolverhampton Wanderers, 1959.

HUDDERSFIELD TOWN

Field: Leeds Road, Huddersfield.
Founded: 1908.
Nickname: "The Terriers."
Most Goals: 97, Second Division, 1919–20.
Most Points: 64, Second Division, 1919–20.
Most Appearances: Billy Smith, 520, 1914–34.
Top Scorer: George Brown, 142, 1921–29.
Titles: Football League, First Division Champions: 1923–24, 1924–25, 1925–26; Second place: 1926–27, 1927–28, 1933–34; Second Division Champions: 1969–70; Second place: 1919–20, 1952–53; F.A. Cup Winners: 1922; Runners-up: 1920, 1928, 1930, 1938.
Club Colors: Blue and white striped shirts, white shorts and stockings.
Alternate Uniform: All yellow.
Record Win: 10–1, vs. Blackpool, 1930.
Record Loss: 0–8, vs. Middlesbrough, 1950.

IPSWICH TOWN

Field: Portman Road, Ipswich, Suffolk.
Founded: 1887.
Nickname: "Town" or "Blues."
Most Goals: 106, Third Division (S), 1955–56.
Most Points: 64, Third Division (S), 1953–54, 1955–56.
Most Appearances: Tom Parker, 428, 1946–57.
Top Scorer: Ray Crawford, 203, 1958–63, 1966–69.
Titles: Football League, First Division Champions: 1961–62; Second Division Champions: 1960–61, 1967–68; Third Division (South) Champions: 1953–54, 1956–57.
Club Colors: Blue shirts with three white stripes down each arm, white shorts, and blue stockings.
Alternate Uniform: White shirts with three black stripes down each arm, black shorts, and black stockings.
Record Win: 10–0, vs. Floriana, Malta (First round, European Cup), 1962.
Record Loss: 1–10, vs. Fulham, 1963.

LEEDS UNITED

Field: Elland Road, Leeds.
Founded: 1919.
Most Goals: 98, Second Division, 1927–28.
Most Points: 67, First Division, 1968–69 (Division record).
Most Appearances: Jack Charlton, 629, 1953–73.
Top Scorer: John Charles, 154, 1948–57 and 1962.
Titles: Football League, First Division Champions: 1968–69, 1973–74; Second place: 1964–65, 1965–66, 1969–70, 1970–71, 1972–73; Second Division Champions: 1923–24, 1963–64; Second place: 1927–28, 1931–32, 1955–56; F.A. Cup Winners: 1972; Runners-up: 1965, 1970, 1973; Football League Cup Winners; 1968; European Fairs Cup Winners: 1968, 1970.
Club Colors: All white with blue and yellow collar and trim.
Alternate Uniform: All yellow with blue and white trim.
Record Win: 10–0, vs. Lyn Oslo (First round, European Cup), 1969.
Record Loss: 1–8, vs. Stoke City, 1934.

LEICESTER CITY

Field: City Stadium, Filbert St., Leicester.
Founded: 1884.
Nickname: "Filberts" and "Foxes."
Most Goals: 109, Second Division, 1956–57.
Most Points: 61, Second Division, 1956–57.
Most Appearances: Adam Black, 530, 1919–35.
Top Scorer: Arthur Chandler, 262, 1923–35.
Titles: Football League, First Division, Second place: 1928-29; Second Division Champions: 1924–25, 1936–37, 1953–54, 1956–57, 1970–71; F.A. Cup, Runners-up: 1949, 1961, 1963, 1969; Football League Cup Winners: 1964; Runners-up: 1965.
Club Colors: Blue shirts with white collars and cuffs, white shorts and stockings.
Alternate Uniform: White shirts with blue trim, blue shorts and stockings.
Record Win: 10–0, vs. Portsmouth, 1928.
Record Loss: 0–12, vs. Nottingham Forrest, 1909.

LIVERPOOL

Field: Anfield Road, Liverpool.
Founded: 1892.
Nickname: "Reds" or "Pool."
Most Goals: 106, Second Division, 1895–96.
Most Points: 62, Second Division, 1961–62.
Most Appearances: Ian Callaghan, 614, 1960–77.
Top Scorer: Roger Hunt, 245, 1959–69.
Titles: Football League, First Division Champions; 1900–01, 1905–06, 1921–22, 1922–23, 1946–47, 1963–64, 1965–66, 1972–73, 1975–76, 1976–77; Second place: 1898–99, 1909–10, 1968–69, 1973–74, 1974–75; Second Division Champions: 1893–94, 1895–96, 1904–05, 1961–62; F.A. Cup Winners: 1965, 1974; Runners-up: 1914, 1915, 1971, 1977; European Cup Winners: 1977; UEFA Cup Winners; 1973, 1976.
Club Colors: All red with white trim.
Alternate Uniform: White shirts with red collars and cuffs, black shorts, white stockings.
Record Win: 11–0, vs. Strömsgodset (European Cup-Winners' Cup) 1974.
Record Loss: 1–9, vs. Birmingham City, 1954.

MANCHESTER CITY

Field: Maine Road, Moss Side, Manchester.
Founded: 1887.
Nickname: "Citizens."
Most Goals: 108, Second Divison, 1926–27.
Most Points: 62, Second Division, 1946–47.
Most Appearances: Alan Oakes, 565, 1959–76.
Top Scorer: Tommy Johnson, 158, 1919–30.
Titles: Football League, First Division Champions: 1936–37, 1967–68; Second place; 1903–04, 1920–21, 1976–77; Second Division Champions: 1898–99, 1902–03, 1909–10, 1927–28, 1946–47, 1965–66; Second place: 1895–96, 1950–51; F.A. Cup Winners: 1904, 1934, 1956, 1969; Runners-up: 1926, 1933, 1955; Football League Cup Winners: 1970, 1976; European Cup-Winners' Cup, Winners: 1970.
Club Colors: Sky-blue shirts, shorts, and stockings with white trim.
Alternate Uniform: White shirts with red and black stripe diagonally across chest, black shorts and stockings.
Record Win: 11–3, vs. Lincoln City, 1895.
Record Loss: 1–9, vs. Everton, 1906.

MANCHESTER UNITED

Field: Old Trafford, Manchester.
Founded: 1878.
Nickname: "Red Devils."
Most Goals: 103, First Division, 1956–57, 1958–59.
Most Points: 64, First Division, 1956–57.
Most Appearances: Bobby Charlton, 606, 1956–73.
Top Scorer: Bobby Charlton, 198, 1956–73.
Titles: Football League, First Division Champions: 1907–08, 1910–11, 1951–52, 1955–56, 1956–57, 1964–65, 1966–67; Second place: 1946–47, 1947–48, 1948–49, 1950–51, 1958–59, 1963–64, 1967–68; Second Division Champions: 1935–36, 1974–75; F.A. Cup Winners: 1909, 1948, 1963, 1977; Runners-up: 1957, 1958, 1976; European Cup Winners: 1968.
Club Colors: Red shirts with white trim, white shorts, black stockings with red tops.
Alternate Uniform: White shirts with three black stripes, black shorts, white stockings.
Record Win: 10–0, vs. Anderlecht (European Cup), 1956.
Record Loss: 0–7, vs. Aston Villa, 1930.

NEWCASTLE UNITED

Field: St. James' Park, Newcastle-upon-Tyne.
Founded: 1882.
Nickname: "Magpies."
Most Goals: 98, First Division, 1951–52.
Most Points: 57, Second Division, 1964–65.
Most Appearances: Jim Lawrence, 432, 1904–22.
Top Scorer: Jackie Milburn, 178, 1946–47.
Titles: Football League, First Division Champions: 1904–05, 1906–07, 1908–09, 1926–27; Second Division Champions: 1964–65; Second place: 1897–98, 1947–48; F.A. Cup Winners: 1910, 1924, 1932, 1951, 1952, 1955; Runners-up: 1905, 1906, 1908, 1911, 1974; European Fairs' Cup Winners: 1969.
Club Colors: Black and white striped shirts, black shorts, black and white stockings.
Alternate Uniform: Yellow shirts, green shorts, yellow and green stockings.
Record Win: 13–0, vs. Newport County, 1946.
Record Loss: 0–9, vs. Burton Wanderers, 1895.

NORWICH CITY

Field: Carrow Road, Norwich.
Founded: 1905.
Nickname: "Canaries."
Most Goals: 99, Third Division (S), 1952–53.
Most Points: 64, Third Division (S), 1950–51.
Most Appearances: Ron Ashman, 590, 1947–64.
Top Scorer: Johnny Gavin, 122, 1945–54; 1955–58.
Titles: Football League, Second Division Champions: 1971–72; Highest League Position: 10th place, First Division, 1975–76; Football League Cup Winners: 1962; Runners-up: 1973, 1975.
Club Colors: Yellow shirts with green trim, green shorts, green stockings.
Alternate Uniform: All white.
Record Win: 10–2, vs. Coventry City, 1930.
Record Loss: 2–10, vs. Swindon Town, 1908.

NOTTINGHAM FOREST

Field: City Ground, Nottingham.
Founded: 1865.
Nickname: "Reds."
Most Goals: 110, Third Division (S), 1950–51.
Most Points: 70, Third Division (S), 1950–51.
Most Appearances: Bob McKinlay, 614, 1951–70.
Top Scorer: Grenville Morris, 199, 1898–1913.
Titles: Football League, First Division Champions: 1977–78; Second place: 1966–67; Second Division Champions: 1906–07 1921–22; Second place: 1956–57; Third Division (South) Champions: 1950–51; F.A. Cup Winners: 1898, 1959.
Club Colors: Red shirts, white shorts, red stockings.
Alternate Uniform: All yellow.
Record Win: 14–0, vs. Clapton, 1890.
Record Loss: 1–9, vs. Blackburn Rovers, 1937.

PRESTON NORTH END

Field: Deepdale, Preston.
Founded: 1881.
Nickname: "The Lilywhites" or "North End."
Most Goals: 100, Second Division, 1927–28 and First Division, 1957–58.
Most Points: 61, Third Division, 1970–71.
Most Appearances: Alan Kelly, 447, 1961–75.
Top Scorer: Tom Finney, 187, 1946–60.
Titles: Football League, First Division Champions: 1888–89 (first champions), 1889–90; Second place: 1890–91, 1891–92, 1892–93, 1905–06, 1952–53, 1957–58; Second Division Champions: 1903–04, 1912–13, 1950–51; Second place: 1914–15, 1933–34; Third Division Champions: 1970–71; F.A. Cup Winners: 1889, 1938; Runners-up: 1888, 1922, 1937, 1954, 1964.
Club Colors: White shirts with blue collars and cuffs, white shorts and stockings.
Alternate Uniform: All yellow.
Record Win: 26–0, vs. Hyde, 1887.
Record Loss: 0–7, vs. Blackpool, 1948.

QUEEN'S PARK RANGERS

Field: South Africa Road, London.
Founded: 1885.
Nickname: "Rangers."
Most Goals: 111, Third Division, 1961–62.
Most Points: 67, Third Division, 1966–67.
Most Appearances: Tony Ingham, 519, 1950–63.
Top Scorer: George Goddard, 172, 1926–34.
Titles: Football League, First Division, Second place: 1975–76; Second Division, Second place: 1967–68, 1972–73; Third Division (South) Champions: 1947–48; Third Division Champions: 1966–67; Football League Cup Winners: 1967.
Club Colors: Blue and white hooped shirts, white shorts, white stockings.
Alternate Uniform: Red and white shirts, black shorts, black stockings.
Record Win: 9–2, vs. Tranmere Rovers, 1960.
Record Loss: 1–8, vs. Mansfield Town, 1965, and Manchester United, 1969.

SHEFFIELD WEDNESDAY

Field: Hillsborough, Sheffield.
Founded: 1867.
Nickname: "Owls."
Most Goals: 106, Second Division, 1958–59.
Most Points: 62, Second Division, 1958–59.
Most Appearances: Andy Wilson, 502, 1900–20.
Top Scorer: Andy Wilson, 200, 1900–20.
Titles: Football League, First Division Champions: 1902–03, 1903–04, 1928–29, 1929–30; Second place: 1960–61; Second Division Champions: 1899–1900, 1925–26, 1951–52, 1955–56, 1958–59; Second place: 1949–50; F.A. Cup Winners: 1896, 1907, 1935; Runners-up: 1890, 1966.
Club Colors: Royal blue and white striped shirts, blue shorts, white stockings.
Alternate Uniform: Yellow and blue shirts, white shorts, yellow stockings.
Record Win: 12–0, vs. Halliwell, 1891.
Record Loss: 0–10, vs. Aston Villa, 1912.

SOUTHAMPTON

Field: The Dell, Milton Road, Southampton.
Founded: 1885.
Nickname: "Saints."
Most Goals: 112, Third Division (S), 1957–58.
Most Points: 61, Third Division (S), 1921–22, Third Division, 1959–60.
Most Appearances: Terry Paine, 713, 1956–74.
Top Scorer: Terry Paine, 160, 1956–74.
Titles: Football League, Third Division (South) Champions: 1921–23; Third Division Champions: 1959–60; Highest League Position: Seventh place, First Division, 1968–69, 1970–71; F.A. Cup Winners: 1976; Runners-up: 1900, 1902.
Club Colors: Red and white striped shirts, black shorts, white stockings.
Alternate Uniform: Gold shirts, blue shorts, gold stockings.
Record Win: 11–0, vs. Northampton, 1901.
Record Loss: 0–8, vs. Tottenham Hotspur, 1936, and Everton, 1971.

SUNDERLAND

Field: Roker Park Ground, Sunderland.
Founded: 1879.
Nickname: "Rokerites."
Most Goals: 109, First Division, 1935–36.
Most Points: 61, Second Division, 1963–64.
Most Appearances: Jim Montgomery, 537, 1962–77.
Top Scorer: Charlie Buchan, 209, 1911–25.
Titles: Football League, First Division Champions: 1891–92, 1892–93, 1894–95, 1901–02, 1912–13, 1935–36; Second place: 1893–94, 1897–98, 1900–01, 1922–23, 1934–35; Second Division Champions: 1975–76; Second place: 1963–64; F.A. Cup Winners: 1937, 1973; Runners-up: 1913.
Club Colors: Red and white striped shirts, black shorts, red stockings.
Alternate Uniform: Blue shirts with red trim, red shorts, blue stockings.
Record Win: 11–1, vs. Fairfield, 1895.
Record Loss: 0–8, vs. West Ham United, 1968.

TOTTENHAM HOTSPUR

Field: 748 High Road, Tottenham, London.
Founded: 1882.
Nickname: "Spurs."
Most Goals: 115, First Division, 1960–61.
Most Points: 70, Second Division, 1919–20.
Most Appearances: Pat Jennings, 472, 1964–77.
Top Scorer: Jimmy Greaves, 220, 1961–70.
Titles: Football League, First Division Champions: 1950–51, 1960–61; Second place: 1921–22, 1951–52, 1956–57, 1962–63; Second Division Champions: 1919–20, 1949–50; Second place: 1908–09, 1932–33; F.A. Cup Winners: 1901, 1921, 1961, 1962, 1967; Football League Cup Winners: 1971, 1973.
Club Colors: White shirts, blue shorts, white stockings.
Alternate Uniform: All yellow, with blue trim.
Record Win: 13–2, vs. Crewe Alexandra, 1960.
Record Loss: 2–8, vs. Derby County, 1976.

WEST BROMWICH ALBION

Field: The Hawthorns, West Bromwich.
Founded: 1879.
Nickname: "Baggies," "Throstles."
Most Goals: 105, Second Division, 1929–30.
Most Points: 60, First Division, 1919–20.
Most Appearances: Tony Brown, 486, 1963–77.
Top Scorer: Ronnie Allen, 208, 1950–61.
Titles: Football League, First Division Champions: 1919–20; Second place: 1924–25, 1953–54; Second Division Champions: 1901–02, 1910–11; Second place: 1930–31, 1948–49; F.A. Cup Winners: 1888, 1892, 1931, 1954, 1968; Runners-up: 1886, 1887, 1895, 1912, 1935; Football League Cup Winners: 1966.
Club Colors: Navy blue and white striped shirts, white shorts and stockings.
Alternate Uniform: Yellow and green striped shirts, green shirts, yellow stockings.
Record Win: 12–0, vs. Darwen, 1892.
Record Loss: 3–10, vs. Stoke City, 1937.

Scotland's goalkeeper Alan Rough makes a save during a match against Wales.

WEST HAM UNITED

Field: Boleyn Ground, Upton Park, London.
Founded: 1900.
Nickname: "Hammers."
Most Goals: 101, Second Division, 1957–58.
Most Points: 57, Second Division, 1957–58.
Most Appearances: Bobby Moore, 544, 1958–74.
Top Scorer: Vic Watson, 306, 1920–35.
Titles: Football League, Second Division Champions: 1957–58, Second place: 1922–23; Highest League Position: First Division, Sixth place, 1926–27, 1958–59, 1972–73; F.A. Cup Winners: 1964, 1975; Runners-up: 1923; European Cup-Winners' Cup, Winners: 1965.
Club Colors: Claret shirts with blue yoke, white shorts and stockings.
Alternate Uniform: White shirts, sky-blue shorts and stockings.
Record Win: 8–0, vs. Sunderland, 1968.
Record Loss: 2–8, vs. Blackburn Rovers, 1963.

WOLVERHAMPTON WANDERERS

Field: Molineaux Grounds, Wolverhampton.
Founded: 1877.
Nickname: "Wolves."
Most Goals: 115, Second Division, 1931–32.
Most Points: 64, First Division, 1957–58.
Most Appearances: Billy Wright, 491, 1946–59.
Top Scorer: Bill Hartill, 164, 1928–35.
Titles: Football League, First Division Champions: 1953–54, 1957–58, 1958–59; Second place: 1937–38, 1938–39, 1949–50, 1954–55, 1959–60; Second Division Champions: 1931–32, 1976–77; Second place: 1966–67; F.A. Cup Winners: 1893, 1908, 1949, 1960; Runners-up: 1889, 1896, 1921, 1939; Football League Cup Winners: 1974.
Club Colors: Old gold shirts, black shorts and old gold stockings.
Alternate Uniform: All white.
Record Win: 14–0, vs. Crosswell's Brewery, 1887.
Record Loss: 1–10 vs. Newton Heath, 1892.

6. SOCCER IN EUROPE

Which nation plays the best soccer in Europe? It all depends on what period in time one is thinking about. No single nation has completely dominated the European soccer scene, but several have had extended periods of success. In the late 1920's and early 1930's it was Austria and manager Hugo Meisl's *Wunderteam.* Then came Vittorio Pozzo's Italian team, winners of both the 1934 and 1938 World Cup titles. The early 1950's belonged to Hungary's "Magical Magyars," a team destroyed when the 1956 Hungarian Revolution drove many of its best players into voluntary exile. Italy and West Germany fielded the most consistently powerful teams in the 1960's and 1970's, with strong competition from Czechoslovakia, the Netherlands, and Yugoslavia.

Individual clubs have also enjoyed long stretches as the best in Europe. In the 1950's Real Madrid was to European soccer what the New York Yankees were to American baseball. Filling its ranks with an international galaxy of stars, the Spanish team won five consecutive European Cups. Benfica of Lisbon was next on top, but was soon deposed by a pair of Italian clubs, AC Milan and Inter-Milan. A pair of Dutch powerhouses, Feyenoord and Ajax, ruled Europe from 1970 through 1973, only to be replaced by Bayern Munich, which enjoyed a three-year reign as the continent's finest team.

Perhaps the best way to get a clear understanding of soccer in Europe is to examine each nation separately beginning, alphabetically, with:

Austria

Until it qualified for the finals of the 1978 World Cup, Austria, a small nation with a population of 7 million people, had not been a power in international soccer since finishing third in the 1954 tournament. From 1912 to the late 1960's its most consistently powerful club was Rapid Vienna, winner of

Roland Hattenberger, a midfield star for both the Austrian national team and the West German club VFB Stuttgart.

twenty-five league championships and nine Austrian Cups. Rapid's chief rival during that era was FK Austria, winner of nineteen cups and eight league titles. Since 1970, T.-S. Innsbruck has won five league championships and two cups.

Belgium

The most prominent name in Belgian soccer for the past forty years has been that of Constant Van den Stock, who earned his reputation first as a player and then, after he had made a fortune in the brewing industry, as president of the Royal Sporting Club Anderlecht.

Anderlecht, located in the suburbs of Brussels, is a multi-sports club that also sponsors basketball, hockey, and track teams. In all, it fields fourteen soccer teams that range from a squad for ten-year-olds to a First Division club that has won sixteen league championships and five Belgium F.A. Cups.

When professionalism was legalized in 1971, Van den Stock opened his checkbook and made the Dutch internation-al striker Rob Rensenbrink one of the best-paid players in Europe by signing him to a seven-year contract that guaranteed the player, among other things, about $100,000 (half of it tax-free) a year and a rent-free villa. In all, Anderlecht has some 300 players on its books, but only seventeen are fulltime professionals. The rest are semipro or amateur members of the club's junior teams.

Belgium is a small nation—it is no more than 200 miles across at its widest point—served by an excellent network of highways, and fans follow their teams from one end of the country to the other. There are three elite clubs, all with national support. Anderlecht is one and the others are Standard Liege, winner of six league titles, and FC Bruges, league champions in 1976 and 1977.

In all, seventeen clubs compete in the First Division of the Belgium League, but since 1960 only one, 1975 champions RWD Molenbeek, has been able to crack the monopoly the elite three have had on the league championship.

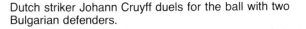

Dutch striker Johann Cruyff duels for the ball with two Bulgarian defenders.

Bulgaria

The Bulgarians have an unenviable reputation for playing the roughest brand of soccer in all of Europe, a reputation that was enhanced by their near crippling of Pelé in the 1966 World Cup. It is said that in league matches, Bulgarian referees will permit fouls that would get players thrown out of the game in other countries.

The Bulgarian League is a state-run "amateur"* affair and has been dominated by CSKA Sofia and Levski Spartak (also of Sofia), which have won nineteen and twelve championships respectively.

Czechoslovakia

Many observers of the international soccer scene were surprised when Scotland edged out Czechoslovakia for a berth in the 1978 World Cup finals, especially after the Czechs had demonstrated their ability by defeating West Germany in the finals of the 1976 European Nations Cup. A comparatively small country with a population of 14 million, the Czechs have a long and proud soccer tradition and were runners-up in both the 1934 and 1962 World Cup finals.

Three clubs from Prague—Sparta, Slavia, and Dulka—have respectively won thirteen, twelve, and nine league championships.

*As in most Eastern European nations, with the notable exceptions of Hungary and Yugoslavia, there are no professional athletes in Bulgaria. All the players have jobs outside of soccer, but often these are jobs in name only and involve little or no work.

Polish striker Grzegorz Lato fends off a Danish defender.

Dulka Prague's Ivo Viktor has long been one of the best goalkeepers in Europe. His team won the 1977 league championship, while Lokomotiv Kosice, which finished fifth in the league, won the Czechoslovakian F.A. Cup.

Denmark

Denmark's best soccer player is Allan Simonsen, a five-foot-six-inch tall, 127-pound striker who was named Europe's Player of the Year in 1977. Simonsen plays for Borussia Mönchengladbach of West Germany, which explains the problem with Danish soccer. Although the nation's soccer federation was formed in 1889, the Danes have lagged behind the rest of Europe in developng the game on a professional level. As a consequence, many of Denmark's best players leave to play elsewhere.

The Danish League was established in 1913, and since then KB Copenhagen has won the championship fourteen times, followed by B 93 Copenhagen and AB Akademisk with nine each.

Finland

Soccer in Finland is played on a totally amateur basis. The Finnish League was formed in 1946, and since then two clubs—Turun Palloseura and Kuopion Palloseura—have won the championship five times each. An F.A. Cup competition was begun in 1955, and Lahden Reipas leads that series with six wins, followed by Valkeakosken Haka with five.

France

For the first time since 1966, France reached the World Cup finals in 1978. The backbone of the national team is provided by St. Etienne, league champions seven times since 1967. Led by defender Gerard Janvion and wing forward Dominique Rocheteau, the club reached the finals of the 1976 European Champions' Cup before losing to Bayern Munich.

The French F.A. Cup has been won by Olympique Marseilles nine times and St. Etienne six times. Michel Platini, a forward who plays for Nancy, has been called the most exciting player in France since Raymond Kopa and Juste Fontaine led the French to a third-place finish in the 1958 World Cup. In 1977 Platini, then twenty-one years old, finished third in the European Player of the Year voting.

East Germany

The East Germans set about to become an international soccer power with the same sort of single-minded determination that brought them to the forefront in such other sports as swimming and track and field—and they have succeeded. In the 1974 World Cup they upset the hosts, and eventual champions, West Germany and two years later, fielding the same team of "amateur athletes," they won a gold medal at the Montreal Olympics.

The East German League began play in 1950, and for many years the leading club was ASK Vorwaerts, winners of six championships. Since 1971, the two most powerful clubs have been FC Magdeburg, winner of three titles, and Dynamo Dresden,* which has won five, including both the 1976 and 1977 championships.

West Germany

For a decade that began in 1966 it could be argued that based on overall performance West Germany had both the best national team and the best club team in Europe, if not in the world.

In 1966 the West Germans finished second in the World

*Here, as in many Eastern European nations, the name "Dynamo" means the club is sponsored by a state-owned power plant.

Cup competition, in 1970 they came in third, and then in 1974 they won the trophy. They also won the European Nations' Cup in 1972 and finished second in 1976.

When West Germany won the World Cup in 1974, six members of its starting eleven also played for Bayern Munich of the Federal German League, or Bundesliga. The six were Franz Beckenbauer, goalkeeper Sepp Maier, Gerd Müller, George Schwarzenbeck, Uli Hoeness, and Paul Breitner, who along with teammate Franz Roth formed the nucleus of a club that won the European Cup in 1974, 1975, and 1976, four Bundesliga championships, and two West German Cups.

Geoffrey Green, a soccer correspondent for the *Times* of London had this to say after watching the Munich team dismantle Atlético Madrid 4–0 to win the 1974 European Cup:

A sharp line divides the British from the Continental and South American styles and argument still rages as to which is the more effective. Nothing could have illustrated this contrast better than the European Cup final between Bayern Munich and Atlético Madrid in Brussels. Nowhere to be seen (in British games) were the classic skills on the ground of Beckenbauer—a boulevardier always, it seems, out for a gentle stroll in the sunshine— Breitner and the others; nor the deadly finishing of the likes of Müller and Hoeness. While the British footballer leads with his body, bringing physical contact to the game and blood to the terraces, the foreigner, by subtle infiltration and technique, leads with his mind . . .

What opponents could not do to Bayern Munich time, the departure of several star players, and the seemingly endless wear and tear of international competition did, and by the mid-1970's another powerhouse club began to dominate the Bundesliga. Borussia Mönchengladbach won the league title in 1975, 1976, and 1977; the UEFA (Union of European Football Associations) Cup in 1975; and finished second in the European Cup in 1977.

This club features among its members such international stars as fullback Berti Vogts, midfield wizard Rainer Bonhof, and the sensational Danish striker Allan Simonsen, who is one of many non-German stars playing in the Bundesliga. Although there are an estimated 3 million soccer players among West Germany's 60 million citizens, there are many wealthy teams in the league that are quite willing to go outside of the country to buy what can't be found at home. Sweden has long been a favorite shopping area for these player-buying sprees, but in recent years West German coaches have been spending a great deal of time watching outstanding British, Belgian, and Yugoslavian players and several of these have already left their native leagues and moved to West Germany.

All this talent made the eighteen-team Bundesliga the

Franz Beckenbauer, in action for Bayern Munich, stages a race for the ball with four Eintracht Frankfurt players.

West German defender Rolf Ruessmann.

highest-scoring league in the Europe in 1976-77 season, with an average of 3.54 goals per game, as compared to 2.80 in Holland and 2.56 in England.

Greece

Since the Greek League was organized in 1928, two clubs have had a near monopoly on the loop title. Olympiakos has won the championship twenty times while its nearest competitor has been Panathinaikos, winners of the league championship a dozen times. The Greek competition has also been controlled by Olympiakos with seventeen victories, followed by AEK Athens with seven, and Panathinaikos with six.

Hungary

In qualifying for the 1978 World Cup finals the Hungarian national team was led by a pair of outstanding strikers, Tibor Nyilasi and Andreas Torocsik, and an exceptional player who alternates between a wing and midfield, Laszlo Fazekas.

Beginning in 1969, Ujpesti Dozsa won seven consecutive league titles until Ferencvaros, Nyilasi's team, won both the league and cup championships in 1976. Since the Hungarian League was formed in 1901, Ferencvaros has won the title a record twenty-two times. Its nearest competitor, with eighteen, is MTK-VM Budapest, a team that last won the league title in 1958.

Republic of Ireland

Although soccer is not the most popular game in Eire—it often takes a back seat to hurling, Irish football, and rugby—the republic's national team has never proved an easy opponent for countries where the sport ranks as number one.

Members of the West German national team frolic on the beach in Rio de Janeiro.

Italian fans cheer their team in a match against England.

In 1976, under the guidance of player-manager Johnny Giles, Eire defeated Poland 2–0 in Poznan and tied England 1–1 in Wembley Stadium.

The governing body of Irish soccer split in 1921 into the Irish F.A. (Northern Ireland) and the F.A. of Ireland. Since then the two national teams have never met, but the luck of the draw has placed both in the same preliminary group for the 1980 European Cup. In order to advance in the competition, the two teams will have to play a home and away series in 1979.

When he heard the news Frank Davis, president of the F.A. of Ireland, said: "The fact that we are playing Northern Ireland may go some way towards bringing the two countries closer together. There have been tentative approaches toward arranging games in the past, but they have never materialized."

Since the Irish League was formed in 1922, Shamrock Rovers have won the championshp twenty times, but their last victory came in 1959. Sligo Rovers won the league championship in 1977, while Dundalk won the F.A. Cup.

Italy

The Italians call the game *il calcio* (or, if they're Roman, *er carcio*), which means "the kick," and there are few places in the world where the ball is kicked about with more intensity. Fan interest is often emotional and at times violent, especially when the national team performs poorly—as it did in the 1974 World Cup.

When Italy reached the finals of the 1978 World Cup it marked the ninth time the Italians have qualified for the tournament. They have only missed the first World Cup, which they declined to enter, and the sixth, the only one they failed to qualify for.

The Italian League was formed in 1898, and since the end of World War II has contained some of the world's finest club teams. The first of the great postwar teams was Torino, winners of the league title in 1946, 1947, and 1948. Then, midway through the 1949 season, a plane carrying the team crashed into a hill near the city of Superga. All seventeen Torino players aboard were killed. Because it was at the top of the standings at the time, the Torino team was voted 1949 league champion.

Italy's two major industrial centers, Milan and Turin, are the home cities for the nation's four most powerful club teams. Inter-Milan has won the league championship eleven times, the World Cup championship twice, and the European Cup twice. Crosstown rival AC Milan has won nine league titles, one world club championship, two European Cups, and two Cup-Winners' Cups.

Although Torino has won eight league championships, the most consistently powerful club in Turin has been Juventus, prize possession of the Agnelli family, a clan that also happens to control the Fiat company and the fortune that comes with it. Juventus has won the league championship a record seventeen times and throughout the 1970's has fielded one of the strongest clubs in Europe. Among its stars are winger Franco Causio and goalkeeper Dino Zoff.

Lazio of Rome, which won the league championship in 1974, is the only club to break the Milan-Turin stranglehold on the league title since 1970.

For many years the richer Italian clubs spent freely through-

Forward Roberto Bettega (center) embraces a teammate after scoring the winning goal in a 3–2 victory that gave Juventus the 1978 Italian League championship over runner-up Laner-ossi Vicenza.

out Europe and South America, buying up the best players wherever they were available. The situation was on the verge of getting out of hand when, in 1965, the Italian Federation voted to ban foreign players from the league. The restriction held firm for thirteen seasons. Then, in 1978, the wealthier clubs lobbied successfully to have the ban lifted on the grounds that it violated the Treaty of Rome, which guarantees full working rights within the European Common Market to all citizens of member countries. It can safely be predicted that in future years Italian soccer will remain a passionate game both on and off the field.

The Netherlands

For a long time the Dutch played some of the best soccer in Europe but were not an important factor in international competition because their two major club teams, Ajax Amsterdam and Feyenoord of Rotterdam, refused to allow their players to play on the same team. When the clubs finally abandoned this narrow-minded attitude, the Netherlands was able to put together a team good enough to finish as runners-up to West Germany in the 1974 World Cup.

The Dutch League has been conducting a championship competition since 1898, and since then Ajax has won the title seventeen times, followed by Feyenoord with a dozen championships. Each has won the world club championship once, and Feyenoord captured the European Champions' Cup in 1970, while Ajax won it in 1971, 1972, and 1973.

The star of that Ajax team was Johann Cruyff, a striker of exceptional talent whose repertoire of skills made him a starter at age seventeen, a full international at nineteen and five years later, in 1971, Europe's player of the year, an honor he won twice more after his transfer to Barcelona for $2.2 million. He was a product of Ajax's youth program, a system that exposes boys to professional coaching as early as age ten, and one that is practiced by many of Europe's top clubs.

After Cruyff's departure to Spain, Ajax went into a brief decline, but by 1977 the club was back on top of the Dutch League.

Norway

The Norwegians last World Cup appearance was in 1938, when they lost in overtime to the eventual champions, Italy. The Norwegian League was organized in 1938, and since then Fredrikstad has won the title nine times, followed by

Juventus forward Franco Causio pushes past a Torino defender. The mustachioed winger is also a mainstay of of the Italian national team.

Italy's Gianni Rivera shouts instructions to a teammate further downfield.

Juan Asensi is a dominant force in midfield for Spain.

Johann Cruyff (right) led Barcelona to a second-place finish behind Real Madrid in 1978, his last season in the Spanish League.

Viking Stavanger with five, including four championships in a row from 1972 through 1975.

Poland

The surprise team of the 1974 World Cup, when they finished third, the Poles qualified again in 1978, with a team managed by Jacek Gmoch and led by striker Grzegorz Lato. Gmoch runs a well-disciplined team, and it has been said that his players move about the field like chessmen on a board. Nevertheless, the Poles have been successful in this approach to the game against some of the world's best teams.

The Polish League began its championship competition in 1921, and since then Ruche Chorzow has won the title eleven times, followed by Gornik Zabrze with ten.

Portugal

Squabbling between the nation's two strongest clubs, Benfica and Sporting Lisbon, has hampered Portugal in international competition. Both often refuse to release their players for international games or, when they do grant releases, allow inadequate practice time with the national team.

In the 1960's, when the then Portuguese colony of Mozambique was supplying it with such players as Mario Coluna, Joaquim Santana, and Eusebio, Benfica fielded one of the world's strongest clubs. It won the European Cup in 1961 and 1962 and finished as runner-up in 1963, 1965, and 1968.

From 1957 through 1977, Benfica won the Portuguese League title fifteen times. Since the league was formed in 1935, Benfica, which tends to draw its fans from Lisbon's working class, has won the championship twenty-three times and the F.A. Cup fifteen times. Sporting Lisbon, which attracts many of its fans from the upper classes, has won the league title fourteen times and the cup eight times.

Romania

King Carol of Romania personally selected his nation's team for the 1930 World Cup finals. The squad won its first game, beating Peru 3–1, but then was eliminated by Uruguay 4–0. So much for royal infallibility. The Romanians have participated in three other World Cup finals, in 1934, 1938, and 1970, but have never made it past the first round—although in their last appearance they did give a good account of themselves before losing to Brazil and England.

The Romanian League has been staging a championship competition since 1910. Since 1963, Dynamo Bucharest has won the title seven times. There are three university teams in the league's First Division and one of them, Craiova, finished third in 1977.

Spain

Real Madrid is more than just a soccer club—it is a Spanish institution. The club owns a forty-acre sports complex of tennis courts, swimming pools, a track-and-field stadium, a

Forward Robby Rensenbrink stars for both the Dutch national team and the Belgian club Anderlecht.

Polish defender Wladyslaw Zmuda launches a pass upfield against Brazil. His club, Slask Wroclaw, finished one point behind Poland's 1978 league champions, Wisla Krakow.

skating rink, and a restaurant. Supporting all this are 60,000 dues-paying members plus a long list of *Madrileños* waiting to join. Membership means a chance to buy tickets for games in the club's 125,000-seat soccer stadium. Participating in any of the club's other activities requires the purchase of bonds at a cost of twenty-five dollars each. To play tennis, for example, a member must buy ten bonds.

The driving force behind this massive enterprise has been Don Santiago Bernabeu, who was captain of Real's soccer team in the 1920's. In 1943 he was elected the club's president and set about building its magnificent stadium, which bears his name, near the heart of Madrid. Once that job was completed, he began to use the club's vast revenues to put together a team worthy of his stadium.

Among the international stars who played for Real in the 1950's were France's Raymond Kopa, Brazil's Didi, Uru-guay's José Santamaria, Argentina's Hector Rial, Hungary's Ferenc Puskas and the man who was the keystone upon whom this brilliant team was constructed—Alfredo Di Stefano.

Born in Buenos Aires in 1926, Di Stefano left Argentina in the late forties as part of a mass exodus of soccer players seeking higher wages in Colombia. In Bogotá, he played for the Milionarios in an outlaw league that hired players from all over South America without paying their home clubs the required transfer fees. As a result of this, Colombia was suspended from FIFA.

When Colombia rejoined soccer's international governing body in 1953, Milionarios was forced to release Di Stefano, who quickly made his way to Spain and Real Madrid, which paid Milionarios a $25,000 transfer fee for his services. It turned out to be the greatest soccer bargain of all time.

Polish midfielder Henyk Kasperczack played in both the
1974 and 1978 World Cup tournaments.

The Real team revolved around Di Stefano, a deep-lying center forward who was nothing short of sensational. He could dribble, he could pass, he could head, he could shoot, he could, as the expression goes, do it all. As team captain he was in complete charge of what happened during the course of a match and more than a trifle arrogant. Teammates played the game his way or they played somewhere else.

Some, like Didi and Kopa, stars in their own right, failed to adjust and left. Others, like Puskas, made their peace and stayed to be part of what many experts insist was the finest club team of all time.

Certainly the record supports this contention. Beginning in 1956, Real won five consecutive European Cups by defeating, year after year, the best teams the rest of Europe had to offer.

For one long stretch, beginning in 1957 and lasting for nearly eight years, they played 120 Spanish League matches in Bernabeu Stadium without losing a single game.*

Between 1954 and 1977, Real won the league championship fifteen times. Its most consistent challengers over that period were Atlético Madrid, Atlético Bilbao, and Barcelona.

Spain's World Cup team qualified in 1978, after surrendering just one goal in a group that contained Romania and Yugoslavia. Outstanding players on the squad were midfielders Juan Asensi, Julio Cardenosa, and Eugenio Leal, and strikers Ruben Cano and Juan Gomez—who in the mid-1970's joined the long list of outstanding forwards who have played for Real Madrid.

*From February 1957, when they lost to Atlético Madrid 3–2, until they were defeated again by Atlético 1–0 in March 1965, Real won 114 and tied 8 league matches at home.

Rob Resenbrink (right) collides with a Bulgarian defender.

Center forward Ralf Edström is a star for both Sweden's national team and his club, IFK Gothenburg.

Sweden

Sweden finished a creditable fifth in the 1974 World Cup and qualified again for the finals in 1978 with a squad led by Roland Sandberg and Ralf Edstrom. Like many outstanding Swedish professionals, Edstrom has spent most of his playing career outside Sweden. In his case, it was with the Dutch League. Other Swedish soccer stars play elsewhere and return home for games with the Swedish national team.

The Swedish League was organized in 1896, and since then IFK Gothenburg, IFK Norrköping, and Malmö FF have each won the championship eleven times.

Switzerland

The Swiss League was formed in 1898, and since then a club called Grasshoppers has won the championship sixteen times, its last title coming in 1971. Grasshoppers' success in 1971 marked the only time since 1965 that the league championship had not been won by either FC Zurich or FC Basel.

Zurich won the title in 1966, 1968, 1974, 1975, and 1976. Basel's winning years were 1967, 1969, 1970, 1972, 1973, and 1977.

Turkey

Although the Fédération Turque de Football was organized in 1923, formalized league play did not begin until 1960. The leading club since then has been Fenerbahce, with seven championships. Trabzonspor won the title in 1976 and 1977.

U.S.S.R.

Because the Soviet Union is so vast the soccer season is governed by climate and geography. In the south the season runs from March to December, in central Russia from April to October, and in the north from May to September.

The outstanding Russian player of the 1970's has been Oleg Blokhin, a winger for Dynamo Kiev and Europe's Player of the Year in 1975. League play began in 1936, and since then Dynamo Moscow has won the championship eleven times, Spartak Moscow nine times, and Dynamo Kiev seven times. Spartak Moscow leads the cup competition with five championships, followed by Torpedo Moscow with five.

Yugoslavia

Always a tough opponent in international matches, the Yugoslav national team's greatest success has come in the Olympic games, where it won the gold medal in 1960 and finished as runner-up in 1948, 1952, and 1956.

Since the Yugoslav League was formed in 1923, Red Star Belgrade has won the championship a dozen times. Hajduk Split has been the next most successful club with eight, followed by Partizan Belgrade with seven.

Borussia Mönchengladbach defender Berti Vogts chases Dynamo Kiev's star forward, Oleg Blotkin.

Leading European Clubs

AJAX AMSTERDAM
Founded: 1900.
Colors: White shirts with two broad red stripes, white shorts.
Home Field: Ajaxstadion.
Championships: World Club: 1972; European Cup: 1971, 1972, 1973; Dutch League: 1918, 1919, 1931, 1932, 1934, 1937, 1939, 1947, 1957, 1960, 1966, 1967, 1968, 1970, 1972, 1973, 1977; Cup: 1917, 1943, 1961, 1967, 1970, 1971, 1972.

ANDERLECHT (Belgium)
Founded: 1908.
Colors: Violet shirts, white shorts.
Home Field: Parc Astrid.
Championships: European Cup-Winners' Cup: 1976; Belgian League: 1947, 1949, 1950, 1951, 1954, 1955, 1956, 1959, 1962, 1964, 1965, 1966, 1967, 1968, 1972, 1974; Cup: 1956, 1972, 1973, 1975, 1976.

ATLETICO BILBAO (Spain)
Founded: 1898.
Colors: Red and white striped shirts, black shorts.
Home Field: Estadio San Mamés.
Championships: Spanish League: 1930, 1931, 1934, 1936, 1943, 1956; Cup: 1901, 1902, 1903, 1910, 1911, 1914, 1915, 1916, 1921, 1923, 1930, 1931, 1932, 1933, 1943, 1944, 1945, 1950, 1955, 1956, 1958, 1969, 1973.

ATLETICO MADRID
Founded: 1903.
Colors: Red and white striped shirts, blue shorts.
Home Field: Estádio Vicente Calderón.
Championships: European Cup-Winners' Cup: 1962; Spanish League: 1940, 1941, 1950, 1951, 1966, 1970, 1973, 1977; Cup: 1960, 1961, 1965, 1972, 1976.

BARCELONA
Founded: 1899.
Colors: Red and blue striped shirts, navy blue shorts.
Home Field: Nou Camp.
Championships: European Fairs Cup: 1955–58, 1958–60, 1966; Spanish League: 1929, 1945, 1948, 1949, 1952, 1953, 1959, 1960, 1974; Cup: 1910, 1912, 1913, 1920, 1922, 1925, 1926, 1928, 1942, 1951, 1952, 1953, 1957, 1959, 1963, 1968, 1971.

BAYERN MUNICH
Founded: 1900.
Colors: Red and white striped shirts, red shorts.
Home Field: Olympiastadion.
Championships: European Cup: 1974, 1975, 1976; European Cup-Winners' Cup: 1967; German League: 1932, 1969, 1972, 1973, 1974; Cup: 1957, 1966, 1967, 1969, 1971.

BENFICA (Portugal)
Founded: 1904.
Colors: Red shirts with white trimmings, white shorts.
Home Field: Estádio da Luz.
Championships: European Cup: 1961, 1962; Portuguese League: 1936, 1937, 1938, 1942, 1943, 1945, 1950, 1955, 1957, 1960, 1961, 1963, 1964, 1965, 1967, 1968, 1969, 1971, 1972, 1973, 1975, 1976, 1977; Cup: 1940, 1943, 1944, 1949, 1951, 1952, 1953, 1955, 1957, 1959, 1962, 1964, 1969, 1970, 1972.

BORUSSIA MONCHENGLADBACH (West Germany)
Founded: 1900.
Colors: White shirts and shorts.
Home Field: Stadion Boekelberg.
Championships: UEFA Cup: 1975; German League: 1970, 1971, 1975, 1976, 1977; Cup: 1960, 1973.

FC BRUGES (Belgium)
Founded: 1894.
Colors: Blue shirts, black shorts.
Home Field: Olympia Stadion.
Championships: Belgian League: 1920, 1973, 1976, 1977, 1978; Cup: 1968, 1970.

MTK BUDAPEST
Founded: 1888.
Colors: White shirts with colored hoops, white shorts.
Home Field: MTK Stadium.
Championships: Hungarian League: 1904, 1907–08, 1913–14, 1916–17, 1917–18, 1918–19, 1919–20, 1920–21, 1921–22, 1922–23, 1923–24, 1924–25, 1928–29, 1935–36, 1936–37, 1951, 1953, 1957–58; Cup: 1909–10, 1910–11, 1911–12, 1913–14, 1922–23, 1924–25, 1931–32, 1951–52, 1968.

FC COLOGNE
Founded: 1901.
Colors: White shirts and shorts.
Home Field: Stadion Cologne.
Championships: German League: 1962, 1964, 1978; Cup: 1968, 1977.

CSKA SOFIA
Founded: 1948.
Colors: Dark red shirts, white shorts.
Home Field: People's Army Stadium.
Championships: Bulgarian League: 1948, 1951, 1952, 1954, 1955, 1956, 1957, 1958, 1959, 1960, 1961, 1962, 1966, 1969, 1970, 1972, 1973, 1975, 1976; Cup: 1951, 1954, 1955, 1960, 1961, 1965, 1969, 1972, 1973, 1974.

DUKLA PRAGUE
Founded: 1948.
Colors: Dark red shirts with yellow sleeves, yellow shorts.
Home Field: Juliska Stadion.
Championships: Czechoslovac League: 1953, 1956, 1958, 1961, 1962, 1963, 1964, 1966, 1977; Cup: 1961, 1965, 1966, 1969.

DYNAMO KIEV
Founded: 1927.
Colors: White shirts, white shorts with blue trimmings.
Home Field: Republic Stadium.
Championships: Russian League: 1961, 1966, 1967, 1968, 1971, 1974, 1975, 1978; Cup: 1954, 1964, 1966, 1974; European Cup-Winners Cup: 1975.

DYNAMO MOSCOW
Founded: 1923.
Colors: White shirts, blue shorts with white trim.
Home Field: Dynamo Stadium.
Championships: Russian League: 1936 (spring), 1937, 1940, 1945, 1949, 1954, 1955, 1957, 1959, 1963; Cup: 1937, 1953, 1967, 1970.

DYNAMO ZAGREB
Founded: 1945.
Colors: Dark blue shirts and shorts.
Home Field: Dynamo Stadium, Maksimir.
Championships: Fairs Cup: 1967; Yugoslav League: 1948, 1954, 1958; Cup: 1951, 1960, 1963, 1965, 1969.

PSV EINDHOVEN (The Netherlands)
Founded: 1913.
Colors: White shirts with red facings, white shorts.
Home Field: Philips Sportpark, Eindhoven.
Championships: Dutch League: 1929, 1935, 1951, 1963, 1975, 1976, 1978; Cup: 1937, 1950, 1974, 1976.

FERENCVAROS (Hungary)
Founded: 1899.
Colors: Green and white striped shirts, white shorts.
Home Field: Nep Stadium.
Championships: Fairs Cup: 1965; Hungarian League: 1903, 1905, 1906–07, 1908–09, 1909–10, 1911–12, 1912–13, 1925–26, 1926–27, 1927–28, 1931–32, 1933–34, 1937–38, 1939–40, 1940–41, 1944, 1948–49, 1962–63, 1964, 1967, 1968, 1976; Cup: 1912–13, 1921–22, 1926–27, 1927–28, 1932–33, 1934–35, 1941–42, 1942–43, 1943–44, 1956–58, 1971–72, 1973–74, 1975–76.

FEYENOORD (The Netherlands)
Founded: 1908.
Colors: Red and white halved shirts, black shorts.
Home Field: Feyenoord Stadium, Rotterdam.
Championships: World Club Championship: 1970; European Cup: 1970; Dutch League: 1924, 1928, 1936, 1938, 1940, 1961, 1962, 1965, 1969, 1971, 1974; Cup: 1930, 1935, 1965, 1969.

FIORENTINA
Founded: 1926.
Colors: Violet shirts, white shorts.
Home Field: Stadio Comunale.
Championships: European Cup-Winners' Cup: 1961; Italian League: 1956, 1969; Cup: 1940, 1961, 1966, 1975.

SV HAMBURG
Founded: 1887.
Colors: White and blue shirts, black shorts.
Home Field: Volksparkstadion.
Championships: German League: 1922 (declined to accept title), 1923, 1928, 1960; Cup: 1963, 1976; European Cup-Winners' Cup: 1977.

INTERNAZIONALE MILAN
Founded: 1908.
Colors: Blue and black striped shirts, black shorts.
Home Field: San Siro.
Championships: World Club Championship: 1964, 1965; European Cup: 1964, 1965; Italian League: 1910, 1920, 1930, 1938, 1940, 1953, 1954, 1963, 1965, 1966, 1971; Cup: 1939.

JUVENTUS
Founded: 1897.
Colors: Black and white striped shirts, white shorts.
Home Field: Stadio Comunale, Turin.
Championships: UEFA Cup: 1977; Italian League: 1905, 1926, 1931, 1932, 1933, 1934, 1935, 1950, 1952, 1959, 1960, 1961, 1967, 1972, 1973, 1975, 1977, 1978; Cup: 1938, 1942, 1959, 1960, 1965.

AC MILAN
Founded: 1899.
Colors: Red and black striped shirts, white shorts.
Home Field: San Siro.
Championships: World Club Championship: 1969; European Cup: 1963, 1969; European Cup-Winners' Cup: 1968, 1973; Italian League: 1901, 1906, 1907, 1951, 1955, 1957, 1959, 1962, 1968; Cup: 1967, 1972, 1973.

OLYMPIQUE MARSEILLE
Founded: 1899.
Colors: White shirts with blue facings, white shorts.
Home Field: Stade Vélodrome.
Championships: French League: 1937, 1948, 1971, 1972; Cup: 1924, 1926, 1927, 1935, 1938, 1943, 1969, 1972, 1976.

PANATHINAIKOS (Greece)
Founded: 1908.
Colors: Green shirts, white shorts.
Home Field: Panathinaikos Stadium, Athens.
Championships: Greek League: 1930, 1949, 1953, 1960, 1961, 1962, 1964, 1965, 1969, 1970, 1972; Cup: 1940, 1948, 1955, 1967, 1969.

RAPID VIENNA
Founded: 1898.
Colors: Green and white striped shirts, black shorts.
Home Field: Hutteldorf.
Championships: Austrian League: 1912, 1913, 1916, 1917, 1919, 1920, 1921, 1923, 1929, 1930, 1935, 1938, 1940, 1941, 1946, 1948, 1951, 1952, 1954, 1956, 1957, 1960, 1964, 1967, 1968; German League: 1941; Wiener Cup: 1919, 1920, 1927, 1946; Austrian Cup: 1961, 1968, 1969, 1972, 1976.

REAL MADRID
Founded: 1902.
Colors: White shirts and shorts.
Home Field: Estádio Santiago Bernabeu.
Championships: World Club Championship: 1960; European Cup: 1956, 1957, 1958, 1959, 1960, 1966; Spanish League: 1932, 1933, 1954, 1955, 1957, 1958, 1961, 1962, 1963, 1964, 1965, 1967, 1968, 1969, 1972, 1975, 1976, 1978; Cup: 1905, 1906, 1907, 1908, 1917, 1934, 1936, 1946, 1947, 1962, 1970, 1974, 1975.

RED STAR BELGRADE
Founded: 1945.
Colors: Red and white striped shirts, white shorts.
Home Field: Red Star Stadium.
Championships: Yugoslav League: 1951, 1953, 1956, 1957, 1959, 1960, 1964, 1968, 1969, 1970, 1973, 1977; Cup: 1948, 1949, 1950, 1958, 1959, 1964, 1968, 1970, 1971.

ST. ETIENNE
Founded: 1920.
Colors: Green shirts, white shorts.
Home Field: Stade Geoffroy-Guichard.
Championships: French League: 1957, 1964, 1967, 1968, 1969, 1970, 1974, 1975, 1976; Cup: 1962, 1968, 1970, 1974, 1975, 1977.

SLOVAN BRATISLAVA (Czechoslovakia)
Founded: 1919.
Colors: Sky blue shirts, dark blue shorts.
Home Field: Tehelne Pole.
Championships: European Cup-Winners' Cup: 1969; Czechoslovac League: 1949, 1950, 1951, 1955, 1970, 1974, 1975; Cup: 1962, 1963, 1968, 1974.

SPORTING LISBON
Founded: 1906.
Colors: Green and white hooped shirts, white shorts.
Home Field: Estádio José Alvalade.
Championships: European Cup-Winners' Cup: 1964; Portuguese League: 1941, 1944, 1947, 1948, 1949, 1951, 1952, 1953, 1954, 1958, 1962, 1968, 1970, 1974; Cup: 1941, 1945, 1946, 1948, 1954, 1963, 1971, 1973, 1974.

STANDARD LIEGE (Belgium)
Founded: 1898.
Colors: Red shirts, white shorts.
Home Field: Stade de Sclessin.
Championships: Belgian League: 1958, 1961, 1963, 1969, 1970, 1971; Cup: 1954, 1966, 1967.

TIROL-SVAROWSKI-INNSBRUCK (Austria)
Founded: 1914.
Colors: Black and green striped shirts, black shorts.
Home Field: Tivoli Stadion.
Championships: Austrian League: 1971, 1972, 1973, 1975, 1977; Cup: 1970, 1973, 1975.

UJPESTI DOZSA (Hungary)
Founded: 1885.
Colors: Lilac shirts with white sleeves and shorts.
Championships: Hungarian League: 1929–30, 1930–31, 1932–33, 1934–35, 1938–39, 1945, 1945–46, 1946–47, 1959–60, 1969, 1970, 1971, 1972, 1973, 1974, 1975, 1978; Cup: 1969, 1970, 1971, 1975.

VASAS BUDAPEST
Founded: 1911.
Colors: Red and blue hooped shirts, blue shorts.
Home Field: Vasa SC Stadion.
Championships: Hungarian League: 1957, 1960–61, 1961–62, 1965, 1966, 1977; Cup: 1954–55, 1973.

7. EUROPEAN CUPS

International championship competition between club teams, so much a fixture of European soccer today, is really the brainchild of a French sports editor who was inspired by the chauvinistic excesses of his English counterparts. The story begins in 1954, one year after the Hungarian national team thrashed England in Wembley Stadium. An English League team, the Wolverhampton Wanderers, played Honved, the Hungarian army team that had several members of the international squad among its starting eleven.

Down by two goals, Wolverhampton staged a tremendous rally to defeat Honved 3–2. One day later several English newspapers proclaimed Wolverhampton "Champions of the World." No one, at least no one outside England, took this claim seriously, but it did set several people to thinking about how a real world champion could be selected.

The European Cup.

Gabriel Hanot, soccer editor of the French daily sports newspaper *L'Equipe* ("The Team"), was among those who gave the matter some serious thought. Realizing that a world championship tournament was impractical, he proposed a competition among the previous season's European league champions to select the best of the best.

The European Cup

Six months after Hanot proposed his plan FIFA approved it, and the Union of European Football Associations (UEFA) agreed to sponsor the competition. By the winter of 1955, the games were underway and the European Cup was a reality. The elimination matches in this tournament are conducted on a home and away basis, with winners chosen on the basis of aggregate goals. The final round consists of a single game staged at a predetermined site.

The European Cup proved such a financial success—with fans flocking to see the best clubs in Europe compete head to head—that a few years later the second of the big three European tournaments, the UEFA Cup, was begun. In 1961 play began in the third tournament in this trio, the European Cup-Winners' Cup.

The First Cup

Since the competition had been the idea of a French journalist it seemed only fitting that a French club, Stade de Rheims, reached the championship game of the first European Cup tournament. Appropriately enough the match was played in Paris, on June 13, 1956, before a highly partisan crowd waiting expectantly to celebrate a Gallic triumph.

As often happens, some uncooperative visitors ruined the party. Rheims' opponent that afternoon was Real Madrid, one of the greatest club teams of all time. Raymond Kopa, a forward of exceptional ability, was the star of the Rheims team. Although he played brilliantly, his efforts were not enough to offset the multiple talents of Real Madrid, whose starting lineup read like a who's who of international soccer.

Toward the end of the contest the French crowd grew restless and began to pelt Real players with paper cups and cushions every time one of them came near the touchlines. It made no difference; Real, led by its Argentine stars Hector Rial and Alfredo Di Stefano, won 4–3.

Even in defeat Raymond Kopa's performance did not go unnoticed by Real's president, Don Santiago Bernabeu. Soon afterward he purchased Kopa's contract and one year later, when Real was in the championship game again, Kopa was wearing the white shirt and shorts of the Madrid club.

A Juggernaut

In 1957 the Italian club Fiorentina fell before Real's juggernaut, and in the following years Real continued to dominate the European Cup championship by defeating AC Milan, Stade de Rheims again, and finally Eintracht Frankfurt. After five years of competition Real Madrid was still the only club ever to win the title.

The 1960 match against Eintracht, an outstanding team in its own right, demonstrated the overwhelming power of the Spanish club. There had been some pregame speculation that Real's two great forwards, Di Stefano and Ferenc

Terry McDermott (far right) scores Liverpool's first goal in his club's 3–1 victory over Borussia Mönchengladbach for the 1977 European Cup. Liverpool won the cup again in 1978, defeating FC Bruges of Belgium for the championship.

Puskas, both thirty-four, might be over the hill. If they were, no one in the crowd of 127,000 that filled Glasgow's Hampden Park noticed.

Di Stefano—elegant, authoritarian, and in complete control of his body—seemed always to be at the center of action. Puskas, a short and stocky Hungarian, functioned as his perfect accomplice. Each complemented the other, and functioning like a perfectly tuned machine, they shredded Eintracht's highly regarded defense.

Before the final whistle sounded, Real had scored seven goals—four were by Di Stefano and three were by Puskas—while holding the German club to three. Not even age could slow this great team.

A New Champion

Real's streak was at last ended in 1961 by Barcelona, the defending Spanish League champions. Led by two Hungarians, Sandor Kocsis and Zoltan Czibor, Barcelona eliminated Real in an early round. After the first game ended in a 1–1 tie, Barcelona won the rematch 2–1 and continued on to the European Cup championship match against Benfica.

The joke in Europe in those days was that a club needed a Hungarian if it hoped to win a championship. Benfica had one; its manager, Bela Guttmann. Kocsis and Czibor each scored a goal for Barcelona in the final, but Benfica scored three times. Although the cup had at last left Spain, it still remained on the Iberian peninsula, moving across the border into Portugal.

Real was back in the championship game the following year with its still potent, but aging, forward line of Puskas, Di Stefano, and Francisco Gento. Benfica was also back, but this time with a brilliant nineteen-year-old striker from Mozambique—Eusebio.

Puskas scored three times for Real, while Eusebio scored twice for Benfica; but Puskas' teammates added no goals, while Eusebio's contributed three as the Portugese team won its second straight European Cup.

Eusebio scored a goal in the 1963 final, but AC Milan spoiled Benfica's hopes for a third consecutive championship by winning 2–1. Both of Milan's goals were scored by its Brazilian center forward, José Altafini. Each had been set up by twenty-year-old Gianni Rivera, who was destined to become one of Italy's greatest soccer players. Rivera had originally been signed by AC Milan when he was only sixteen for a reported $300,000.

Rivera's chief rival during this period was Alessandro Mazzola of Inter-Milan. He was the son of Valentino Mazzola, who had been the captain both of the Italian national team and the Torino team whose run of five consecutive Italian championships was ended by the tragic air disaster that claimed the life of the elder Mazzola and sixteen of his teammates.

Teamed with Luis Suarez, an outstanding Spanish striker,

Alessandro Mazzola led Inter-Milan to European Cup titles in 1964 and 1965.

European Tournament Results

THE EUROPEAN CUP
(Open to all European national champions)

1956	Real Madrid 4, Stade de Rheims 3	1968	Manchester United 4, Benfica 1
1957	Real Madrid 2, Fiorentina 0	1969	AC Milan 4, Ajax Amsterdam 1
1958	Real Madrid 3, AC Milan 2	1970	Feyenoord 2, Glasgow Celtic 1
1959	Real Madrid 2, Stade de Rheims 0	1971	Ajax Amsterdam 2, Panathinaikos 0
1960	Real Madrid 7, Eintracht Frankfurt 3	1972	Ajax Amsterdam 2, Internazionale Milan 0
1961	Benfica 3, Barcelona 2	1973	Ajax Amsterdam 1, Juventus 0
1962	Benfica 5, Real Madrid 3	1974	Bayern Munich 4, Atlético Madrid 0
1963	AC Milan 2, Benfica 1		(after first game was tied at 1–1)
1964	Internazionale Milan 3, Real Madrid 1	1975	Bayern Munich 2, Leeds United 0
1965	Internazionale Milan 1, Benfica 0	1976	Bayern Munich 1, St. Etienne 0
1966	Real Madrid 2, Partizan (Belgrade) 1	1977	Liverpool 3, Borussia Mönchengladbach 1
1967	Glasgow Celtic 2, Internazionale Milan 1	1978	Liverpool 1, FC Bruges 0

Mazzola helped Inter-Milan reach the final of the 1964 European Cup. Inter-Milan's opponent, making its seventh appearance in the championship game of this ten-year-old tournament, was Real Madrid. Puskas and Di Stefano were still with the team, but time at last had begun to take its toll. The Madrid team was able to score only once, while the Milan team scored three times. Two of its goals were knocked in by Mazzola, who wept openly after the match while recalling that it had been his father's dream that a European club championship might some day be established.

Inter-Milan won again in 1965, defeating Benfica 2–1. One year later, Real Madrid was back in the championship match, this time without Puskas and Di Stefano. The two stars were not missed, as Real won its sixth European Cup, beating Partizan of Belgrade 2–1.

British Champions

Glasgow Celtic became the first team from Great Britain to win the European Cup in 1967, beating Inter-Milan 2–1. One year later Manchester United became the second, turning back Benfica 4–1 in a thrilling overtime match.

There had been a controversial rule change prior to the 1967–68 tournament. It called for away goals to count double in the event teams were tied in aggregate goals after their home and away series. This change took some of the sparkle from the competition since it encouraged teams to play cautiously at home, lest they surrender too many goals.

The first club to benefit from the new rule was 1968 runner-up Benfica, which won a first-round series with the Irish club Glentoran because of it. Playing in Ireland, the two clubs battled to a one-goal draw. A return match in Lisbon ended in a scoreless tie, but Benfica advanced because the goal it had scored in Ireland was now worth two goals.

The Dutch Takeover

In 1969, AC Milan won the title by defeating Ajax Amsterdam 4–1. Then in 1970 a club from Rotterdam, Feyenoord, defeated Glasgow Celtic 2–1 in the championship, as the Dutch began their four-year domination of the tournament.

With Johann Cruyff on the left wing and Johann Neeskens in midfield, Ajax Amsterdam was the class of Europe in the early 1970's. In the 1971 final against the Greek club Panathinaikos, which was managed by Ferenc Puskas, Ajax earned one goal and then got another as a gift when a Greek defender accidentally kicked the ball past his own goalie into the net. It was all the Dutch club needed to win 2–0.

The following season Ajax was, if anything, better. With a new manager, Stefan Kovacs (yet another Hungarian), Ajax defeated Dynamo Dresden, Olympique Marseille, Arsenal, and Benfica enroute to the final. In the championship match against Inter-Milan, the Dutch defense smothered the Italian offense—which included such outstanding forwards as Alessandro Mazzola and Roberto Boninsegna—while their offense set up Cruyff for a pair of goals, as Ajax won 2–0.

Johnny Rep, an aggressive and talented midfielder, joined Ajax the following season and scored the only goal in the 1973 title match against Juventus of Turin.

A Bavarian Dynasty

Ajax hopes for a fourth consecutive European Cup were dashed by CSKA Sofia in the second round of the 1973–74 tournament, while the eventual champion got off to a very shaky beginning. Bayern Munich faced a lightly regarded Swedish club, Atvidaberg, in the opening round and at home easily won 3–1. But playing before their hometown fans, Atvidaberg won the rematch by the identical score—which meant the series would have to be decided by a penalty-shot contest, with each team getting five opportunities to score.

The contest was staged immediately after the second game and the West Germans won it 4–3, despite the roars of a highly partisan Swedish crowd. Bayern continued its advance to the championship game by winning home and away series against Dynamo Dresden, CSKA Sofia, and Ujpesti Dozsa. The Munich team's final opponent was Atlético Madrid.

The match was played in Brussels before 65,000 spectators who watched the teams play a 1–1 tie in regulation time followed by a scoreless overtime period. A rematch was played two nights later, and this time the 65,000 in attendance watched Bayern dismantle the Spanish club 4–0, with two goals each by Gerd Müller and Uli Hoeness.

Bayern's opponent in the 1975 championship match was Leeds United, and thousands of that club's fans crossed the Channel to attend the game in Paris. Müller and Franz Roth each scored for Bayern, while goalie Sepp Maier played brilliantly to shut out the English club. After the match, Leeds' fans rioted and as a result the club was banned from European competition the following season.

In 1976, Bayern won its third straight title by beating St. Etienne 1–0 on a goal off a free kick by Franz Roth.

The Kop Triumphs

Thirty-two clubs were entered in the 1976–77 tournament, which had grown so large that the eventual champion would have to play nine matches—this in addition to its regular domestic-league schedule and F.A. Cup competition.

One of the entrants, defending English League champion Liverpool, had something extra going for it: the support of that unique 12,000-voice wall of noise called the Kop. If ever the noun "fan" truly means fanatic it is here, for the members of the Kop, dressed in the red-and-white club colors of Liverpool, are as vocal a group of supporters as any team could ever hope to have.

Any visiting club taking the pitch at Anfield Road will know the fury of the Kop, which roars in delight when Liverpool has the ball and snarls with menace at an opponent's every move. Most English clubs are used to the Kop, but some foreign clubs visiting Anfield Road have been so intimidated that their games have suffered.

With the Kop cheering them on, Kevin Keegan and his Liverpool mates advanced to the finals with victories over Sweden's Malmö, Northern Ireland's Crusaders, Turkey's Trabzonspor, St. Etienne, and Zurich. Their opponent in the final was the new West German powerhouse, Borussia Mönchengladbach.

The game was played in Rome on May 25, 1977. Borussia's great Danish striker, Allan Simonsen, scored his team's only goal while Terry McDermott, Tommy Smith, and Phil Neal each scored for Liverpool, which won 3–1 and took the European Cup home to its cheering Kop.

The 1978 championship match was played in London and once again Liverpool won the cup, defeating FC Bruges of Belgium 1–0. The game's lone goal was scored by Scottish international Kenny Dalglish in the sixty-fourth minute of play.

THE UEFA CUP

This competition began in 1955 with a tongue twister of a title. It was originally called the International Inter-City Industrial Fairs Cup and was supposed to be a tournament between all-star teams representing cities that sponsored trade fairs.

After a very shaky beginning (it took five years to complete the first two tournaments), the format was changed to allow individual clubs into the competition. By 1961, the Fairs Cup was open to any club that finished among the top four in its native league—provided the team was not also entered in another international cup tournament.

For the 1966–67 season it was agreed, after several experiments with different formats, that the championship would be staged as a two-game home and away series. The team with the highest goal aggregate would be declared champion.

Dynamo Zagreb defeated Leeds United for the 1967 title by winning 2–0 in Yugoslavia and then playing Leeds to a scoreless tie in England. One year later, Leeds tried again and succeeded, defeating the Hungarian club Ferencvaros for the title.

The cup remained in England the following season, when Newcastle United took the home leg of the championship series over Hungary's Ujpesti Dosza 3–0 and then followed up with a 3–2 victory on the road to win the title by an aggregate score of 6–2.

For the 1969–70 tournament, the field was increased to sixty-four teams as more and more clubs recognized the financial rewards of international play. The final pitted England's Arsenal against Belgium's Anderlecht.

Playing in Brussels, Anderlecht won 3–1, but Arsenal came back at Old Highbury with a 3–0 triumph to take the cup with a 4–3 aggregate score. In 1971, the cup stayed in England when Leeds United defeated Juventus. This series ended in a 3–3 tie, but because Leeds had scored two goals in Turin while Juventus had only scored one away from home, Leeds was awarded the title.

A New Name

To the delight of sportswriters everywhere the tournament was renamed the UEFA Cup for the 1971–72 season, which produced a championship series between two English clubs: the Wolverhampton Wanderers and Tottenham Hotspur. Martin Chivers scored two goals to give Tottenham a 2–1 victory at home. The rematch ended in a 1–1 tie, so Tottenham won the title with a 3–2 aggregate.

England continued to control the championship in 1973, when Liverpool defeated Borussia Mönchengladbach in the title series. Kevin Keegan supplied the spark Liverpool needed to win at home, scoring a pair of goals in the 3–0 victory. The West Germans won their home game 2–0, giving Liverpool a one-goal aggregate victory.

Any hopes England had for winning a seventh straight UEFA Cup were extinguished in the 1974 series by the Dutch club Feyenoord. Tottenham Hotspur reached the finals and

West Ham United's Alan Sealey and Martin Peters cheer after Sealey scores in 1965 Cup-Winners' victory over Munich 1860.

Willie Johnston of the Glasgow Rangers, surrounded by two Moscow Dynamo defenders, scores the first of his two goals in the 1972 Cup-Winners' Cup final.

played the Dutch to a 2–2 tie at White Hart Lane. It was a lucky draw for the Spurs; they got one goal from fullback Mike England and a second when van Daele of Feyenoord accidentally kicked the ball into his own goal.

Playing in Rotterdam, the Dutch team was clearly superior and won 2–0—a victory that was marred when Tottenham Hotspur fans rioted in the stands after their team had been outplayed on the field.

Borussia Mönchengladbach faced the Dutch club Twente Enschede in the 1975 championship series. After the two teams battled to a scoreless tie in Düsseldorf, the German club was simply too strong in the return match and scored an overpowering 5–1 triumph.

Liverpool won its second UEFA Cup in 1976, in a hard-fought series against the Belgian club Bruges. Bruges took a one-goal lead in the first match, played in Liverpool, when Raoul Lambert sent a shot whistling into the nets after only

four minutes of action. Eight minutes later, Bruges had a two-goal advantage when Julion Cools scored. At that point, Liverpool's defense tightened and the Belgians were shut out for the rest of the afternoon.

With the Kop screaming its support, Liverpool took charge in the second half. After fourteen minutes, Ray Kennedy scored, two minutes later Jimmy Case tied, and after another three minutes Kevin Keegan converted a penalty shot to give Liverpool a 3–2 victory. In the return match, Bruges' Lambert and Liverpool's Keegan each scored one goal and the match ended in a 1–1 tie. Liverpool took the cup with a 4–3 aggregate score.

The rule that causes away goals to count double when both teams have the same aggregate gave Juventus the UEFA Cup in 1977. Playing against Atlético Bilbao in Spain, the Italian club lost 2–1. Atlético failed to score in Turin, losing 1–0, and Juventus' away goal provided the margin of victory.

UEFA Cup

(A special committee from UEFA selects the entrants)

1958	Barcelona 6, London (represented by Chelsea) 0	1969	Newcastle United 3, Ujpesti Dozsa (Hungary) 0
	London 2, Barcelona 0		Ujpesti Dozsa 2, Newcastle United 3
1959	No competition	1970	Anderlecht 3, Arsenal 1
1960	Birmingham City 0, Barcelona 0		Arsenal 3, Anderlecht 0
	Barcelona 4, Birmingham City 1	1971	Juventus 2, Leeds United 2
1961	AS Roma 2, Birminghan City 0		Leeds United 1, Juventus 1 (Leeds won on away-goal rule.)
	Birmingham City 2, AS Roma 2	1972	Wolverhampton Wanderers 1, Tottenham Hotspur 2
1962	Barcelona 1, Valencia 1		Tottenham Hotspur 1, Wolverhampton Wanderers 1
	Valencia 6, Barcelona 2	1973	Liverpool 3, Borussia Mönchengladbach (West Germany) 0
1963	Dynamo Zagreb 2, Valencia 1		Borussia Mönchengladbach 2, Liverpool 0
	Valencia 2, Dynamo Zagreb 0	1974	Tottenham Hotspur 2, Feyenoord 2
1964	Real Zaragoza 2, Valencia 1 (only one game played)		Feyenoord 2, Tottenham Hotspur 0
1965	Ferencvaros 1, Juventus 0 (only one game played)	1975	Borussia Mönchengladbach 2, Twente Enschede 0
1966	Barcelona 1, Real Zaragoza 0		Twente Enschede 1, Borussia Mönchengladbach 5
	Real Zaragoza 4, Barcelona 2 (Barcelona won on away-goal rule under which goals scored away from home are weighted as two goals instead of the usual one.)	1976	Liverpool 3, FC Bruges (Belgium) 2
			FC Bruges 1, Liverpool 0
		1977	Juventus 1, Atlético Bilbao 0
1967	Dynamo Zagreb 2, Leeds United 0		Atlético Bilbao 2, Juventus 1 (Juventus won on away-goal rule.)
	Leeds United 0, Dynamo Zagreb 0		
1968	Ferencvaros 0, Leeds United 0	1978	PSV Eindhoven (Netherlands) 0, Bastia (France) 0
	Leeds United 1, Ferencvaros 0		PSV Eindhoven 3, Bastia 0

THE CUP-WINNERS' CUP

This competition is open to winners of national cup competitions. If a nation's cup winner is also its league champion, it will enter the European Cup while the runner-up will compete for this slightly less prestigious prize.

The first edition of this tournament was staged during the 1960–61 season with Glasgow and Fiorentina reaching the final, which was, for the first and only time, conducted as a two-game home and away series. Fiorentina won the first game in Glasgow 2–1, and then won the rematch in Florence, 2–0, to take the title. The highlight of this game was a spectacular goal by Fiorentina's Swedish star Kurt Hamrin, who beat three Rangers to the ball near the sideline and then unleashed a powerful shot as he tumbled out of bounds amidst a group of photographers.

In 1962 the championship match was to be a single contest between Fiorentina and Atlético Madrid, but when the score was still tied 1–1 after regular and extra time a rematch had to be staged. Because of scheduling conflicts, four months passed before the two clubs met again. This time Atlético Madrid won easily, 3–0.

The most interesting aspect of the following season's tournament was the early matchup between AC Napoli, the Italian Cup winners, and Bangor City, a nonleague club that managed to win the Welsh Cup. After the home and away series, the two clubs were tied with three goals each and a playoff game was required. Napoli won this match 2–1, but it was only after the game was over that the club's fans discovered the lowly status of their team's opponent. Even though they had won, the club's players and officials were showered with abuse upon their return to Naples.

In the 1962 title game, Atlético Madrid's hopes for a second straight win were crushed by Tottenham Hotspur 5–1.

A second game was required to decide the championship in 1963, after Sporting Lisbon and MTK Budapest played to a 3–3 tie. The Portuguese club won this match 1–0.

West Ham United faced Munich 1860 in the next championship match. With Bobby Moore leading an impenetrable defense and Alan Sealey scoring two late goals, the English club won 2–0.

One year later, the West Germans got some revenge when Borussia Dortmund defeated Liverpool 2–1 in overtime. In 1967, there was another Anglo-German final and Bayern Munich edged Glasgow Rangers 1–0 on a goal by Roth.

Two goals by Kurt Hamrin was all the scoring AC Milan needed when they shut out SV Hamburg to win the title in 1968. One year later, Czechoslovakia's Slovan Bratislava won the championship with a 3–2 victory over Barcelona.

The Cup-Winners' Cup crossed the Channel in 1970 and remained in Great Britain for three years. Manchester City was the first to win it, defeating the Polish club Gornik Zabrze 2–1 during a torrential rainstorm in Vienna. The deciding goal came on a penalty shot by Francis Lee.

Chelsea celebrated its 1970 F.A. Cup triumph, the club's first ever, by winning the 1971 Cup-Winners' Cup championship. It wasn't an easy win for the London club. Its opponent was Real Madrid, and after 120 minutes of soccer (including extra time) the score was tied 1–1. But in the rematch a few days later, the brilliant midfield play of Charlie Cooke and goals by John Dempsey and Peter Osgood gave the team from Stamford Bridge its first European trophy.

En route to the 1972 championship, Glasgow's Rangers defeated Sporting Lisbon, Torino, and Bayern Munich to set up a meeting with Moscow Dynamo in Barcelona. It was a rough contest and the more than 20,000 Scottish fans in the stadium heaped a constant barrage of verbal abuse on referee Ortiz de Mendibi.

Late in the contest, with their team leading 3–2, the Scots stormed out onto the field and attacked several Russian players while joyfully carrying many of the Rangers about on their shoulders. Although there were several minutes left to play, the referee ordered the game abandoned. The Rangers were awarded the cup, but because of their fans' behavior they were unable to defend it, having been barred for one year from any European competition.

England had a chance to retain possession of the cup in 1973, when Leeds United reached the final against AC Milan. Violence also marred this contest, when late in the game Leeds players began to assault members of the Milan team. Leeds claimed the real villain was an incompetent referee who failed to call some flagrant Italian fouls. After Leeds lost 1–0, its fans could perhaps take some consolation in the fact that the Greek referee was later banned by his own federation and suspended by FIFA.

One year later, AC Milan lost the cup to the East German club FC Magdeburg by a score of 2–0. The cup moved even farther east in 1975 when Dynamo Kiev completely outplayed the Hungarian club Ferencvaros to win the final 3–0.

The Belgian club Anderlecht brought the cup back to Western Europe in 1976, by defeating West Ham United. The English club took an early lead on a goal by Pat Holland, but three goals by Rob Rensenbrink and a fourth by Van der Elst were too much to overcome, and Anderlecht led 4–2 when the final whistle sounded.

Anderlecht reached the championship match again in 1977, but this time lost to SV Hamburg 2–0. One year later, Anderlecht became the first club to recapture the title by defeating FK Austria 4–0.

Atlético Bilbao goalkeeper Iribar (dark shirt) punches the ball away from three Manchester City attackers in the 1969 Cup-Winners' Cup final.

Cup-Winners' Cup

1961	Fiorentina 4, Glasgow Rangers 1		1970	Manchester City 2, Gornik Zabrze (Poland) 1
1962	Atlético Madrid 3, Fiorentina 0		1971	Chelsea 2, Real Madrid 1
1963	Tottenham Hotspur 5, Atlético Madrid 1		1972	Glasgow Rangers 3, Dynamo Moscow 2
1964	Sporting Lisbon 1, MTK Budapest 0		1973	AC Milan 1, Leeds United 0
1965	West Ham United 2, Munich 1860 0		1974	FC Magdeburg (East Germany) 2, AC Milan 0
1966	Borussia Dortmund 2, Liverpool 1		1975	Dynamo Kiev 3, Ferencvaros (Hungary) 0
1967	Bayern Munich 1, Glasgow Rangers 0		1976	Anderlecht (Belgium) 4, West Ham United 2
1968	AC Milan 2, SV Hamburg 0		1977	SV Hamburg 2, Anderlecht 0
1969	Slovan Bratislava 3, Barcelona 2		1978	Anderlecht 4, FK Austria 0

THE EUROPEAN NATIONS CHAMPIONSHIP

The Glasgow Rangers parade the 1972 Cup-Winners' Cup
before their fans in Ibrox Stadium.

This is a tournament between national teams conducted on a quadrennial basis midway between World Cups. The first competition was limited to eighteen nations and took two years to complete, with the Soviet Union winning the championship by defeating Yugoslavia on July 10, 1960 in Paris by a score of 2–1. Key to the Soviet victory was the masterful play of goalkeeper Lev Yachin.

The second European Championship began in 1962 with twenty-six nations entered. After two years of elimination matches, the Soviet Union reached the title game again. Spain provided the opposition and had the advantage of playing before a highly partisan crowd in Madrid on June 21, 1964. This time the goalkeeping star was Spain's Iribar, whose crucial saves helped his team achieve a 2–1 victory.

By the time the next tournament began there were thirty-one nations entered, and for the first time the Soviet Union did not reach the final game. The Soviets were eliminated not by being outscored, but by being outlucked. They faced Italy in a semifinal match played in Naples, and when both teams failed to score in both regulation and extra time, officials from FIFA ordered that the match be decided by a tossed coin. Italy won the toss and advanced to the title game against Yugoslavia.

That game was played in Rome on June 8, 1968 and ended in a scoreless tie. There was no coin toss to decide the winner this time. Instead a rematch was played two days later, and with goals by Pietro Anastasi and Luigi Riva, Italy won 2–0 as goalkeeper Dino Zoff shut out the opposition. In the nine games Italy played in this tournament, Zoff surrendered only three goals and recorded seven shutouts.

West Germany emerged as the class team of Europe during the 1970–72 competition, putting on a series of convincing exhibitions of how overwhelming the concept of "total football" could be if a team had the necessary talent to support the theory.

With Franz Beckenbauer operating from his position as sweeper, Paul Breitner at a fullback spot, Gunter Netzer in midfield, and Europe's goal poacher par excellence Gerd Müller up front, the Germans were unstoppable. They brushed past England 3–1 before an unusually subdued Wembley throng in the quarterfinals, topped Belgium 2–1 in the semifinals, and then, with Müller scoring twice, dazzled the Soviet Union 3–0 in the championship match that was played in Brussels on June 18, 1972.

Favored to win the next tournament, West Germany had a difficult time in reaching the title game. After its first quarterfinal match with Spain ended in a draw, the Germans were forced into a replay, which they won 2–0.

In the semifinal round, Yugoslavia carried West Germany into extra time before finally submitting 4–2 to set up a final game between the Germans and Czechoslovakia. This match was played in Belgrade on June 20, 1976 and after extra time was tied at two goals apiece.

The title was then decided in a penalty-shot competition, with each team taking five shots. West Germany was able to convert on only three of its attempts, while the Czechs converted all five to win the championship.

The Next Tournament

Thirty-two nations have entered the 1980 European Championship. All the teams—except for the automatically qualified host country, Italy—have been assigned to one of seven groups. Group matches will be played on a round-robin basis, with the winners advancing to the final stages of the tournament, which will be held in Italy in June of 1980. The groupings for this competition are as follows:

GROUP 1

England
Denmark
Rep. of Ireland
Bulgaria
N. Ireland

GROUP 2

Belgium
Norway
Austria
Scotland
Portugal

GROUP 3

Yugoslavia
Cyprus
Romania
Spain

GROUP 4

The Netherlands
Iceland
Poland
E. Germany
Switzerland

GROUP 5

Czechoslovakia
Luxemburg
Sweden
France

GROUP 6

U.S.S.R.
Finland
Hungary
Greece

GROUP 7

W. Germany
Malta
Wales
Turkey

8. SOUTH AMERICAN SOCCER

Although there are four times as many people and twelve times as many registered soccer players in Europe, there is nothing second-rate about the quality of soccer played in South America. Indeed, in head-to-head competition South American national teams and local clubs have more than held their own against European opponents.

Of the fifteen World Club championships played between European Cup champions and winners of the Copa Liberta-dores ("Liberators' Cup"), South American clubs have won eight. This despite the fact that hundreds of the continent's best players have been drawn away to higher paying positions with top European clubs.

Two South American nations won five of the first ten World Cup tournaments. Brazil took the title in 1958, 1962, and 1970; finished second in 1950; third in 1938; and fourth in 1970. Uruguay, with a population of less than three million people, has won two World Cups (in 1930 and in 1950) and finished fourth twice (in 1954 and in 1970).

The South American soccer federation is the Confederación Sudamericana de Futbol (CONMEBOL), which consists of ten member nations.

Argentina

A retired general had died in Córdoba at the age of eighty; a few bombs had exploded in Bogotá, and of course the Argentine football team was continuing its violent progress through Europe.

Graham Greene
The Honorary Consul

For decades the Argentines were the bad boys of international soccer, favoring such a rough-and-tumble style of play that England's Sir Alf Ramsey was once moved to describe

Argentina's Ardiles hitches a ride on the shirt of Scotland's Archie Gemmill.

them as "animals." That reputation may be just history now, and if it is the credit can go to one man—Cesar Luis Menotti, the coach who guided Argentina to its 1978 World Cup championship.

After taking office in 1976, Menotti, then thirty-six, said, "My country's football needs major restructuring. Perhaps if we can win the World Cup my way it could inspire a revision of the philosophy of the game. Perhaps it would take the emphasis away from the cynical and the violent. Perhaps."

If there is to be a revolution in Argentine soccer it will come because Menotti gave players like midfielder Osvaldo Ardiles a chance to exploit their natural talents. Looking like a refugee from a 1920's movie about the tango, with his high cheekbones and slicked-back hair, Ardiles seems to glide up and down the field, making passes and creating goals.

Other Argentine standouts include goalkeeper Ubaldo Fillol, defender Daniel Passarella, and forwards Daniel Ber-

toni, Mario Kempes, and Leopoldo Luque.

British sailors introduced soccer to Argentina in 1860, and seven years later the Buenos Aires Football Club was formed. Then, as the British-owned railway system snaked its way through the countryside, new clubs were established in the hinterlands. Two of the oldest, Quilmes (formed in 1887) and Rosario (1889), are still members of the Argentine League, which was organized in 1891.

Although Argentina has developed some of the world's finest soccer players, it has had trouble keeping many of them at home. The most famous of these expatriate athletes was Alberto Di Stefano, who spent most of his playing years with Real Madrid. But Di Stefano is only one of hundreds of Argentine soccer players who have crossed the ocean to find fame and fortune in Europe.

Until the Italian League banned foreign players in 1965, several hundred Argentinians played in Italy. Since then,

Osvaldo Ardiles joined the English club Tottenham Hotspur after Argentina won the 1978 World Cup.

Willie Johnston of Scotland (dark shirt) tries to make peace with an Argentine player.

Spain has become the favorite destination for Argentine players seeking higher rewards for their talents. In 1977, thirty-five Argentinians were playing in Spain, while others filled spaces in the ranks of French and West German clubs.

Among those playing in Europe are Carlos Babbington, Argentina's midfield star in the 1974 World Cup, who plays for the West German club Wattenscheid 09; fullback Enrique Wolff, who plays for Real Madrid; forward Mario Kempes, on the Valencia team, and forward Oswaldo Piazza, who plays for St. Etienne.

Despite all these defections, enough talented players stay home to field a half dozen of the strongest club teams in the world. The six, which have dominated league play since the 1930's, are Boca Juniors, Estudiantes, Independiente, Rac-

ing Club, River Plate, and San Lorenzo. Since 1958, only Huracán, the winners in 1973, and Newells Old Boys, the 1974 champions, have broken the stranglehold these six clubs have had on the league title.

The South American club championship is the Copa de los Libertadores. The tournament began in 1960, and since then Independiente has won it six times—a record that includes four consecutive victories, beginning with the 1972 tournament. Estudiantes has won the championship three times, and Boca Juniors won the title in 1977, defeating Brazil's Cruzeiro in a three-game series that was finally decided by penalty shots after the third match ended in a scoreless tie.

Of the twenty-two South American championships played since 1916, Argentina has won twelve.

Brazil

Soccer appeals to us because it is a game of elegant aggressiveness. We don't like violent sports, but the agility and trickiness required in soccer we appreciate. You can see this trait even in our business dealings. We don't admire hard work so much. But we do admire a successful trick.

Dr. A.H. Fuerstenthal
São Paulo psychiatrist

As the good doctor implies, the best of Brazil's footballers are masters of the dribble, the fake, and the perfect pass to set up an unexpected shot on goal. Names like Pelé, Didi, Garrincha, Jairzinho, and Rivelino have become synonymous with amazing individual skills seldom equaled anywhere else in the world.

Brazilians begin to hone these skills at an early age, many on the beaches of Ipanema, Botafogo, Leblon, or that four-mile-long stretch of oceanside sand called Copacabana. Those who are good enough will be invited to join one of the junior teams sponsored by the professional clubs. The youngest boys, those between ten and twelve, will compete in the Dente de Leite ("milk tooth") Division, then the Infantil (for twelve- to sixteen-year-olds), the Juvenil B (fourteen- to sixteen-year-olds), and the Juvenil A (sixteen- to eighteen-year-olds). When they become eighteen, the best will join Brazil's 7,300 registered professional soccer players.

Each of Brazil's twenty-one states has its own soccer federation, but all of them are members of the Confederaco Brasilia de Deportes (CBD), an overall authority for all sports in the nation.

The CBD controls Brazil's national team—and as the record would indicate, does a thorough job. Prior to Brazil's first World Cup victory in 1958, the CBD prepared a forty-page dossier on conditions the team could expect in Sweden, and for months before the tournament Brazil's players ate only Swedish food. In 1977, the CBD purchased a ranch fifty miles north of Brazil and converted it into a training camp for the national team, which is always one of the world's best.

Brazil's strongest leagues are located in the states of Rio and São Paulo. The top clubs in Rio have been, over the years, Fluminense, Flamengo, Vasco da Gama, and Botafogo. Cruzeiro, a powerful team from Belo Horizonte, also competes in the Rio League. São Paulo's top clubs have been Palmeiras, São Paulo, Corinthians, and the club Pelé starred for from 1956 to 1974—Santos.

With Pelé as a drawing card, Santos became the most-traveled club team in the world, visiting sixty-five different nations in its globetrotting expeditions. Ironically soccer's greatest star is not Brazil's most capped player. That honor is held by Djalma Santos, a hard-tackling fullback who starred for Palmeiras and was selected to play for the national team 110 times, as compared to Pelé's 108 caps.

Brazil's two brightest new stars in the 1970's are Zico and Zeze. Zico, called the "White Pelé" by many of his countrymen, became his nation's highest-paid athlete in 1977, when Flamengo signed him to a contract worth $225,000 a year. West German team manager Helmut Schoen has described Zico as "the most exciting Brazilian player of his generation," and France's coach Michel Hidalgo called him "the most creative playmaker in world soccer today."

Zeze, who as a seventeen-year-old striker was added to the national squad in 1978, is a teammate of Rivelino's on the Fluminense club. Comparisons with past greats are popular in Brazil, and national team coach Claudio Coutinho has referred to Zeze as "the new Garrincha."

Argentine and Scottish players get their heads together in a fight for the ball.

Willie Johnston launches a shot at Argentina's goal.

Bolivia

Often called the Tibet of South America, this mountainous, landlocked nation has never been one of the continent's major soccer powers. Bolivia had a chance to qualify for the 1978 World Cup by winning the wild-card berth shared by South America and Europe. The Bolivians had finished third in South America's second qualifying round, losing to Brazil 8–0 and Peru 5–0.

In a home and away series with Hungary the Bolivians lost 6–0 in Budapest and 3–2 in La Paz. There is little chance the national team will show any great improvement in the near future because the majority of Bolivia's best young players leave the country for more lucrative careers elsewhere.

The two leading club teams in Bolivia are Guabria, from the plains of Santa Cruz de la Sierra, and Bolivar, of La Paz. Bolivia's last appearance in the final round of the World Cup was in 1950, when it lost to Uruguay 8–0.

Chile

The host nation for the 1962 World Cup, when it finished a surprising third, Chile has had a checkered history in international competition. It qualified for the 1974 World Cup finals when, for political reasons, the Soviet Union refused to play the Chilean national team in Santiago. But Chile was eliminated in the opening round of the finals when the national team lost to both East and West Germany.

The captain of Chile's national team, centerback Elias Figueroa, was named South America's Player of the Year in 1974, 1975, and 1976, while playing for the Brazilian club Internacional de Porto Alegre. In 1977, he returned to Chile to join Santiago's Palestino club.

Palestino is one of the nation's four top clubs. The other three are Everton of Viña del Mar, Unión Español, and Colo Colo, named after an Indian liberation hero. Former Honved and Real Madrid star Ferenc Puskas served as head coach of

But goalkeeper Mario Gatti makes the save.

Colo Colo for several years in the mid-1970's.

In 1973, Colo Colo became the first Chilean club to reach the final of the Copa Libertadores. Independiente of Argentina won the cup.

Colombia

The biggest soccer news in Colombia is that the nation has been selected to host the finals of the 1986 World Cup. Colombia last attracted the attention of soccer fans around the globe in the early 1950's when it established an outlaw professional league that signed foreign players without paying any transfer fees. FIFA suspended the league and in reaction to international pressure it surrendered the hijacked players in 1953.

Colombians favor a defensive style of soccer and their referees are among the strictest in South America, brooking little violence and handing out fines and suspensions without hesitation.

The nation's leading clubs are Independiente Santa Fe, Milionarios of Bogotá, Deportivo Cali, and Nacional Medellín. With Argentine coach Osvaldo Zubeldia and six Argentine players, Nacional won the Colombian championship in 1977.

Ecuador

There are thirty clubs playing in the Ecuadorian League, which is divided into two divisions. Over the years the three best have been Emelec and Liga Deportiva Universiaria, both of Quito, and Deportivo of Cuenca.

In early 1977, the Ecuadorian national team played Uruguay in Montevideo. With the score tied at 1–1 after seventy-five minutes of play, the referee sent off two Ecuadorian players, and, after violent protests from their teammates, sent the other nine players off as well.

Later that year, in an effort to improve standards of play and develop players who can better control their emotions, Ecua-

151

dor's Soccer Federation went to the unusual length of importing a dozen referees from neighboring South American countries to officiate at local league games.

Paraguay

Paraguay's main problem is similar to one shared by many South American nations, and that is simply finding a method of keeping its best athletes at home. In 1977, eighteen of Paraguay's best players were playing in Spain, while other Paraguayans found employment elsewhere in Latin America.

The Paraguayan F.A. was founded in 1906, and since then the nation's top clubs have been Olimpia, Sportivo Lugueño of Luque, and Asunción.

Peru

After a surprisingly good performance in the 1970 World Cup—where they were eliminated by Brazil 4–2 in the quarterfinals—the Peruvians failed to qualify in 1974, but were back in the finals in 1978.

Throughout the 1970's the national team was built around such players as midfielder Teofilo Cubillas, winger Juan José Munante, and defenders Julio Melendez and Hector Chumpitaz. In 1975, Peru won the South American championship.

The leading clubs in Peru are Alianza of Lima and Alfonso Ugarte of Puno. The nation's outstanding player in the 1960's and early 1970's was Ramon Mifflin, captain of the Peruvian national team and a teammate of Pelé's both at Santos and in New York with the Cosmos.

Uruguay

No nation of similar size can boast the proud soccer history that Uruguay has established since its soccer association was founded in 1900. Winners of the Olympic Games of 1924 and 1928, winners of the World Cup twice and the South

Brazil's Jairzinho on the attack against Argentina.

Jairzinho on the loose.

Midfielder Roberto Rivelino (center) was the captain of Brazil's 1978 World Cup team.

American championship seven times, this tiny country with only 550 registered professionals has indeed compiled an impressive record.

Because of its small size and lack of financial resources, Uruguay has had trouble keeping many of its top players in the country. For example, since starring in the 1970 World Cup, when Uruguay reached the semifinals, midfielder Pedro Rocha has played for São Paulo. Because Brazilian teams are allowed to field only one foreign player in their starting lineups, Rocha took out Brazilian citizenship papers in 1977, prompting a Montevideo newspaper to denounce him as a traitor.

One of Uruguay's top clubs, Peñarol, began life in the late nineteenth century as the Central Uruguayan Railway Cricket Club. It has won the Copa Libertadores three times (in 1960, 1961, and 1966) and the World Club championship twice, over Benfica in 1961 and over Real Madrid in 1966.

The other leading club teams are Cerro of Montevideo,

Defensor, and Nacional. In 1976, Defensor became the first club other than Peñarol or Nacional to win the Uruguayan championship in forty-five years.

Venezuela

Soccer was not really all that popular here until overseas oil companies arrived in the mid-1950's and brought with them workers who helped the game reach the same status that baseball has with Venezuelan athletes and fans. Still, as of 1977, almost 45 per cent of Venezuela's professional soccer players were foreigners. Among them was the great Brazilian forward Jairzinho, who played for the Caracas club Deportiva Galicia.

The two top clubs in the Venezuelan League have been Deportiva Galicia and Deportiva Portuguesa. In 1977, Portuguesa reached the semifinal round of the Copa Libertadores before being eliminated by two Brazilian clubs, Internacional Porto Alegre and the eventual champion, Cruzeiro.

Rio's Copacabana Beach serves as a soccer field for thousands of Brazilian youngsters.

Rivelino and his teammates celebrate a goal against Poland.

TOURNAMENTS

The Copa Libertadores

Begun in 1960 to determine South America's club champion, this tournament has produced some thrilling games, several stellar individual performances, and enough zany on- and off-field antics to fill a three-act farce.

At the start it was called the Champion Clubs Cup and showed few signs of surviving for more than a couple of seasons. Three members of CONMEBOL (the South American soccer confederation) boycotted the first competition, claiming that it interfered with their regular league schedules. Other nations, including Brazil, failed to enter their top clubs and often those that did allowed those clubs to hold back some of their best players.

The competition was contested on a home and away basis with the Uruguayan club Peñarol winning the title in both 1961 and 1962. But lack of fan interest made for low gate receipts and put the tournament in serious financial straits.

Help arrived in 1962 when the great Brazilian team Santos and its superstar Pelé entered the tournament. All over South America there was standing room only when Pelé and his teammates came to town to take on the local defending champion. In one season the tournament went from near collapse to complete success.

The 1962 competition reached its climax in a hectic championship series between Santos and Peñerol. Although Pelé was sidelined with an injury, Santos won the first match, played in Montevideo, 2–1. Game two was staged in São Paulo and was delayed for ninety minutes when someone threw a rock from the stands and knocked the referee unconscious. Even when revived, his brain must have still been addled because he allowed play to continue after time had expired.

What happened next resembled something out of a Gilbert and Sullivan operetta. When the Chilean referee was knocked out Peñarol led Santos, still playing without Pelé, 3–2. After the match resumed, Santos tied the score and everyone went home thinking the Brazilians had won the cup with an aggregate goal edge of 5–4. Everyone that is except the referee. In his official report on the match he ruled that the game had already ended before Santos scored its last goal.

Chaos ensued, tempers flared, threats were exchanged, and two nations considered declaring war on Chile. Finally, cooler heads prevailed and it was decided to stage a playoff match at a neutral site. Both sides agreed on Buenos Aires and this time, with Pelé restored to full health and playing brilliantly, Santos scored a decisive 3–0 victory.

Santos won again, without any untoward incidents, the following year. The Argentine club Independiente won the next two championships, defeating Uruguay's Nacional in 1964 and Peñarol in 1965.

In 1966, the tournament was renamed the Copa Libertadores de Sud America and was expanded to include two teams from each nation—the league champions and the runners-up.

In 1966, the title was taken by Peñarol, and in 1967 Racing Club of Argentina won the championship. Another Argentinian, Daniel Onega of River Plate, scored fifteen goals before his team was eliminated in the 1967 competition.

Racing Club's victory began a decade during which Argen-

tine teams won nine out of ten championships. Estudiantes de la Plata won in 1968, 1969, and 1970; Uruguay's Nacional broke the streak in 1971; and then Independiente took the next four championships. The Argentine clubs were helped by a rule that automatically admits the defending champion to the semifinal round of the following year's competition.

Throughout this period the Copa Libertadores was plagued by violence both on the field and in the stands. The worst incident occurred in 1970, when the final game between Estudiantes and Peñarol erupted into a no-holds-barred brawl between players and reserves from both teams.

Independiente's bid for a fifth consecutive title was dashed in the semifinal round by River Plate, a club that carried Argentina's banner into the 1976 final against the Brazilian club Cruzeiro. After each club won at home, a playoff match was staged in Santiago, and the Brazilians won 3–2. During the course of this tournament Cruzeiro played thirteen games, winning ten, tying two, and losing only one.

Six teams reached the semifinal round of the 1977 tournament and were divided into two groups to play a round-robin schedule. In Group I, Boca Juniors of Argentina finished ahead of Deportivo Cali (Colombia) and Libertad Asunción (Paraguay). Group II was dominated by defending champion Cruzeiro. The club from Belo Horizonte defeated Venezuela's Portuguesa twice and defeated and tied another Brazilian club, International Porto Alegre.

The first game of the championship series was played in Buenos Aires and won by Boca Juniors 1–0. Cruzeiro won the return match in Belo Horizonte by an identical score so a playoff game was staged in Montevideo.

With both teams scoreless after regulation and extra time, the game was decided on penalty kicks with each team receiving five opportunities to score. Boca Juniors converted all of its attempts and when goalkeeper Raul Gatti stopped Cruzeiro's fifth shot the Argentine club won the 1977 edition of the Copa Libertadores.

The Copa Sudamericana

As the Copa Libertadores gained in popularity this competition among national teams fell on hard times and has only been staged once since 1967. That was in 1975, when Peru defeated Colombia for the title.

The competition has had a sporadic history and has been conducted twenty-one times since Uruguay won the first tournament in 1917. Argentina leads the championship derby with eight victories, followed closely by Uruguay with seven. Brazil has won the cup three times, while Peru has won twice, and Bolivia and Paraguay once each.

World Club Championship

The competition between the winners of the European Cup and the Copa Libertadores has had a short, turbulent, and not altogether happy history. In 1977 Liverpool, the European champions, declined an invitation to compete in this tournament and it remains questionable that the competition will resume any time in the near future.

Violence and a series of ugly incidents have soured many European clubs toward the tournament, and on several occasions the European Cup winner has simply refused to compete, sending a runner-up team in its place. Although there had been several fights in the first seven tournaments, things really started to get out of control in 1967, when Glasgow Celtic played Racing Club of Argentina.

The first match was played in Glasgow and after several fist fights Celtic was ahead 1–0 when the game finally ended. The return match was played in Buenos Aires, but even before it got underway Celtic goalkeeper Ronnie Simpson was knocked out of action by a bottle thrown from the stands. Racing Club won the game 2–1 after four Celtic players and two Argentinians had been tossed out for fighting.

Since the aggregate score was tied at 2–2, a third game was necessary. Despite official fears it ended with everyone still alive and Racing on top 1–0.

In 1968 Estudiantes de la Plata fought it out with Manchester United, winning at home 1–0 and playing to a draw in England. In that match George Best and Estudiantes' Medina were ejected for brawling. The Argentines took the title with one win and a tie.

Almost from the opening whistle there was open warfare when AC Milan met Estudiantes in 1969. Playing in Italy, Milan won 3–0—with one of its goals being scored by Combin, an Argentine-born forward.

During the return match in Buenos Aires, Combin was viciously tackled while driving toward the goal and was carried off with a broken leg. Estudiantes won the game 2–1, but lost the title by an aggregate goal score of 4–2.

Brazil's star forward, Zico.

If anything, conditions worsened in 1970 when Feyenoord of Rotterdam traveled to Buenos Aires to play Estudiantes. The Dutch sustained a constant battering but overcame a two-goal deficit to leave Argentina with a 2–2 tie and then win the return match in Holland, 1–0, to take the title.

Ajax Amsterdam, the 1971 European Cup winners, bypassed its chance to play the Uruguayan Club Nacional so the Greek team Panathinaikos went in its place. After the first game ended 1–1, Nacional took the second game—and the title—2–1.

In 1972 Ajax had a change of heart and agreed to meet Argentina's Independiente. Using their feet to kick the ball and their fists for survival, the Dutch escaped from Buenos Aires with a 1–1 tie and then smashed Independiente 4–0 in the return match.

Ajax could have had a chance to defend its title in 1973, but the team's management decided to step aside in favor of Italy's Juventus. The tournament was limited to a single game, played in Rome and won by Independiente 1–0.

Bayern Munich passed up its chance to play in 1974, so Atlético Madrid went in its place and defeated Independiente with a 2–1 aggregate. The competition was suspended in 1975, but resumed again in 1976 when Bayern Munich defeated Independiente. Liverpool declined an invitation to compete in 1978, so runner-up Borussia Mönchengladbach played Argentina's Boca Juniors, who won the title.

Zico (left) on the attack against West Germany.

COPA LIBERTADORES

1960	Peñarol (Argentina)	1969	Estudiantes
1961	Peñarol	1970	Estudiantes
1962	Santos (Brazil)	1971	Nacional (Uruguay)
1963	Santos	1972	Independiente
1964	Independiente (Argentina)	1973	Independiente
1965	Independiente	1974	Independiente
1966	Peñarol	1975	Independiente
1967	Racing Club (Argentina)	1976	Cruzeiro (Brazil)
1968	Estudiantes (Argentina)	1977	Boca Juniors (Argentina)

SOUTH AMERICAN CHAMPIONSHIP

1917	Uruguay	1926	Uruguay	1953	Paraguay
1919	Brazil	1927	Argentina	1955	Argentina
1920	Uruguay	1937	Argentina	1957	Argentina
1921	Argentina	1939	Peru	1959	Argentina
1922	Brazil	1942	Uruguay	1963	Bolivia
1923	Uruguay	1947	Argentina	1967	Uruguay
1924	Uruguay	1949	Brazil	1975	Peru

WORLD CLUB CHAMPIONSHIP

1960	Real Madrid (Spain)	1969	AC Milan (Italy)
1961	Peñarol (Uruguay)	1970	Feyenoord (Netherlands)
1962	Santos (Brazil)	1971	Nacional (Uruguay)
1963	Santos	1972	Ajax (Netherlands)
1964	Internazionale Milan (Italy)	1973	Independiente
1965	Internazionale Milan	1974	Atlético Madrid (Spain)
1966	Peñarol	1975	Not played
1967	Racing (Argentina)	1976	Bayern Munich
1968	Estudiantes (Argentina)	1977	Not played
		1978	Boca Juniors

Brazil's 1970 World Cup champions.

Brazilian players embrace after scoring a goal against
West Germany.

9. CANADA, MEXICO, AND THE CARIBBEAN

The Confederación Norte-Centroamericana y del Caribe de Futbol (CONCACAF) is the governing soccer federation for North and Central America and the Caribbean. The United States is a member of this federation. Among its other members are:

Canada

Ice hockey, baseball, and Canadian football have, until quite recently, ranked ahead of soccer with the Dominion's sports fans and athletes. Then, just as it did south of the border, the game enjoyed a sudden surge of popularity in the 1970's. With two strong members in the North American Soccer League—the Vancouver Whitecaps and the Toronto Metros—the future of the sport in Canada appears to be a bright one.

Toronto was the home of Canada's first soccer team. It was formed back in 1876 as part of the Charlton Cricket Club. Although there have been teams in all the provinces, the sport only flourished in British Columbia, and when Canada entered its first World Cup competition—an elimination round for the 1958 tournament—most of its team's members were from this western province.

The Canadians gave a good account of themselves, defeating the United States by scores of 5–1 and 3–2 before being eliminated by Mexico.

Twenty years later it was again Canada that eliminated the United States from the World Cup. The two nations had finished in a tie behind Mexico in a preliminary round of the CONCACAF tournament and a playoff game was staged in

Haiti to decide which team would advance, along with Mexico, to the next round.

The Canadian team, coached by Eckhard Krautzun, won the match 3–0 with goals by Brian Budd, Bob Lenarduzzi, and Bob Bolitho. Canada ultimately finished third in the six-team final round.

Although they defeated Surinam 2–1 and Guatemala by the same score, the Canadians were tied with Haiti 1–1 and beaten by El Salvador 2–1 and Mexico 3–1.

El Salvador

After qualifying for the 1970 World Cup finals, following a short but bloody war with Honduras, El Salvador was eliminated in the first round, surrendering nine goals while scoring none. Since then the nation has developed an extensive youth soccer program that is largely supported by the country's two major clubs, Aguila and Alianza.

Guatemala

The three strongest clubs in Guatemala are Aurora FC, the Club Comunicaciones, and Municipal, which won the CONCACAF Champions' Tournament in 1973.

Haiti

CONCACAF's representative in the 1974 World Cup finals, Haiti has many strong clubs. Among the best are Viollet, Aigle Noir, Victory, Don Bosco de Petionville, and the Racing Club, which won the 1966 edition of the CONCACAF Champions' Tournament.

Honduras

This nation has a large youth program with over 75,000 youngsters registered with junior leagues. The most successful clubs in the professional league have been Club España and Club Olimpia.

Mexico

The First Divison of the Mexican League stages one of the most hotly contested championships in the world before large and enthusiastic crowds. The top clubs include Guadalajara, Toluca, Cruz Azul, Atlético Español, Universtaad, and Club America.

In qualifying for the 1978 World Cup finals the Mexican team, coached by Ignacio Trellez, was led by such outstanding forwards as Victor Rangel, Hugo Sanchez, Francisco Solis, and Pedro Damian. The team's midfield leader was Leonardo Cuellar.

Mexico advanced to the finals by winning a six-nation playoff tournament that included Canada, El Salvador, Guatemala, Haiti, and Surinam. The competition was staged in Mexico City and Monterrey over an eighteen-day period in October of 1977.

The Mexicans won all five of their games, outscoring the opposition twenty goals to five. Haiti finished second in the tournament with a record of three wins, one loss, and a tie.

Surinam

Surinam, formally Dutch Guiana, has a ten-club league. The major clubs are Robin Hood, Voorward, and Transval, winners of the 1974 CONCACAF Champions' Tournament.

Trinidad and Tobago

This two-island nation has produced some outstanding players, including Steve David, the North American Soccer League's scoring champion in 1975 and 1977. Before coming to the United States, David was a policeman in Trinidad.

Other natives of the islands who have done well in the States are Lincoln Phillips, who is now coach of the Howard University team, and Warren Archibald, a speedy winger who played ten seasons in the NASL.

Hugo Sanchez of Mexico in action against El Salvador.

Tunisian midfielder Tarak Dhiab (white shirt) scores in the
4–1 victory against Egypt that earned the Tunisian team a trip
to Argentina for the 1978 World Cup finals.

OCEANIA

Before this century is over the African continent may well be producing as many outstanding teams as Europe or South America. Certainly the athletic potential is there. What had been lacking in the past was quality coaching and adequate financial support, two problems that were beginning to be solved in the 1970's.

In the past many of Africa's finest players found fame and fortune in Europe. Undoubtedly the most famous of these is Eusebio, "the Black Panther," who starred for Benfica in the 1960's and was the leading scorer in the 1966 World Cup finals when he knocked in nine goals for Portugal.

Eusebio is a native of Mozambique, as are Joaquim Santana, Mario Coluna, and goalkeeper Costa Pereira, all of whom helped make Benfica one of the most powerful club teams in the world.

Selif Keita, a native of Mali, joined the French club St. Etienne in 1968 and became the team's leading scorer. He later played for Valencia and Sporting Club of Lisbon. Many African players still leave for Europe each season, but as local leagues and clubs improve, that number will start to decrease over the next decade.

The first team from the African continent to make any sort of international impression was a squad from Egypt that traveled to Italy for the 1934 World Cup. The Egyptians met Hungary in Naples and scored two goals. Unfortunately goalkeeper Moustafa Kamel surrendered four, and a few days later the team sailed for home.

It was not until 1970 that another team from Africa reached the World Cup finals. For many years Morocco had been importing European coaches to help develop local clubs. The most important of these was former Yugoslavian coach Blagoje Vlidinic, who took over as manager of the national team in 1969 and one year later took it to Mexico. The team did better than anyone expected, playing Bulgaria to a 1–1 draw and losing to West Germany 2–1 and Peru 3–0.

Soon afterwards Vlidinic moved south to Zaïre, where President Mobutu Sese Seko had launched a full-scale campaign, supported by a generous budget, to improve the quality of his national team. Whatever Vlidinic did must have worked, for by 1974 Zaïre had become the first black nation to reach the World Cup finals.

Against such soccer powers as Scotland and Brazil, Zaïre performed reasonably well, losing by scores of 2–0 and 3–0. When it came up against Vlidinic's old team, Yugoslavia, it was a different story. Perhaps the Yugoslavians were out to impress their former coach, or maybe the Africans just had a terrible day. Whatever the reason, Zaïre was routed 9–0.

In 1978 Tunisia represented the thirty-eight-nation African Football Confederation in the World Cup finals, after winning a three-nation playoff with Egypt and Nigeria. Tunisia was coached by Mejid Chetali, who built his team around goalkeeper Sadok Gassi Attouga and defender Labidi Kamal.

Asia

Money may or may not be able to buy happiness, but the leaders of several oil-rich states in the thirty-one-nation Asian Football Confederation are out to prove it can purchase some excellent soccer teams—or at least the means to build those teams.

This confederation is the most diverse in FIFA, stretching from Israel and Iraq in the Middle East to Japan and Indonesia in the Pacific and to Thailand and Hong Kong in the Far East.

Glutted with petrodollars, several of the Middle Eastern members have been attempting to buy their way into the world's soccer elite. Kuwait hired Brazilian coach Mario Zaglo, the United Arab Emirates put up a sheik's ransom to lure Don Revie away from England's national team, and Saudi Arabia's royal family announced in 1976 that it was prepared to spend $50 million over a three-year period to upgrade its nation's soccer program.

So far the most successful big spender has been Iran. When its team qualified for the 1978 World Cup finals each member of the twenty-man squad was paid, as had been promised beforehand, $100,000.

Iran won the right to compete in the finals by defeating Kuwait 2–1 before 90,000 wildly cheering supporters in Teheran's sparkling new Aryamehr Stadium. The most devoted of those fans was Iran's Crown Prince Reza, who a few months earlier had laid out $10,000 for a team victory party when Iran defeated Australia.

Although they may have been the strongest, the Iranians were not the first Asian team to reach the finals. In 1938 the Dutch East Indies, now Indonesia, competed in Italy and were eliminated in the first round 6–0, by Hungary.

In 1954 South Korea was eliminated in the first round, following defeats by Hungary and Turkey by the lopsided scores of 9–0 and 7–0. Twelve years later, in England, North Korea was the tournament's surprise team. Nobody was more surprised than the Italian team that lost a 1–0 decision to the Koreans and flew home to a welcoming committee armed with rotten fruit and vegetables.

The Koreans were finally eliminated by Portugal 5–3, but not before men like Yang Sung Kook, Pak Suen Jin, and Li Dong Woon gave Asian soccer new respect and a tremendous boost in the Far East. Japan was one nation inspired by the Koreans' success, and by 1968 the Japanese had produced a team good enough to win a bronze medal at the Olympic Games. Japan also provided that competition with its top goal scorer, striker Kunishege Kamamoto.

Today, with financial support from such industrial giants as Honda, Japanese interest in soccer is at an all-time high; the nation now has 2,676 high school teams, as compared to fewer than 200 in 1965. Japan's professional league has two divisions of ten teams each. Most of the clubs are industry sponsored and have such names as the Toyota Textile Machines, the Osaka Yanmar Diesel, and the Mitsubishi Football Club of Tokyo.

Israel further enhanced the confederation's prestige with its performance in the 1970 World Cup. With a team built around striker Mordechai Shpigler, who later played for the Cosmos, Israel tied both Sweden and Italy and lost only to Uruguay.

The Israeli Soccer League was formed in 1952 and has developed several clubs that have proved themselves in international competition. Among the best are Hapoel Petah-Tiquva, Hapoel Tel Aviv, and Maccabi-Tel Aviv.

Asia's largest nation, the People's Republic of China, is not a member of FIFA because of its insistence that Taiwan be expelled as a precondition of its joining. In the fall of 1977 China's national team toured the United States, playing three games with the U.S. national team, and one each with the Cosmos and the Tampa Bay Rowdies.

The two national teams tied their first game 1–1, but the United States won the next two by scores of 1–0 and 2–0. The Cosmos and China played to a 1–1 tie, and then the Chinese recorded their lone victory of the tour by defeating the Tampa Bay Rowdies 2–1.

Oceania

Soccer in Australia has come a long way since that sad day in 1951 when the Aussies' national team lost to England 17–0, a record defeat in international play.

Until a fourteen-club national league was organized in 1977, soccer in Australia was played on a regional-league basis. The game's development has been hampered in the past by the popularity of rugby (*the* game in New South Wales and Queensland) and Australian Rules Football, which is the most popular sport in the nation's other states.

Soccer received a much-needed boost from the performance of Australia in the 1974 World Cup. The Socceroos, as the team is called, competed in the Asian Zone and defeated South Korea 1–0 to advance to the finals—where they lost to East Germany 2–0, West Germany 3–0, and played Chile to a scoreless tie.

Although the Australian National League is a semiprofessional organization, it contains some outstanding players. Among the best are defender Doug Utjesenovic and forwards Attila Abonyi, John Kosmina, and John Nyskohus. All four are members of the Socceroos.

New Zealand has a twelve-team league that has been dominated by three clubs; Christchurch United, Auckland's Mount Wellington, and Diamond United of Wellington. As in Australia, soccer has traditionally ranked behind rugby in attracting fans and athletes, but has made tremendous gains in the 1970's.

Moktar Dhouib of Tunisia in action against Egypt.

Forward Temine Lahzami (hands upraised) celebrates his
team's victory over Egypt.

11. SOCCER IN THE UNITED STATES

How did it happen? How did a game that for more than a century was either simply ignored or dismissed as something "foreign" suddenly catch America's attention and become our fastest-growing team sport? The answer, as it always seems to be the case with questions like this, is not an easy one to arrive at.

To begin with there is what can best be described as the "kid factor." For example, if someone gave a young child a soccer ball in the 1960's he or she would most probably receive in return a look of complete bewilderment. What do I do with this thing? Throw it through a hoop, hit it over a net—surely you don't just kick it?

That was in the 1960's. Flash ahead one decade and you find Little League baseball and football struggling for survival in many parts of the country while hundreds of thousands of youngsters flock to organized soccer programs.

Item: In 1963 a Catholic priest tried to organize a youth soccer league in the town of Massapequa on New York's Long Island. After being able to recruit only eight players on his own, he had to go to a local grammar school and plead for boys who had been cut from the football team. Thirteen years later there were 2,200 youths eighteen years old and under playing organized soccer in Massapequa. One afternoon the football coach walked up to the priest and said, "Give me anyone you cut from your soccer teams. I need them for football."

Item: In 1970 Miami's Orange Bowl Committee decided to sponsor a junior soccer tournament over the Christmas holidays. It was to be a relaxed, laid-back affair; a few kids playing soccer in the sunshine while their parents watched. Forget relaxed. Forget laid back. By 1977, 2,000 boys and girls representing ninety-six teams from Canada to Puerto Rico were competing in the three-day tournament. The tournament involved 162 games and utilized twenty-five fields. Said Aristides Sastre, president of the Dade County Youth Soccer Association: "We had more than two hundred and fifty applications from out of town. We try to get as much representation as we can, so in areas where several teams apply we ask the state associations to hold a playoff and we invite the winner."

On the night of August 14, 1977, 77,691 fans filled New Jersey's Giants Stadium to watch the Cosmos play the Ft. Lauderdale Strikers. It was the largest crowd ever to watch a soccer game in North America up to that time.

Item: In 1964 the American Youth Soccer Organization consisted of nine teams in and around Inglewood, California. In 1978, it had 8,750 teams playing in twenty-one states. When a rival group, the United States Youth Soccer Association, was formed it had 30,000 youngsters enrolled. By 1978, that number had grown to nearly a quarter of a million.

A map of the nation with shaded areas showing concentrations of youth soccer activities would have a definite mottled effect. The darkened sections would include the Pacific Northwest and many areas of California, St. Louis, large chunks of Texas and Florida, a good portion of Minnesota, several dotted areas in and around Chicago, and most of the northeastern states, especially Connecticut, New York, and the suburbs of Washington, D.C.

That's an indication of what has happened, which brings us to why it happened. To begin with, there are no size requirements in soccer. Pelé is of average size and weight, five-foot-nine inches tall and 160 pounds. Jim McAlister of the Seattle Sounders, the NASL's Rookie of the Year in 1977, stands five-foot-eight and weighs a mere 140 pounds. Dennis Tueart of the Cosmos is the same height and weighs 154 pounds,

and the list could go on and on, but the point is that while an athlete may be too small to play professional football or basketball, he is hardly ever too small to play pro soccer.

In July of 1977, *Newsweek* examined the sudden surge of popularity soccer was enjoying with the nation's youth and came up with the following explanation:

In Little League baseball, the strongest kid usually pitches while smaller teammates stand idly in the field. Football places even greater emphasis on size and power. But when eleven kids begin kicking a ball, hardly anything matters but a willingness to keep running. And no individual ends up striking out with the bases loaded, fumbling or otherwise ruining his coach's temperament and his own weekend. "In soccer you don't have these crazy coaches yelling 'Stick 'im, hit 'im' all the time," says one New Jersey 10-year-old. An appreciative Washington, D.C., 6-year-old adds that the rules of the game are delightfully simple: "Go to the bathroom before practice and keep your pants zipped up."

The number of children playing in organized soccer leagues passed the one million mark in the late 1970's.

Even four-year-olds found that they could play soccer.

Another point to be mentioned, and an important one, is that soccer is an inexpensive game to play. Twenty-two kids can be kept busy with one fifteen-dollar ball, about the price of one football helmet—if you can get it wholesale.

"Soccer players do it for ninety minutes," is one of the NASL's promotional slogans and another reason children like the game—because the action is almost nonstop from start to finish. It also seems to be a sport kids stick with. In 1971, there were 2,2l7 high schools with varsity soccer teams. Seven years later that figure was close to 7,000, and that doesn't include the growing number of girls' teams.

Of course the natural successor to girls' teams are teams for women, and there are plenty of those in California, Florida, and Texas. In and around Dallas there are over a thousand active members of the North Texas Women's Soccer Association, and the league expects to double in size over the next decade.

"Before you leap to the conclusion that we are all female truck drivers and candidates for the Green Bay Packers defensive line," explained league member Ann Smith, "let me assure you we are not. The majority of these women are over thirty, wives, mothers, working women, career women. The rewards? An increased sense of well-being from conditioning and improvement of skills, and camaraderie, something women have not often experienced."

Boom at the Top

While all this growth was taking place at the grass-roots level, professional soccer was also undergoing a metamorphosis. In 1969 the North American Soccer League was tottering on the brink of oblivion. Down to just five clubs, twelve less than it had in 1968, the league was being run in a two-room office by a staff of three people, including the commissioner. The only requirement for acquiring a new franchise was the ability, and willingness, to lose a great deal of money over a short period of time.

Then came the boom, and by 1978 the NASL needed half a floor in a building on New York's Avenue of the Americas to house its fulltime staff of twenty-seven employees. Anyone interested in purchasing a new franchise had to pay $1 million for the privilege and on top of that demonstrate an ability to sustain operating losses of $300,000 a year for five years.

Instead of laughing at that offer organizations in Boston, Denver, Detroit, Houston, Memphis, and Philadelphia found it too good to refuse and came up with both the money and the proof of their financial stability. The league, which had eighteen members in 1977, was up to twenty-four in 1978.

Of course, the picture was not one of total success, and before the 1978 season began four franchises were moved. The Connecticut team was switched to Oakland; the St. Louis Stars went to Anaheim and became the California Surf; the

The number of girls and women who play soccer increases every year.

Las Vegas Quicksilvers were reborn as the San Diego Sockers; and Team Hawaii went to Oklahoma where it was named the Tulsa Roughnecks.

Pelé and Promo

Two factors lifted the NASL up to big-league status. One was the arrival of Pelé, the other a thorough, well-thought-out marketing and promotional campaign.

It took a great deal of money to lure Pelé out of retirement in Brazil, some skillful negotiating on the part of former Cosmos president Clive Toye, and the intervention of former Secretary of State Henry Kissinger.

Kissinger, a devoted soccer fan who used to have European league scores delivered to him via diplomatic pouch, was called upon to soothe some ruffled Brazilian feathers when the Yankee dollar took away a man considered a national treasure in Brazil.

Pelé supplied the NASL with instant credibility and the kind of publicity money can't buy. Within weeks after his arrival, Pelé was at the White House showing President Ford how to kick a soccer ball, chatting on national television with Johnny Carson, and drawing huge crowds of paying spectators wherever he and the Cosmos played.

Meanwhile the league's various members were doing some heavy marketing and promotional work of their own.

"We're selling the team the way Procter & Gamble sells soap," said Martin J. Ritberg, vice president for sales for the Tampa Bay Rowdies.

Dallas, one of the more promotion-minded clubs, had two parachutists drop into Ownby Stadium during the playing of the national anthem. In the 1977 off-season, the Tornado sent six players to challenge local high-school faculty members to volleyball games. The soccer players, who were not allowed to use their hands in the matches, won twenty-three of the twenty-five games played.

The Seattle Sounders offered a prize to the fan who correctly guessed how high a soccer ball would bounce after it was dropped from the top of the 58,000-seat Kingdome Stadium. "Players in other sports ignore the fans," said Brian Runnels, Sounders marketing director. "We send our team running into the stands after a game to pass out flowers in appreciation of the fans' support."

A Key Date

On June 19, 1977 a NASL game between Tampa Bay and the Cosmos drew 62,349 fans to Giants Stadium in East Rutherford, New Jersey. "When they write the history of soccer in this country," said Kurt Lamm, general secretary of the United States Soccer Federation (USSF), "that afternoon will be day one in all the books."

Wherever Pelé played in the United States he attracted large crowds of admirers.

Never had so large a crowd witnessed a soccer game in this country. To prove it was no fluke, 57,191 paying customers showed up the following Sunday to watch the Cosmos play the Los Angeles Aztecs. A few miles away, just across the Hudson River, the New York Yankees were playing the Boston Red Sox in a key American League game before a smaller crowd. Soccer had now reached the point where in head-to-head competition it could outdraw baseball.

About the only thing that was not yet truly big league about the NASL were the players' salaries. Major league baseball players average $76,000 a season, football players $55,000, hockey players $96,000, and basketball players $143,000. The payroll average in the NASL in 1978 was $19,000 for a thirty-game, four-month regular season, but when the salaries of such high-priced superstars as Franz Beckenbauer and Giorgio Chinaglia are subtracted the average falls to around $10,000 a season.

Of course, that is still more than players earned a few years ago. In 1971 Jorge Siega was paid $1,000 a month by the Cosmos, and he was the team's highest-paid player. Some of his teammates received as little as $75 a game, but were asked not to admit it for fear of embarrassing the league and the team. That was the same year Warner Communications purchased the Cosmos for $10,000. By 1978 the franchise was estimated to be worth more than $5 million.

Borrowed Players

For more than half of the NASL's players, the comparatively low salaries cause no extreme hardship because they play here in the spring and summer months and then often return to participate in the European league seasons, which are played during the rest of the year. For the league's American players it is a different story, and as more and more become good enough to play professional soccer one can expect to see a strong players' association similar to those in other major sports.

In 1978 more than 55 per cent of the players on NASL rosters were foreign-born, and some European clubs have begun to worry about a possible draining away of their best athletes in the future.

"Mansfield Boss Blasts Those Damn Yankees," read a headline in the *London Daily Mirror* in February of 1978. "It's time we took an even tougher line to stop American clubs from pinching so many players," Mansfield Town manager Peter Morris was quoted as saying. "I've tried to make seven signings in as many weeks, but most players I've talked to seem preoccupied with going to the states."

If there is anything that can stop this importation of foreign talent it is the development of American soccer players. In a move that provoked a great deal of controversy league teams began to sign undergraduates off college campuses—in a few cases players have been signed shortly after they finished high school.

The Sounders signed Jim McAlister following his graduation from Seattle's Kennedy High School. Gary Etherington, a product of the Annandale, Virginia, youth soccer program, was signed by the Cosmos after his graduation from Mt. Vernon High School.

The Cosmos also signed two college undergraduates; goalkeeper David Brcic (pronounced Bur-sek), from St. Louis University, and forward Rick Davis, from the University of California at Santa Clara. Both signed contracts that allowed them to preserve their amateur status so that they can compete in the 1980 Olympics. This is a device that allows players to receive room, board, travel expenses, a fifty-dollar-a-week allowance, plus a fee for "not being able to seek other self-employment" because of their Olympic amateur status. If the players wished to attend college in the off-season, the Cosmos promised to pay their tuition.

Speaking about the signings, which enraged many college coaches, Cosmos coach Eddie Firmani said, "The colleges are just not turning out the numbers and the quality of players we need. They play only three months a year—maybe twenty games of mediocre competition by our standards. Developing kids need year-round training. By the time a boy's twenty-two and getting out of school, he's wasted four years in which he might have been developing toward the pros. We're moving toward the system followed elsewhere in the world, of club junior teams, with proper coaching and training. It's something like the farm systems in baseball and hockey."

Etherington, Brcic, and Davis spent the winter of 1977–78 in Italy, where they trained with the junior members of AC Milan.

World Cup Hopes

It is young players who form the backbone of the United States national team. In July of 1976 the USSF hired Walt Chyzowych to coach the national team, and he has set out to create a squad with the future, specifically the 1982 World Cup finals, in mind.

Chyzowych was born in the city of Lvov in the Ukraine and came to the United States when he was seven. In 1964 he began coaching the soccer team at the Philadelphia College of Textiles and Sciences. Over twelve seasons his teams compiled a 128–37–13 record, competed in six National Collegiate Athletic Association (NCAA) championship tournaments, and produced a dozen all-American players.

After his team was eliminated by Canada in a preliminary round of the 1978 World Cup, Chyzowych began to reorganize the squad. After watching all the NASL teams in action he invited thirty players, all U.S. citizens, to a camp and then selected a young team, a group that will have an average age of twenty-six when the next World Cup tournament rolls around in 1982.

That competition will be held in Spain and there has been speculation that the size of the final field will be doubled to include thirty-two nations, giving the U.S. an excellent chance of reaching the finals for the first time since 1950.

First Tournament Win

In September of 1977, Chyzowych's young team won the Soccer Festival of the Americas. It was the first international tournament ever won by a U.S. national team. To win, the team had to defeat clubs from Ecuador, Colombia, and Peru.

Four of Pelé's more devoted fans.

Pelé's teammates carry him off the field following his final game, an exhibition match between the Cosmos and his former Brazilian club, Santos.

Among the outstanding players for the American team were goalkeepers Arnold Mausser and Alan Mayer, forwards Gary Etherington, Rick Davis, and Greg Villa, and defender Dave D'Errico.

After it was all over Chyzowych said, "We never won anything in the past and here we are winning a tournament and scoring eight goals in three games. It used to take us several years to score eight goals."

Actually the United States did fairly well during its first international competition, but that was a long time ago—in 1886 to be exact. At that time a team selected by the American Football Association began a two-year series with a squad from Canada. After six matches each team had two wins, two losses, and two ties.

The Beginnings

Years earlier, in 1869, a football game was played in New Jersey between teams from Princeton and Rutgers. It is still regarded as the first college football game ever played, but the ball used that day was round and the rules employed were those of soccer as it was then played.

Instead of adopting soccer as their primary varsity sport, student athletes at Princeton, Rutgers, and other eastern colleges elected to alter the rules of rugby and over the years the game of football evolved. It was probably inevitable. Soccer was an English sport and we were a new and growing nation anxious to shake off European influences and make our own mark in the world. Football was a game that could honestly wear the tag, "Made in the U.S.A."

Not that there weren't any serious attempts to popularize soccer. There were—it's just that they never quite succeeded. In 1912, a Scottish sportsman, Sir Thomas Dewar, donated a large silver trophy to be awarded to America's national champion. In 1913 the Brooklyn Field Club defeated Brooklyn Celtic 2–1 to win the Dewar's Cup, which is still the top prize for the nation's semipro and amateur clubs.

For the next five years competition for the trophy, officially called the National Challenge Cup, was dominated by a team sponsored by Bethlehem Steel. The company's president, Charles M. Schwab, spent a small fortune trying to make soccer a big-league sport in this country. Raiding clubs both at home and abroad, he put together a team good enough to win the Dewar's Cup four times.

He could have saved his money for all this mattered to the general American public. Soccer was still considered a game played by immigrants, and the children of many of these players were anxious to shed any foreign identification by adopting such native games as baseball and football.

The Name Game

The sport's governing body did little to help matters. Affiliated with FIFA in 1913 as the United States Football Association, it took the organization thirty-two years to admit "football" did not mean soccer to most Americans. After much soul-searching and debate the name was finally changed, in 1945, to the United States Soccer Football Association.

Twenty-nine years later the other shoe was at last dropped; in 1974 the word "football" was abandoned and the organization was renamed the United States Soccer Federation.

Over the years the sport was really kept alive by hyphenated teams, such as the Greek-Americans, Italian-Americans, Hungarian-Americans, and so forth. Most competed in leagues up and down the East Coast. The strongest of these was the German-American Football Association, founded in 1923 and still going strong in the New York-New Jersey area.

The U.S. national team won two of three matches with the People's Republic of China in 1977.

Several players in the NASL have come out of this league, including Tampa Bay Rowdies goalkeeper Arnold Mausser, who played for Blau-Weiss Gotchee, and Cosmos defender Werner Roth, a former member of the German-Hungarians.

The outstanding American-born player of the pre-World War II era was probably Bill Gonsalvés, a native of Fall River, Massachusetts. A member of the U.S. team in both the 1930 and 1934 World Cup tournaments, Gonsalvés began playing professionally in 1925 with the Fall River Rovers. A midfielder, his playing career lasted for twenty-seven years, many of them with the Brooklyn Hispaños, one of the East Coast's strongest clubs in the 1930's.

Professional Growth

Although relatively few people know it, the nation has had a professional soccer league since 1933 when the American Soccer League (ASL) was formed. For many decades it was at best a semipro operation, then in 1976 it began to attract some media attention with the appointment of former basketball great Bob Cousy as league commissioner. The ASL had an average game attendance of 2,100 in 1977 and entered the 1978 season with ten clubs and its major-league pretensions still unrealized.

A more ambitious attempt to popularize professional soccer was made in 1960 by promoter Bill Cox, who sponsored the International Soccer League (ISL). This was actually just a summer tournament involving teams from South America and Europe that for its best games would draw crowds of about 15,000 to New York's old Polo Grounds, vacated when the baseball Giants moved to San Francisco.

Cox, who at one time had owned baseball's Philadelphia Phillies, was able to keep the ISL alive for six seasons before heavy financial losses forced him to abandon the project. Despite its eventual failure, the ISL did arouse the interest of many American businessmen in the possibility of creating a successful soccer league. Unfortunately too many people got the same idea at once and in 1966, one year after the ISL folded, there were three groups with grandiose plans for soccer in the United States.

A Confusing Season

Before the 1967 summer season began two of the groups agreed to merge and form the United Soccer Association—the USA. The other group decided to go its own way and called itself the National Professional Soccer League.

Each group approached the problem of selling soccer to

American sports fans from opposite directions. The USA imported entire clubs from Europe and South America and assigned them to various cities. Cerro of Montevideo went to New York, the Wolverhampton Wanderers became a Los Angeles team, while Chicago got Cagliari of Sardinia.

Two of the more interesting assignments were the placing of Dublin's Shamrock Rovers in Boston and Northern Ireland's Glentoran in Detroit. One did not need a degree in foreign relations to predict what would happen when these two clubs staged a mid-season meeting in Boston. As might be expected, it was less a soccer match than a reenactment of the Battle of the Boyne.

Equally exciting, for fans of guerrilla warfare, was the clash in Yankee Stadium between Cagliari (Chicago) and Cerro (New York). The city's Italian soccer fans turned out by the thousands for this match waving tricolored flags and greeting the Sardinian team members like long lost brothers.

Several fights broke out on the field as players took turns fouling each other while the Italian members of the crowd taunted the Uruguayan team with shouts of, *"Bestia!"* ("animal"), *"Brutta bestia!"* ("ugly animal") and finally, when things got really ugly, *"Mascalzone!"* ("rascal").

Before the game was over Italian fans stormed onto the field and chased the referee. They caught and kicked him until a squad of police came to the rescue. The incident did attract a great deal of press attention—but not the sort USA promoters were hoping for.

Meanwhile, the NPSL was having troubles of its own. Rather than importing entire clubs, this league had chosen instead to bring over individual players, forgetting that just because they both play soccer doesn't mean a Brazilian and a Yugoslavian can communicate, especially with an English coach as the go-between.

This polyglot league produced few outstanding games but many wonderful stories. A favorite concerns Ruben Navarro, an Argentine fullback who played for the Philadelphia Spartans. After a winning game he decided to throw a victory party. Not realizing that in Pennsylvania liquor is sold only at state-run shops, Navarro stopped off at a supermarket and bought a case of liquid bottled like champagne. He and his teammates must have had a terrific time at the party, drinking all that nicely bottled bubble bath.

Before the summer was over, every club in both leagues, twenty-two in all, had lost money. Only two choices remained, collapse or merge. The second option was taken and in 1968 the North American Soccer League was born.

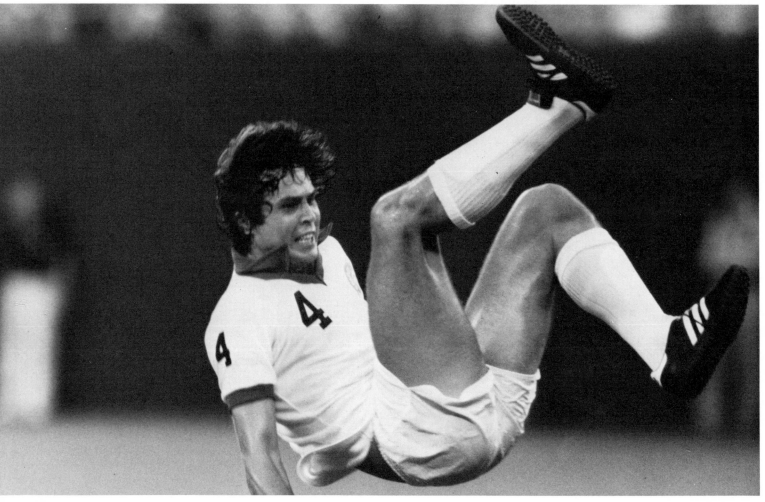

Cosmos defender Werner Roth is a former member of the New York metropolitan area's German-American (now Cosmopolitan) League.

English international Dennis Tueart of the Cosmos is one of many British stars playing in the NASL.

United States Collegiate Champions

NCAA Division One

Champion	Runner-up	
1959—St. Louis	5–2	Bridgeport
1960—St. Louis	3–2	Maryland
1961—West Chester State	2–0	St. Louis
1962—St. Louis	4–3	Maryland
1963—St. Louis	3–0	Navy
1964—Navy	1–0	Michigan State
1965—St. Louis	1–0	Michigan State
1966—San Francisco	5–2	Long Island
1967—St. Louis Michigan State	0–0	(co-champions; game called due to bad weather)
1968—Maryland Michigan State	2–2	(co-champions; game called after two overtimes)
1969—St. Louis	4–0	San Francisco
1970—St. Louis	1–0	UCLA
1971—Howard*	3–2	St. Louis
1972—St. Louis	4–2	UCLA
1973—St. Louis	2–1 (OT)	UCLA
1974—Howard	2–1 (OT)	St. Louis
1975—San Francisco	4–0	Southern Illinois-Edwardsville
1976—San Francisco	1–0	Indiana
1977—Hartwick	2–1	San Francisco

* Title vacated by Howard for alleged use of ineligible players

NCAA Division Two

Champion	Runner-up	
1972—Southern Illinois Edwardsville	1–0	Oneonta State
1973—Missouri-St. Louis	3–0	Fullerton State
1974—Adelphi	3–2	Seattle Pacific
1975—Baltimore	3–1	Seattle Pacific
1976—Loyola-Baltimore	2–0	New Haven
1977—Alabama A&M	2–1	Seattle Pacific

NCAA Division Three

Champion	Runner-up	
1974—Brockport State	3–1	Swarthmore
1975—Babson College	1–0	Brockport State
1976—Brandeis	2–1 (OT)	Brockport State
1977—Lock Haven	1–0	Cortland State

National Association of Intercollegiate Athletics (NAIA)

Champion	Runner-up	
1959—Pratt Institute	4–3 (OT)	Elizabethtown
1960—Elizabethtown Newark Engineering	2–2 (OT)	(co-champions)
1961—Howard	3–0	Newark Engineering
1962—East Stroudsburg State	4–0	Pratt Institute
1963—Earlham College Castleton State		(co-champions; finals not held because of snow)
1964—Trenton State	3–0	Lincoln
1965—Trenton State	5–2	Earlham College
1966—Quincy College	6–1	Trenton State
1967—Quincy College	3–1	Rockhurst
1968—Davis & Elkins	2–1 (OT)	Quincy
1969—Eastern Illinois	1–0 (OT)	Davis & Elkins
1970—Davis & Elkins	2–0	Quincy
1971—Quincy	1–0	Davis & Elkins
1972—Westmont	2–1 (OT)	Davis & Elkins
1973—Quincy	3–0	Rockhurst
1974—Quincy	6–0	Davis & Elkins
1975—Quincy	1–0	Simon Fraser
1976—Simon Fraser	1–0	Rockhurst
1977—Quincy	4–0	Keene State

Junior College Champions
NJCAA CHAMPIONS

1961—Dean Junior College, Franklin, Mass.
1962—Mitchell College, New London, Conn.
1963—Mercer Junior College, Trenton, N.J.
1964—Mitchell College
1965—Monroe Community College, Rochester, N.Y.
1966—Nassau Community College, Garden City, N.Y.
1967—Florissant Valley Community College, St. Louis, Mo.
1968—Mercer Junior College
1969—Florissant Valley Community College
1970—Florissant Valley Community College
1971—Florissant Valley Community College
1972—Meramec Community College, St. Louis, Mo.
1973—Florissant Valley Community College
1974—Essex Community College, Baltimore County, Maryland
1975—Florissant Valley Community College
1976—Meramec Community College
1977—Ulster Community College, N.Y.

American Soccer League Champions

1934 Kearny Irish	1957 New York Hakoah
1935 Philadelphia Germans	1958 New York Hakoah
1936 New York Americans	1959 New York Hakoah
1937 Kearny Scots	1960 Colombo
1938 Kearny Scots	1961 Ukranian Nationals
1939 Kearny Scots	1962 Ukranian Nationals
1940 Kearny Scots	1963 Ukranian Nationals
1941 Kearny Scots	1964 Ukranian Nationals
1942 Philadelphia Americans	1965 Hartford S.C.
1943 Brooklyn Hispanos	1966 Roma S.C.
1944 Philadelphia Americans	1967 Baltimore St. Gerard's
1945 New York Brookhattan	1968 Ukranian Nationals
1946 Baltimore Americans	1968 Washington Darts
1947 Philadelphia Americans	1969 (First Summer Season)
1948 Philadelphia Americans	Washington Darts
1949 Philadelphia Americans	1970 Philadelphia Ukranians
1950 Philadelphia Nationals	1971 New York Greeks
1951 Philadelphia Nationals	1972 Cincinnati Comets
1952 Philadelphia Americans	1973 New York Apollo
1953 Philadelphia Nationals	1974 Rhode Island Oceaneers
1954 New York Americans	1975 Boston Astros-
1955 Uhrik Truckers	New York Apollo
1956 Uhrik Truckers	1976 Los Angeles Skyhawks
	1977 New Jersey Americans

The National Open Challenge Cup

(Open to professional and amateur teams belonging to the United States Soccer Federation)

1914 Brooklyn Field Club	1946 Chicago Vikings
1915 Bethlehem Steel	1947 Ponta Delgada
1916 Bethlehem Steel	1948 Simpkins of St. Louis
1917 Fall River Rovers	1949 Morgan, Pennsylvania
1918 Bethlehem Steel	1950 Simpkins of St. Louis
1919 Bethlehem Steel	1951 German Hungarian
1920 Ben Millers	1952 Harmarville, Pennsylvania
1921 Robbins Dry Dock	1953 Falcons, Illinois
1922 Scullin Steel	1954 New York Americans
1923 Patterson	1955 Eintracht, New York
1924 Fall River	1956 Harmarville, Pennsylvania
1925 Shawsheen	1957 Kutis of St. Louis
1926 Bethlehem Steel	1958 Los Angeles Kickers
1927 Fall River	1959 San Pedro Canvasbacks
1928 New York Nationals	1960 Philadelphia Ukrainian
1929 Hakoah All-Stars	1961 Philadelphia Ukrainian
1930 Fall River	1962 New York Hungaria
1931 Fall River	1963 Philadelphia Ukrainian
1932 New Bedford	1964 Los Angeles Kickers
1933 Stix, Baer & Fuller	1965 New York Ukrainian
1934 Stix, Baer & Fuller	1966 Philadelphia Ukrainian
1935 Central Breweries	1967 New York Greek-Americans
1936 Philadelphia Americans	1968 New York Greek-Americans
1937 New York Americans	1969 New York Greek-Americans
1938 Sparta of Chicago	1970 Elizabeth, New Jersey
1939 St. Mary's Celtic of Bklyn.	1971 New York Hota
1940 Baltimore S.C.	1972 Elizabeth, New Jersey
1941 Pawtucket	1973 Los Angeles Maccabees
1942 Gallatin of Pennsylvania	1974 New York Greek-Americans
1943 Brooklyn Hispano	1975 Los Angeles Maccabees
1944 Brooklyn Hispano	1976 San Francisco Athletic Club
1945 Brookhattan	1977 Los Angeles Maccabees

The National Amateur Cup

(Open to amateur teams belonging to the United States Soccer Federation)

1924 Fleisher Yarn	1951 German Hungarian
1925 Toledo	1952 Raiders
1926 Defenders	1953 Ponta Delgada
1927 Heidelberg	1954 Beadling
1928 Swedish-Americans	1955 Heidelberg Tornados
1929 Heidelberg	1956 Kutis, St. Louis
1930 Raffies	1957 Kutis, St. Louis
1931 Goodyear	1958 Kutis, St. Louis
1932 Cleveland Shamrock	1959 Kutis, St. Louis
1933 German-American	1960 Kutis, St. Louis
1934 German-American	1961 Kutis, St. Louis
1935 W. W. Riehl	1962 Carpathia Kickers
1936 Brooklyn S.C.	1963 Italian-Americans
1937 Trenton Highlander	1964 Schwaben
1938 Ponta Delgada	1965 German Hungarian
1939 St. Michael	1966 Chicago Kickers
1940 Morgan Strasser	1967 Hartford Italians
1941 Fall River	1968 Chicago Kickers
1942 Fall River	1969 British Lions
1943 Morgan Strasser	1970 Chicago Kickers
1944 Eintracht	1971 Kutis, St. Louis
1945 Eintracht	1972 Busch, St. Louis
1946 Ponta Delgada	1973 Philadelphia Inter
1947 Ponta Delgada	1974 Philadelphia Inter
1948 Ponta Delgada	1975 Chicago Kickers
1949 Elizabeth	1976 Milwaukee Bavarians
1950 Ponta Delgada	1977 Denver Kickers

12. THE NORTH AMERICAN SOCCER LEAGUE

If 1967 was a bad year for those who sought to promote soccer in North America, then 1968 can only be described as catastrophic. The season began with high hopes, seventeen clubs, and a contract with the CBS television network. It ended with owners counting huge losses, twelve clubs deciding not to return for another season, and CBS using its option to cancel the tv contract.

The Atlanta Chiefs won the NASL championship in 1968, defeating the San Diego Toros. The league's high scorer was John Kowalik, a Polish international who scored thirty goals in twenty-eight games. He was also credited with nine assists and under the league's procedure of awarding two points for a goal and one for an assist, Kowalik finished the season with sixty-nine points, two more than San Diego's Cirilio Fernández—an outstanding player who also scored thirty goals but had only seven assists.

This season is also memorable for the introduction of a point system to decide league standings that is still in use. Each winning team receives six points toward its season standings. Bonus points are awarded on the following basis. Both winners and losers receive one point in the standings for each goal they score up to a maximum of three goals. Thus, a winning team that scores three or more goals receives nine points in the league standings. Losing teams can get a maximum of three points (for three or more goals) in the standings. Until 1974, if a game ended in a tie each team received three points plus any bonus points earned.

The Cosmos star center forward, Giorgio Chinaglia, celebrates in the rain after scoring a goal.

Hard Times

Someone once said that if things can get worse they will, and in 1969 they did. The league now consisted of just five clubs: Kansas City, Atlanta, Dallas, St. Louis, and Baltimore, each playing a sixteen-game season.

Since this was a make or break year for the NASL expectations were scaled down, fewer foreign players were imported, and a great deal of emphasis was placed on promoting and selling soccer, especially with youth clinics and other grass-roots efforts to popularize the game.

As there was no playoff in 1969, Kansas City won the league championship with a little help from the point system. Atlanta actually had a better won-lost-tied record, finishing at 11–2–3, but scored fewer goals than Kansas City, which finished with a 10–2–4 record. The final standings showed Kansas City with 110 points, one more than Atlanta.

The season's scoring champion was one of the great names in American sports, Kaiser "Boy Boy" Motaung of Atlanta who had sixteen goals and four assists for thirty-six points, one more than George Benitez of Kansas City.

Baltimore dropped out for the 1970 season, but two new franchises—the Washington Darts and the Rochester Lancers—joined the league. The six clubs were divided into two three-team divisions, Northern and Southern, with each team playing a twenty-four-game schedule.

At season's end the two new franchises had each won their division title and played a two-game championship series,

Goalie Shep Messing leaps over the head of Washington Diplomats forward Peter Silvester (11) and punches the ball away from his goal.

Sounders forward Jimmy Robertson heads downfield.

won by Rochester with an aggregate goal margin of 4–3. Kirk Apostolidis of Dallas and Carlos Metidieri of Rochester shared the scoring honors with thirty-five points each, although Apostolidis scored sixteen goals to Metidieri's fourteen. Leroy DeLeon of Washington also finished the season with sixteen goals, but had just one assist for a point total of thirty-three.

New York Joins

Kansas City called it quits before the 1971 season, while the New York Cosmos, the Toronto Metros, and the Montreal Olympics joined to give the NASL two four-club divisions.

Fans needed a computer to follow their favorite team because of a new and complicated schedule that allowed games against such foreign clubs as Portuguese Rio of Brazil and Apollo of Greece to count in the standings. After regular season play was concluded, there was a four-team championship playoff involving the two top teams in each division. In the final round, the Dallas Tornado defeated Atlanta in a three-game series to win the championship. Carlos Metidieri of Rochester won the scoring title, while Randy Horton of New York finished second.

There was only one change in the league makeup for the 1972 season; the Washington Darts moved south and became the Miami Toros. In an effort to cut financial losses, the

Cosmos winger Steve Hunt loses the ball to Bernie Fagan of the Los Angeles Aztecs.

league played an abbreviated fourteen-game schedule. In the championship game the New York Cosmos defeated the St. Louis Stars 2–1. Randy Horton of the Cosmos was the league's scoring leader with nine goals and four assists.

The following season was a crucial one for the NASL. A new franchise, the Philadelphia Atoms, was added and the league was divided into three divisions of three teams each. All the clubs played a nineteen-game regular season.

A new offside rule was instituted by adding an extra line to each half of the field, thirty-five yards from the goal line. An attacker could not now be whistled offside unless he was within this new line.

The Yanks Are Coming

Philadelphia raided the college ranks and hired Al Miller of Hartwick College as its head coach. Miller had compiled a 64–10–2 record at the small upstate New York institution and had helped make Hartwick one of the nation's leaders in intercollegiate soccer.

As his number-one choice in the 1973 draft of college players, Miller selected goalkeeper Bob Rigby—a graduate of his own alma mater, East Stroudsburg State College in Pennsylvania. It proved to be a brilliant choice as Rigby shut out six opponents and completed his first campaign with a remarkable 0.62 goals against average.

Other American-born starters on the Atoms roster were former Naval Academy all-American Lt. Casey Bahr; ex-Philadelphia Textile star Barry Barto; and defender Bobby Smith, a graduate of Rider College.

To round out his squad, Miller imported such outstanding English players as Chris Dunleavy, Jim Fryatt, and Andy "the Flea" Provan, a five-foot-five, 140-pound striker who finished the season with eleven goals.

The Atoms were what the NASL had been waiting for since its birth. Completing the regular season with nine victories, two losses, and eight ties the club had an average home attendance of 11,382—a new league record.

In the championship game, Philadelphia faced the Dallas Tornado, a team with a sparkling new American-born star of its own. He was Kyle Rote, Jr., son of the former S.M.U. and New York Giants football great, who had won the league scoring title with thirty points in this his first season.

A crowd of 18,825 in Texas Stadium saw the Atoms defeat Dallas 2–0 as the Philadelphia club became the first expansion team ever to win a major American sports title in its initial season.

Unfortunately this happy tale has an unhappy postscript. In the ensuing seasons the Atoms' fortunes soured, and after the 1976 campaign the club went out of business. In 1978 it was replaced by a new club, the Philadelphia Fury.

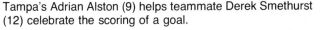

Tampa's Adrian Alston (9) helps teammate Derek Smethurst (12) celebrate the scoring of a goal.

No More Ties

Two franchises, Montreal and Atlanta, dropped out before the 1974 season began and eight new ones—Los Angeles, Baltimore, Boston, Washington, D.C., San Jose, Seattle, Denver, and Vancouver—joined. The NASL now had fifteen clubs divided into four divisions, with each team playing twenty games.

The league did some tinkering with the rules and came up with a rather complicated system for eliminating tie games. If the score was tied after regulation time, each team would receive five penalty kicks and the team converting the most kicks would be declared the winner.

If the score remained tied after each team took five shots, penalty kicks would be alternated until one team converted and the other failed. A team winning in this manner would be awarded a "tie-win" and instead of receiving six points in the league standings would be credited with just three plus one for each goal up to three. The losing team would get one point for each goal up to three.

The new rule was employed in the championship match between the Los Angeles Aztecs and the Miami Toros. After regulation time the score was tied at 3–3, but the Aztecs won the penalty-shot contest and the match.

Help from Abroad

Hartford, Chicago, Portland, San Antonio, and Tampa Bay signed on for the 1975 season—and so did an impressive array of outstanding foreign players.

The biggest headlines concerned New York's signing of Pelé. His first match in a Cosmos uniform, an exhibition game

Kyle Rote, Jr., is one of the NASL's first native-born stars.

against Dallas, was televised nationally and Pelé delighted everyone by scoring one goal himself and setting up a second for teammate Mordechai Sphigler, who had starred for Israel in the 1970 World Cup.

The Cosmos were not the only NASL club to import outstanding players from overseas. Boston sent its agents to Portugal and they came back with Eusebio and Antonio Simoes. Tampa Bay coach Eddie Firmani signed English First Division stars Stewart Scullion, Clyde Best, and Derek Smethurst. English goalkeeper Peter Bonetti came to St. Louis, a team built around such talented homegrown players as Gary Rensing, Pat McBride, Al Trost, Denny Vaninger, and Mike Seerey.

The league tinkered with the rules again and changed the method of deciding tie games. In the process the confusing "tie-win" category was also eliminated from the standings. Tie games would now be decided in a fifteen-minute sudden-death overtime period. If neither team scored, penalty shots would be used to select a winner. The winning team would then receive a full six points in the league standings.

Tampa Bay's Rowdies won the championship game, defeating the Portland Timbers 2–0 thanks to a pair of brilliant individual efforts by Haitian defender Arsène Auguste and Clyde Best.

Auguste scored first with a tremendous boot from thirty yards out. Then, with just two minutes left in the game, Best took the ball at midfield, raced down the left wing, and finally sent a swerving shot past Timbers' goalkeeper Graham Brown. The game, christened Soccer Bowl I, was played before a capacity crowd of 17,000 in San Jose's Spartan Stadium.

More New Stars

Giorgio Chinaglia, star striker from the Roman club Lazio, joined the Cosmos in 1976. English international Rodney Marsh signed with Tampa Bay, and Northern Ireland's George Best became a member of the Los Angeles Aztecs.

Many of these foreign stars found the style of play in the NASL much more attractive than the game played in their native leagues. "Skilled players in England don't go to the top. They just fade away," said Derek Smethurst, currently in his second season with Tampa. "It's the runners and kickers that come through over there. The thirty-five-yard line gives forwards more space and enough room to operate. In the NASL strikers can attack without worrying about being offsides."

The Toronto Metros-Croatia had the league's most ungainly name and two of its best players when the Canadian club was able to purchase Eusebio and midfielder Wolfgang Sühnholz from the financially strapped Boston club. Toronto finished second in its division, behind the Chicago Sting, but because of the expanded playoff system the Metros were able to reach Soccer Bowl II with victories over Rochester, Chicago, and Tampa Bay.

The Metros' opponents were the Minnesota Kicks, a team built around several excellent British players. This group included Geoff Barnett, Ron Webster, Alan Merrick, Frank Spraggon, and Alan West. Minnesota was favored to win the title match, played in Seattle's Kingdome, but Toronto was overpowering and scored a 3–0 victory.

A Year to Remember

When the 1977 season was over an awards ceremony was held and various honors distributed. Seattle's Jim McAlister was named Rookie of the Year, Ft. Lauderdale's Ron New-

Tampa's Rodney Marsh goes on the attack.

Two of soccer's all-time greats: Pelé and, in hot pursuit, George Best.

Minnesota Kicks forward Ade Coker joined the NASL in 1974 and by the end of the 1977 season had scored thirty-three goals.

Cosmos defender Bobby Smith gets a grip on Washington forward Mark Liveric.

Seattle goalkeeper Tony Chursky makes a save off the foot of Washington's Gary Darrell.

man walked off with a plaque that said he was Coach of the Year, and the Cosmos' Franz Beckenbauer won the election for the season's Most Valuable Player.

Five months earlier, before the season began, none of these three seemed destined to win any awards, at least not in the NASL. Twenty-year-old Jim McAlister had just been promoted from Seattle's reserve squad and was still an unknown quantity. Ron Newman was the recently hired coach of a team that had won only six games in 1976; and as for Beckenbauer, why he was still playing for Bayern Munich in West Germany.

McAlister did enter the new season with sound credentials, for the Seattle Sounders are recognized as having one of the finest training programs in the NASL, a reserve system that specializes in nurturing young North American-born soccer talent. McAlister, who had begun playing junior-league soccer at the age of seven in Seattle, spent most of the 1976 season with the Sounders' reserve team. Occasionally, when the game's outcome was no longer in doubt, he would be inserted as a substitute in a regular-league match. These opportunities did not come very often, for when the season ended McAlister had compiled a mere ninety-six minutes of playing time with Seattle's first team.

When the 1977 campaign began, Seattle coach Jimmy Gabriel took a chance and started McAlister at left back. Twenty-six games later "Little Mac," as the five-foot-eight,

140-pound McAlister is known to his fans, had compiled 2,015 minutes of playing time and the Sounders were on their way to Soccer Bowl '77.

The journey had not been an easy one. As a matter of fact, Seattle got off to a terrible start, losing six of its first eight games and failing to score a goal in four of those losses.

That was in April and May. In June, the Sounders did a complete about-face and won six of their next eight matches. July began with a 1–0 loss to Vancouver, but Seattle came back one match later and beat the Cosmos by the same score. McAlister was injured in that game, suffering a concussion as the result of a collision with Cosmos midfielder Terry Garbett. Not a man to convalesce, McAlister was back in Seattle's starting lineup three games later.

The Sounders continued to be an up and down sort of team. With forward Tommy Ord scoring three goals, for the first hat trick in Seattle history, they rolled over the Bicentennials of Connecticut 4–1. One game later, they played dead as the Rochester Lancers romped to a 3–0 victory. When the regular season came to an end, Seattle's record stood at 14 and 12. Ahead were the championship playoffs.

Vancouver's Whitecaps were the first obstacle to be overcome. The Whitecaps, who had finished second in the Pacific Conference's Western Division (one point ahead of Seattle), went down 2–0 as Milt Machin and Ord each scored once for the Sounders.

Pelé goes airborne while Tampa's Mike Connell looks on.

A two-game series with the Minnesota Kicks was next. Game one was tied 1–1 at the end of regulation time and was won by Seattle in overtime on a goal by Dave Butler. Ord produced the lone goal in game two, and Seattle advanced to face the high-scoring Aztecs of Los Angeles.

Living up to their press clippings, the Aztecs displayed their offensive prowess in the opening moments of game one and took a quick lead on a goal by Bobby McAlinden. It proved to be the last goal Seattle goalkeeper Tony Chursky would surrender in this series.

While Los Angeles was being shut out, Seattle responded with goals by Jimmy Robertson, Steve Buttle, and Mickey Cave. The second match was played in Seattle's Kingdome before a crowd of 56,256. A header by Jocky Scott after fourteen minutes of play was all the Sounders needed for a 1–0 win and a trip to Soccer Bowl '77.

A Winning Coach

At the conclusion of the 1976 season the Miami Toros had a 6 and 18 record and little hope for the future. One year later the team had a new home—Ft. Lauderdale—a new name—the Strikers—a new coach—Ron Newman—and new hope.

Newman had compiled a remarkable record during the short history of the NASL. After thirteen years as a profession-

al soccer player in England, he had crossed the Atlantic in 1967 and joined the Atlanta Chiefs, then coached by current NASL commissioner Phil Woosnam. In 1968, Atlanta won the league championship and Newman was the team's MVP.

The following season Newman became head coach of the Dallas Tornado, a team with a 2–26–4 record in 1968. Two years later the Tornado were NASL champions.

In 1976 Newman left Dallas to take over as coach of the American Soccer League's Los Angeles Skyhawks. The Skyhawks lost only two of twenty-four games and won the league championship. For his efforts Newman was named the ASL's Coach of the Year.

When Ft. Lauderdale offered Newman an opportunity to return to the NASL he accepted the challenge. One of his early moves was to lure Gordon Banks out of retirement. Banks had been England's goalkeeper when it won the 1966 World Cup and had been elected England's Footballer of the Year in 1972. That same year he was involved in an auto accident that cost him the sight of one eye and forced him out of competitive soccer.

Banks thought his playing days were over, but Newman was convinced he could still play and finally persuaded the thirty-eight-year-old goalkeeper to come to Florida and give the game another try.

Giorgio Chinaglia and Tampa's Radomir Stefanovick in a race for the ball.

Ft. Lauderdale's Ron Newman was named the NASL's Coach of the Year in 1977.

Time proved Newman's assessment of Banks's talent correct. In twenty-six regular season games the experienced English goalie recorded nine shutouts and his goals against average was 1.12, second only to Ken Cooper of Dallas, whose average was a remarkable 0.90.

"Some of the saves he made couldn't have been done better with two eyes," said Newman. "Gordon doesn't dive around like a nineteen-year-old goalkeeper, but he's always at the right place at the right time, making everything look so easy."

Surrendering a mere twenty-nine goals in twenty-six games, the Strikers finished with a 19 and 7 record, the best won-and-lost mark in the NASL for 1977.

Dallas defender Steve Pecher takes a well-earned breather.

The Kaiser Is Coming

Could the team that brought Pelé out of retirement bring a man currently regarded by many as the world's best player to the United States? Is the Pope Catholic? Is Paris a city? Don't ask silly questions.

So Franz Beckenbauer—Europe's Footballer of the Year in 1976, captain of West Germany's 1974 World Cup champions, and a man called "the Kaiser" by Bayern Munich fans because of his ability to take charge of a game—joined the Cosmos. He could not have come at a better time, for when he arrived the best soccer team money could buy was in a state of disarray.

After nine games the Cosmos' record stood at 5 and 4 and there was confusion both on and off the field. Beckenbauer landed at Kennedy Airport on May 24th and four days later started a game in Tampa against the Rowdies. Maybe he was still suffering from jet lag, for his presence failed to help the Cosmos, who lost 4–2 and looked terrible in the process.

Five days later Tampa coach Eddie Firmani resigned amidst rumors he was going to the Cosmos. Everyone concerned denied these rumors, saying they were constructed out of thin air and insisting that Cosmos coach Gordon Bradley would finish the season with his team. Then on July 7th the denials ceased and Firmani was named the Cosmos' head coach.

Portland's Stewart Scullion tries to elude Gordon Fearnley of the Ft. Lauderdale Strikers.

Coach Eddie Firmani left Tampa in the middle of the 1977 season to join the Cosmos.

The Cosmos were 12 and 8 at the time and had been attracting huge crowds at home. Brazilian defenders Nelsi Morais and Rildo had joined their back line, adding extra strength and talent to the Cosmos defense. On offense Pelé was displaying his old brilliance with a trio of hat tricks, scoring three goals each in games against Ft. Lauderdale, Tampa, and Los Angeles.

Firmani's arrival did not pass without incident. Bradley had been popular with many of his players and there was some internal dissension. One argument ended with winger Steve Hunt on the floor, the victim of a well-aimed uppercut by teammate Giorgio Chinaglia.

Before things got out of hand, Firmani asserted his authority and made some quick changes. The first was to switch

Neil Cohen, a Dallas native, stars on defense for the Tornado.

Beckenbauer from his traditional role as a sweeper and place the Kaiser in a midfield position. It was a move dictated by the NASL's offside rule.

In West Germany, indeed everywhere else in the world, the midfield stripe is the offside line. A major ingredient of the Beckenbauer magic was his uncanny ability to launch devastating attacking forays from this stripe. But with the offside line only thirty-five yards up from his goal line Beckenbauer had been forced to hang back, increasing the length of his attacking runs and reducing their number.

To replace Beckenbauer at the sweeper position Firmani obtained the services of Carlos Alberto, captain of Brazil's 1970 World Cup champions and a former Santos teammate of Pelé's.

At season's end the Cosmos had a 15–11 won-lost record and were second in the Eastern Division of the Atlantic Conference behind the amazing Ft. Lauderdale Strikers.

Tampa provided the Cosmos with their first playoff test and they responded by passing with flying colors, posting a 3–0 victory with two goals by Pelé and one by Chinaglia.

Four days later, on August 14th, Ft. Lauderdale came to Giants Stadium in East Rutherford, New Jersey, to play game one of a two-match series. It was a night to remember, for that contest was witnessed by 77,691 spectators, the largest crowd ever to watch a soccer game in North America.

"They are selling standing-room seats," reported an overly enthusiastic pressbox announcer. His reaction was excusable since the crowd seemed to lift the spirits of everyone

Carlos Alberto (25) of the Cosmos, one of the NASL's premier defenders, captained Brazil's World Cup-winning team in 1970.

connected with the Cosmos organization, especially the players. Playing like men possessed, they delighted the partisan throng and destroyed the Strikers.

Chinaglia scored three goals, Steve Hunt got a pair, and Beckenbauer, Tony Field, and Gary Etherington contributed one each. Add them all up and it comes to eight goals, five more than the Strikers were able to manage.

Ft. Lauderdale's pride was on the line for the return match, and the inspired Strikers played brilliantly before an overflow crowd in Lockhart Stadium. The Cosmos trailed 2–1 with only six minutes left to play, but then Chinaglia beat Banks to the ball in Ft. Lauderdale's penalty area and fired it into the net.

The match ended with the score tied 2–2, and when neither team managed a goal in the fifteen-minute overtime a shoot-out was necessary. This was a new device the NASL had insituted to decide tie games. Each team selects five players, who take turns trying to score. They begin at the thirty-five-yard line and receive five seconds to maneuver and shoot.

The opposing goalkeeper has no restrictions on his moves within the regular rules of play.

The shoot-out really boils down to a contest between goalkeepers, a test of their skills under pressure-cooker conditions. The Cosmos converted their first four attempts while Shep Messing stopped the Strikers' shooters twice, sending his team into the next round of the playoffs against the Rochester Lancers.

The Cosmos won both matches in this series, by scores of 2–1 and 4–1, and moved on to the championship game against the Seattle Sounders.

Soccer Bowl '77

Long before the Cosmos had begun to shatter attendance records it had been decided to hold this title match in Portland, Oregon, and it was too late to make any changes now. So on the damp and drizzly afternoon of August 28th, 35,548 fans filled Portland's Civic Stadium and along with a national

Ken Cooper of Dallas was the NASL's top goalkeeper in 1977.

Franz Beckenbauer of the Cosmos was the NASL's Most Valuable Player in 1977.

Derek Smethurst of Tampa scored fifty-seven goals during his first three seasons in the NASL.

Lenny Glover of the Tampa Bay Rowdies heads the ball away from the Cosmos' Bobby Smith.

Steve Hunt scored the Cosmos' first goal in Soccer Bowl '77.

Pelé and Franz Beckenbauer embrace after the Cosmos won the 1977 NASL championship.

television audience settled back to watch what proved to be quite a game.

It was to be the last championship match of Pelé's twenty-two-year playing career and according to one teammate, fullback Bobby Smith, "You could see how badly Pelé wanted it. His eyes were hungry, man."

Of course Seattle had no intention of making Pelé's competitive finale a happy occasion. Marking him closely throughout the first half, Seattle defenders seemed intent on sending Pelé sprawling onto the artificial turf every time he touched the ball. Equally well marked were his high-scoring teammates, Chinaglia and Field.

When it appeared that only a Seattle mistake could get the Cosmos a goal, fate selected Sounders goalkeeper Tony Chursky—who had turned in such an outstanding performance against the Los Angeles Aztecs in the playoffs—to commit that costly error.

Following an acrobatic save of a shot by Steve Hunt, Chursky turned his back on the Cosmos winger and tried to roll the ball to a teammate. Hunt charged in, tipped the ball away, and then raced toward the goal with Chursky alongside. Both players tumbled into the net together with the ball and with nineteen minutes gone the Cosmos were up by one.

Four minutes later, three Sounders combined to tie the score. First Jocky Scott took the ball away from Beckenbauer near the Cosmos goal. Quickly he passed it to Mickey Cave, who just as swiftly knocked it over to Tommy Ord on his right.

Shep Messing dived for the ball, but Ord's shot zipped under him for the equalizer.

Several times in the second half the gloomy afternoon was brightened when Pelé ignited brief flashes of his old form. Once he broke loose for an open shot that sailed over the bar. Another time he dribbled past three defenders only to have the ball stripped away by Mike England's sliding tackle. A goal by Pelé would have provided the match with a storybook ending, but it was not to be. Instead it was left to the opportunistic Hunt, who had scored the Cosmos' first goal, to set up the clincher.

He did this by sending a perfectly timed floater to Chinaglia, who was positioned in front of Seattle's goal. The six-foot-one forward leaped high, flicked his head, and scored his tenth goal in six postseason games. With twelve minutes left, the Cosmos led 2–1.

Neither team scored again and later, in the chaos of celebration that engulfed the Cosmos dressing room, Pelé was once again the center of attraction. In situations such as this, Pelé has always had the knack of doing and saying just the right thing. So as reporters and well-wishers gathered around he lifted a bottle of champagne to his lips, took several healthy gulps and said, "Oh, God is very nice to me."

A beautiful sentiment from a man who more than any other individual made soccer big league in the United States. Pelé, to paraphrase his own words, had indeed been very nice to the NASL.

NASL Standings Through the Years

1968 STANDINGS

Eastern Conference

Atlantic Division	Won	Lost	Tied	GF	GA	Bonus Pts	Total Pts
Atlanta	18	7	6	50	32	48	174
Washington	15	10	7	63	53	56	167
New York	12	8	12	62	54	36	164
Baltimore	13	16	3	42	43	41	128
Boston	9	17	6	51	69	49	121

Lakes Division							
Cleveland	14	7	11	62	44	58	175
Chicago	13	10	9	68	68	59	164
Toronto	13	13	6	55	69	48	144
Detroit	6	21	4	48	65	40	88

Western Conference

Gulf Division	Won	Loss	Tied	GF	GA	Bonus Pts	Total Pts
Kansas City	16	11	5	61	43	47	158
Houston	14	12	6	58	41	48	140
St. Louis	12	14	6	47	59	40	130
Dallas	2	26	4	28	109	28	52

Pacific Division							
San Diego	18	8	6	65	38	60	186
Oakland	18	8	6	71	38	59	185
Los Angeles	11	13	8	55	52	49	139
Vancouver	12	15	5	51	60	49	136

Playoff Results

Eastern Conference
  Atlanta 1, Cleveland 1.
  Atlanta 2, Cleveland 1 (sudden death overtime)
Western Conference
  San Diego 1, Kansas City 1.
  San Diego 1, Kansas City 0 (overtime)
League Championship
  Atlanta 0, San Diego 0.
  Atlanta 3, San Diego 0

Top Goal Scorers

	Goals	Assists	Pts
John Kowalik (Chicago)	30	9	69
Cirilio Fernández (San Diego)	30	7	67
Ilija Mitic (Oakland)	18	12	48
Henry Klein (Vancouver)	20	4	44
Iris DeBrito (Toronto)	21	2	44

1969 STANDINGS

	Won	Lost	Tied	GF	GA	Bonus Pts	Total Pts
Kansas City	10	2	4	53	28	38	110
Atlanta	11	2	3	46	20	34	109
Dallas	8	6	2	32	31	28	82
St. Louis	3	11	2	24	47	23	47
Baltimore	2	13	1	27	56	27	42

Top Goal Scorers

	Goals	Assists	Pts
Kaiser Motaung (Atlanta)	16	4	36
George Benitez (Kansas City)	15	5	35
Ilija Mitic (Dallas)	11	4	26

1970 STANDINGS

Northern Division	Won	Lost	Tied	GF	GA	Bonus Pts	Total Pts
Rochester	9	9	6	41	45	39	111
Kansas City	8	10	6	42	44	34	100
St. Louis	5	17	2	26	71	24	60

Southern Division							
Washington	14	6	4	52	29	41	137
Atlanta	11	8	5	53	33	42	123
Dallas	8	12	4	39	39	32	92

Playoff Results:

Rochester 3, Washington 0.
Washington 3, Rochester 1

Top Goal Scorers

	Goals	Assists	Pts
Kirk Apostolidis (Dallas)	16	3	35
Carlos Metidieri (Rochester)	14	7	35
Leroy DeLeon (Washington)	16	1	33
Art Welch (Atlanta)	12	8	32
Manfred Seissler (Kansas City)	11	7	29

1971 STANDINGS

Northern Division	Won	Lost	Tied	GF	GA	Bonus Pts	Total Pts
Rochester	13	5	6	48	31	45	141
New York	9	10	5	51	55	48	117
Toronto	5	10	9	32	47	32	89
Montreal	4	15	5	29	58	26	65

Southern Division							
Atlanta	12	7	5	35	29	33	120
Dallas	10	6	8	38	24	35	119
Washington	8	6	10	36	34	33	111
St. Louis	6	13	5	37	47	35	86

Playoff Results:

Semifinals (best-of-three-series)
Rochester 2, Dallas 1 (overtime).
Dallas 3, Rochester 0.
Dallas 2, Rochester 1 (overtime).
Atlanta 1, New York 0 (overtime).
Atlanta 2, New York 0
Championship Games (best-of-three series)
Atlanta 2, Dallas 1 (overtime).
Dallas 4, Atlanta 1.
Dallas 2, Atlanta 0

Top Goal Scorers

	Goals	Assists	Pts
Carlos Metidieri (Rochester)	19	8	46
Randy Horton (New York)	16	5	37
Casey Frankiewicz (St. Louis)	14	5	33
Jorge Siega (New York)	9	9	27
Manfred Seissler (Rochester)	10	7	27

1972 STANDINGS

Northern Division	Won	Lost	Tied	GF	GA	Bonus Pts	Total Pts
New York	7	3	4	28	16	23	77
Rochester	6	5	3	20	22	19	64
Montreal	4	5	5	19	20	18	57
Toronto	4	6	4	18	22	17	53

Southern Division							
St. Louis	7	4	3	20	14	18	69
Dallas	6	5	3	15	12	15	60
Atlanta	5	6	3	19	18	17	56
Miami	3	8	3	17	32	17	44

Playoff Results:

Semifinals
St. Louis 2, Rochester 0
New York 1, Dallas 0
Championship Game
New York 2, St. Louis 1

Top Goal Scorers

	Goals	Assists	Pts
Randy Horton (New York)	9	4	22
Michael Dillon (Montreal)	8	2	18
Paul Child (Atlanta)	8	1	17
Warren Archibald (Miami)	6	5	17
Willie Roy (St. Louis)	7	2	16

1973 STANDINGS

Eastern Division	Won	Lost	Tied	GF	GA	Bonus Pts	Total Pts
Philadelphia	9	2	8	29	14	26	104
New York	7	5	7	31	23	28	91
Miami	8	5	6	26	21	22	88

Northern Division							
Toronto	6	4	9	32	18	26	89
Montreal	5	10	4	25	32	22	64
Rochester	4	9	6	17	27	17	59

Southern Division							
Dallas	11	4	4	36	25	33	111
St. Louis	7	7	5	27	27	25	82
Atlanta	3	9	7	23	40	23	62

Playoff Results:

Semifinals
Dallas 1, New York 0.
Philadelphia 3, Toronto 0.
Championship Game
Philadelphia 2, Dallas 0

Top Goal Scorers

	Goals	Assists	Pts
Kyle Rote, Jr. (Dallas)	10	10	30
Warren Archibald (Miami)	12	5	29
Andy Provan (Philadelphia)	11	6	28
Gene Geimer (St. Louis)	10	5	25
Ilija Mitic (Dallas)	12	1	25

1974 STANDINGS

Northern Division

	Won	Lost	Tie-Wins	GF	GA	Bonus Pts	Total Pts
Boston	10	9	1	36	23	31	94
Toronto	9	10	1	30	31	30	87
Rochester	8	10	2	23	30	23	77
New York	4	14	2	28	40	28	58

Eastern Division

	Won	Lost	Tie-Wins	GF	GA	Bonus Pts	Total Pts
Miami	9	5	6	38	24	35	107
Baltimore	10	8	2	42	46	39	105
Philadelphia	8	11	1	25	25	23	74
Washington	7	12	1	29	36	25	70

Central Division

	Won	Lost	Tie-Wins	GF	GA	Bonus Pts	Total Pts
Dallas	9	8	3	39	27	37	100
St. Louis	4	15	1	27	42	27	54
Denver	5	15	0	21	42	19	49

Western Division

	Won	Lost	Tie-Wins	GF	GA	Bonus Pts	Total Pts
Los Angeles	11	7	2	41	36	38	110
San Jose	9	8	3	43	38	40	103
Seattle	10	7	3	37	17	32	101
Vancouver	5	11	4	29	30	28	70

(Baltimore and San Jose qualified for quarterfinals as "wild card" teams.)

Playoff Results:

Quarterfinals
   Dallas 3, San Jose 0.
   Boston 1, Baltimore 0.
Semifinals
   Los Angeles 2, Boston 0.
   Miami 3, Dallas 1.
Championship Game
   Los Angeles 4, Miami 3 (tie breaker)

Top Goal Scorers

	Goals	Assists	Pts
Paul Child (San Jose)	15	6	36
Peter Silvester (Baltimore)	14	3	31
Douglas McMillan (Los Angeles)	10	10	30
John Rowlands (Seattle)	10	8	28
Steven David (Miami)	13	0	26

1975 STANDINGS

Northern Division

	Won	Lost	GF	GA	Bonus Pts	Total Pts
Boston	13	9	41	29	38	116
Toronto	13	9	39	28	36	114
New York	10	12	39	38	31	91
Rochester	6	16	29	49	28	64
Hartford	6	16	27	51	25	61

Eastern Division

	Won	Lost	GF	GA	Bonus Pts	Total Pts
Tampa Bay	16	6	46	27	39	135
Miami	14	8	47	30	39	123
Washington	12	10	42	47	40	112
Philadelphia	10	12	33	42	30	90
Baltimore	9	13	34	52	33	87

Central Division

	Won	Lost	GF	GA	Bonus Pts	Total Pts
St. Louis	13	9	38	34	37	115
Chicago	12	10	39	33	34	106
Denver	9	13	37	42	31	85
Dallas	9	13	33	38	29	83
San Antonia	6	16	24	46	23	59

Western Division

	Won	Lost	GF	GA	Bonus Pts	Total Pts
Portland	16	6	43	27	42	138
Seattle	15	7	42	28	39	129
Los Angeles	12	10	42	33	35	107
Vancouver	11	11	38	28	33	99
San Jose	8	14	37	48	35	83

Playoff Results:

Quarterfinals
   St. Louis 2, Los Angeles 1 (tie breaker).
   Miami 2, Boston 1 (overtime).
   Tampa Bay 1, Toronto 0.
   Portland 2, Seattle 1 (overtime)
Semifinals
   Portland 1, St. Louis 0.
   Tampa Bay 3, Miami 0
Soccer Bowl
   Tampa Bay 2, Portland 0

Top Goal Scorers

	Goals	Assists	Pts
Steven David (Miami)	23	6	52
Gordon Hill (Chicago)	16	7	39
Derek Smethurst (Tampa Bay)	18	3	39
Peter Withe (Portland)	16	6	38
Uri Banhoffer (Los Angeles)	14	9	37

1976 STANDINGS

Northern Division

	Won	Lost	GF	GA	Bonus Pts	Total Pts
Chicago	15	9	52	32	42	132
Toronto	15	9	38	30	33	123
Rochester	13	11	36	32	36	114
Hartford	12	12	37	56	35	107
Boston	7	17	35	64	32	74

Eastern Division

	Won	Lost	GF	GA	Bonus Pts	Total Pts
Tampa Bay	18	6	58	30	46	154
New York	16	8	65	34	52	148
Washington	14	10	46	38	42	126
Philadelphia	8	16	32	49	32	80
Miami	6	18	29	58	28	63

Southern Division

	Won	Lost	GF	GA	Bonus Pts	Total Pts
San Jose	14	10	47	30	39	123
Dallas	13	11	44	45	39	117
Los Angeles	12	12	43	44	36	108
San Antonio	12	12	38	32	35	107
San Diego	9	15	29	47	28	82

Western Division

	Won	Lost	GF	GA	Bonus Pts	Total Pts
Minnesota	15	9	54	33	48	138
Seattle	14	10	40	31	39	123
Vancouver	14	10	38	30	36	120
Portland	8	16	23	40	23	71
St. Louis	5	19	28	57	28	58

Playoff Results

Qualifying Round
    Washington 0, New York 2
    Los Angeles 0, Dallas 2
    Vancouver 0, Seattle 1
    Rochester 1, Toronto 2
Quarterfinals
    Tampa Bay 3, New York 1
    San Jose 2, Dallas 0
    Chicago 2, Toronto 3 (overtime)
    Minnesota 3, Seattle 0
Semifinals
    Tampa Bay 0, Toronto 2
    Minnesota 3, San Jose 1
Soccer Bowl
    Toronto 3, Minnesota 0

Top Goal Scorers

	Goals	Assists	Pts
Giorgio Chinaglia	19	11	49
Derek Smethurst	20	5	45
Pelé	13	18	44
Mike Stojanovic	17	7	41
Alan Willey	16	6	38

1977 STANDINGS

Atlantic Conference

	Won	Lost	GF	GA	Bonus Pts	Total Pts
Northern Division						
Toronto	13	13	42	38	37	115
St. Louis	12	14	33	35	32	104
Rochester	11	15	34	41	33	99
Chicago	10	16	31	43	28	88
Connecticut	7	19	34	65	30	72
Eastern Division						
Ft. Lauderdale	19	7	49	29	47	161
Cosmos	15	11	60	39	50	140
Tampa Bay	14	12	55	45	47	131
Washington	10	16	32	49	32	92

Pacific Conference

	Won	Lost	GF	GA	Bonus Pts	Total Pts
Western Division						
Minnesota	16	10	44	36	41	137
Vancouver	14	12	43	46	40	124
Seattle	14	12	43	34	39	123
Portland	10	16	39	42*	38	98
Southern Division						
Dallas	18	8	56	37	53	161
Los Angeles	15	11	65	54	57	147
San Jose	14	12	37	44	35	119
Hawaii	11	15	45	59	40	106
Las Vegas	11	15	38	44	37	103

Playoff Results:

First Round
August 10 at Los Angeles
    Los Angeles 2, San Jose 1 (Attendance 4,308)
August 10 at Vancouver
    Seattle 2, Vancouver 0 (Attendance 21,915)
August 10 at New York
    New York 3, Tampa Bay 0 (Attendance 57,828)
August 10 at St. Louis
    Rochester 1, St. Louis 0 (Shootout) (Attendance 7,137)
Division Championships
1st Round
August 14 at Minnesota
    Seattle 2, Minnesota 1 (overtime) (Attendance 35,889)
August 14 at Los Angeles
    Los Angeles 3, Dallas 1 (Attendance 5,295)
August 14 at New York
    New York 8, Ft. Lauderdale 3 (Attendance 77,691)
August 13 at Rochester
    Rochester 1, Toronto 0 (Shootout) (Attendance 14,152)
August 17 at Dallas
2nd Round
    Los Angeles 5, Dallas 1 (Attendance 18,489)
August 17 at Ft. Lauderdale
    New York 3, Ft. Lauderdale 2 (Shootout) (Attendance 14,152)
August 17 at Seattle
    Seattle 1, Minnesota 0 (Attendance 42,091)
August 16 at Toronto
    Rochester 1, Toronto 0 (Attendance 8,062)
Conference Championships
1st Round
August 21 at Los Angeles
    Seattle 3, Los Angeles 1 (Attendance 9,115)
August 21 at Rochester
    New York 2, Rochester 1 (Attendance 20,005)
2nd Round
August 25 at Seattle
    Seattle 1, Los Angeles 0 (Attendance 56,256)
August 24 at New York
    New York 4, Rochester 1 (Attendance 73,669)
Soccer Bowl '77
August 28 at Portland
    New York 2, Seattle 1 (Attendance 35,548)

1977 Leading NASL Scorers

Player-Team	Games	Goals	Assists	Points
Steve David, Los Angeles	24	26	6	58
Derek Smethurst, Tampa Bay	21	19	4	42
George Best, Los Angeles	20	11	18	40
Giorgio Chinaglia, New York	24	15	8	38
Mike Stojanovic, Rochester	24	14	5	33
Mickey Cave, Seattle	22	12	6	30
Alan Willey, Minnesota	20	14	1	29
Pelé, New York	25	13	3	29
Paul Child, San Jose	26	13	3	29
Kyle Rote, Jr., Dallas	24	11	6	28
Derek Possee, Vancouver	16	11	5	27
Rodney Marsh, Tampa Bay	24	8	11	27
Drago Vabec, Toronto	15	11	4	26
Ron Futcher, Minnesota	20	11	4	26
Buzz Parsons, Vancouver	25	10	6	26
Steve Hunt, New York	23	8	10	26
Stewart Scullion, Portland	24	11	3	25
John O'Hare, Dallas	21	10	3	23
Alan Green, Washington	16	9	5	23
Tommy Ord, Seattle	21	8	7	23
Brian Tinnion, Hawaii	26	7	9	23

1977 NASL Goalkeepers Statistics

Player-Team	Minutes*	Saves	Goals	Shutouts	Average
Ken Cooper, Dallas	2,100	120	21	8	0.90
Gordon Banks, Ft. Lauderdale	2,329	147	29	9	1.12
John Jackson, St. Louis	1,526	103	20	7	1.18
Zeljko Bilecki, Toronto	2,239	185	30	10	1.21
Geoff Barnett, Minnesota	2,165	117	30	8	1.25
Tony Chursky, Seattle	2,200	143	31	7	1.27
Alan Mayer, Las Vegas	1,997	152	31	7	1.40
Mick Poole, Portland	1,932	132	30	3	1.40
Mike Hewitt, San Jose	2,225	135	35	8	1.42
Shep Messing, Cosmos	1,737	155	28	4	1.45
Jack Brand, Rochester	2,373	167	39	6	1.48
Mervyn Cawston, Chicago	2,370	179	40	3	1.52
Arnie Mausser, Vancouver	2,386	149	44	8	1.66
Eric Martin, Washington	2,192	123	41	4	1.68
Paul Hammond, Tampa Bay	2,184	174	41	4	1.69
Peter Fox, Hawaii	2,282	187	52	1	2.05
Gene DuChateau, Connecticut	1,546	140	38	1	2.21
Bob Rigby, Los Angeles	1,680	137	46	1	2.46

*(need 1,170 minutes to qualify)

NORTH AMERICAN SOCCER LEAGUE DIRECTORY

CALIFORNIA SURF
Address: P.O. Box 4449, Anaheim, California 92803.
General Manager: Paul Deese.
Coach: Jim Sewell.
Colors: White and light blue with dark blue and lime green trim.

CHICAGO STING
Address: Suite 1525, 333 N. Michigan Ave., Chicago, Illinois 60601.
General Manager: Jim Walker.
Coach: Willy Roy.
Colors: Black and yellow.

COLORADO CARIBOUS
Address: 2460 West 26th Ave., Denver, Colorado 80211.
General Manager: Joe Echelle.
Coach: Dave Clements.
Colors: White, tan, and black.

THE COSMOS
Address: 75 Rockefeller Plaza, New York, N.Y. 10019.
General Manager: Krikor Yepremian.
Coach: Eddie Firmani.
Titles: NASL Champions 1972, 1977, 1978.
Colors: Green and white.

DALLAS TORNADO
Address: 6116 N. Central Expressway, Dallas, Texas 75206.
General Manager: Fred Hoster.
Coach: Al Miller.
Titles: NASL Champions 1971.
Colors: Red and white.

DETROIT EXPRESS
Address: Pontiac Silverdome, 1200 Featherstone Road, Pontiac, Michigan 48057.
General Manager: Roger Faulkner.
Coach: Ken Furphy.
Colors: Orange and blue.

FORT LAUDERDALE STRIKERS
Address: Suite 405, 5100 N. Federal Highway, Ft. Lauderdale, Florida 33308.
General Manager: Beau Rogers.
Coach: Ron Newman.
Colors: Red and yellow.

HOUSTON HURRICANE
Address: 5085 Westheimer Road, Houston, Texas 77056.
General Manager: Hans Von Mende.
Coach: Timo Liekoski.
Colors: White, red, and orange.

LOS ANGELES AZTECS
Address: 9171 Wilshire Blvd., Beverly Hills, California 90210.
General Manager: Rudy Larusso.
Coach: Tommie Smith.
Titles: NASL Champions 1974.
Colors: Orange and white.

MEMPHIS ROGUES
Address: 2200 Union Avenue, Memphis, Tennessee 38104.
General Manager: Bill Marcum.
Coach: Eddie McCreadie.
Colors: Red and white.

MINNESOTA KICKS
Address: 7200 France Ave. So., Minneapolis, Minnesota 55435.
General Manager: Freddie Goodwin.
Coach: Freddie Goodwin.
Colors: Orange and blue.

NEW ENGLAND TEA MEN
Address: 34 Mechanic Street, Foxboro, Massachusetts 02543.
General Manager: Bob Keating.
Coach: Noel Cantwell.
Colors: Gold and red.

OAKLAND STOMPERS
Address: 7901 Oakport Blvd., Oakland, California 94621.
General Manager: Dick Berg.
Coach: Ken Bracewell.
Colors: Blue, yellow, and white.

PHILADELPHIA FURY
Address: Veteran Stadium, Philadelphia, Pennsylania 19148.
General Manager: Bob Ehlinger.
Coach: Alan Ball.
Colors: Burgundy, white, and gold.

PORTLAND TIMBERS
Address: 10151 SW Barbur Blvd., Portland, Oregon 97219.
General Manager: Keith Williams.
Coach: Don Megson.
Colors: Green and gold.

ROCHESTER LANCERS
Address: 812 Wilder Bldg., Rochester, New York 14614.
General Manager: Richard Kraft.
Coach: Don Popovic.
Titles: NASL Champions 1970.
Colors: White shirts, shorts, and socks.

SAN DIEGO SOCKERS
Address: San Diego Stadium, San Diego, California 92108.
General Manager: Marvin Milkes.
Coach: Hubert Volgelsinger.
Colors: Gold Shirts, shorts, and socks.

SAN JOSE EARTHQUAKES
Address: 2025 Gateway Place, San Jose, California 95110.
General Manager: Tony Kovac.
Coach: Terry Fisher.
Colors: Red shirts, shorts, and socks.

SEATTLE SOUNDERS
Address: 300 Metropole Bldg., Seattle, Washington 98104.
General Manager: Jack Daley.
Coach: Jim Gabriel.
Colors: White shirts, shorts, and socks.

TAMPA BAY ROWDIES
Address: 1311 N. West Shore Blvd., Tampa, Florida 33607.
General Manager: Charles Serednesdky.
Coach: Gordon Jago.
Titles: NASL Champions 1975.
Colors: White, yellow, and green.

TORONTO METROS
Address: 1678 Bloor Street West, Toronto, Canada.
General Manager: J.I. Albrecht.
Coach: Ivan Sangulian.
Titles: NASL Champions 1976.
Colors: Red, blue, and white.

TULSA ROUGHNECKS
Address: P.O. Box 35190, Tulsa, Oklahoma 75135.
General Manager: Noel Lemon.
Coach: Alex Skotarek.
Colors: Red, black, and white.

VANCOUVER WHITECAPS
Address: 885 Dunsmuir Street, Vancouver, British Columbia.
General Manager: John Best.
Coach: Tony Waiters.
Colors: White, red, and black.

WASHINGTON DIPLOMATS
Address: Robert F. Kennedy Stadium, Washington, D.C. 20003.
General Manager: John Carbray.
Coach: Gordon Bradley.
Colors: Red and white.

13. SOCCER SUPERSTARS

Genius cannot readily be explained in any field of human endeavor. This is a fact that is as true in sports as it is in music, science, or literature. There are some athletes who are just special, who send a quiver of anticipation through a crowd just by trotting out onto the field, because they bring with them the possibility of something extraordinary taking place.

A Dutch fan recalls watching a match between the Netherlands and Belgium in 1975 that illustrates this point. "It had been a rather dull match," he remembered, "but Johann Cruyff was playing for Holland that afternoon so there was always the chance of something thrilling happening before the game was over. Sure enough, late in the second half Cruyff got the ball, eluded two defenders, and raced toward Belgium's goal. When the keeper came out in an attempt to stop him, Cruyff never even slowed down. In what could have been a well-rehearsed movement from a ballet he flicked the ball over the goalie's head, glided past, recovered the ball, and then blasted it into the net. It was the kind of play kids on sandlots daydream about, but one that only a handful of the very best professionals can ever hope to accomplish."

Singling out certain players and saying they are the best is at best an arbitrary process. Who can say with any certainty if the men who starred in the 1920's and 1930's could maintain their levels of excellence in the game as it is played today? To be honest, no one will ever know the answer to this question and therefore such judgments must rest in the realm of speculation.

With that in mind, what follows is a collection of soccer players who have been judged outstanding by their peers, by the press, and by the fans. No doubt some important names will be missing, for no listing like this can ever be completely comprehensive. The game of soccer is simply too big, is played in too many places by too many people to make a really accurate and inclusive accounting of the all-time greats possible.

So instead of being a complete list this then is a limited collection of some of the stars of the past and present who, no matter where or when they played, had that something special that made them stand out and be noticed.

The Goalkeepers

GORDON BANKS: He became the starting goalkeeper for England's national team in 1960 at the age of twenty-one and, except when sidelined by illness or injury, held that position for twelve years. An aggressive goalkeeper, Banks was never afraid to range far out of his net to stop a breakaway. His willingness to come out and challenge an attacker sometimes resulted in painful collisions, and Banks suffered many injuries—but more often than not he would be back in position after a few minutes of first aid from the trainer.

Banks joined the professional ranks at the age of nineteen, signing on with Chesterfield in 1958. One year later he was transferred to Leicester City, where he spent eight seasons, and then to Stoke City for seven. During the 1966 World Cup finals, Banks played in six matches and allowed just three goals, one on a penalty shot. Playing in the 1970 World Cup, he made a sensational save of a header by Pelé, flying across the goalmouth from one end to the other and then tipping the ball over the bar. "I hated him for a brief moment," Pelé said

Johann Cruyff in action for the Netherlands against Uruguay in the 1974 World Cup.

Gordon Banks (right) working out with Peter Shilton when both were playing for Stoke City in England.

afterwards, "because he made what I consider the greatest save I have ever seen."

In 1972, Banks was involved in a serious auto accident and lost the sight of one eye. He retired from soccer for several seasons and then made a comeback in 1977, at the age of thirty-eight, with the Ft. Lauderdale Strikers of the NASL. At the end of that season he was voted the league's Player of the Year by the Professional Soccer Reporters' Association.

GILMAR: Born dos Santos Meves in 1930, Gilmar was chosen to become goalkeeper for the Brazilian national team in 1955. When Brazil won the World Cup three years later he played seven matches, shut out Austria, England, the U.S.S.R., and Wales and allowed only four goals.

When Brazil won the World Cup again in 1962 Gilmar was, if anything, even better—recording a total of seventy-three saves during the course of the tournament. In all, he appeared for Brazil one hundred times and surrendered only ninety-five goals. Most of Gilmar's club career was spent in the São Paulo League, where he played for Santos and Corinthians.

PAT JENNINGS: An excellent way to start an argument in a London pub is to compare the relative merits of Pat Jennings and Gordon Banks. Born in Newry in Northern Ireland's County Down, Jennings started out as a Gaelic football

player, and this rough-and-tumble game gave him the kind of temperament so important to the personal makeup of an aggressive goalkeeper.

"When I finally started to get really interested in soccer," he once recalled, "I was confident that I could be a good goalie, because I feel that goalies should come out with no fear of being hurt. I never had any fear, and that is what I think caught the attention of scouts who used to watch our schoolboy games."

Jennings was Northern Ireland's goalkeeper through most of the 1960's and 1970's and played over 400 English League games with Tottenham Hotspur. He was the Spurs' goalie when they won the F.A. Cup in 1967, the League Cup in 1971 and 1973, and the UEFA Cup in 1972. In 1973, Jennings was elected England's Footballer of the Year.

One of his greatest personal triumphs came during the 1967 Charity Shield match between Tottenham Hotspur, the F.A. Cup winners, and Manchester United, the league champions. After making a save, Jennings sent a kick booming downfield. Aided by a strong wind, the ball flew straight toward Manchester's goal. When United goalkeeper Alex Stepney came out to catch it the ball landed, bounced high over his head and into the goal.

"I felt both proud and embarrassed," Jennings said afterwards. "I know just how I would have felt if it had been the other goalie putting the ball past me. It's something you often dream of but never really expect to see happen. After all, a

Brazilian goalkeeper Gilmar makes a save during a 1963 match against England.

goalie scoring one goal is like a forward scoring 500."

Jennings was still playing First Division soccer in 1978, protecting the goalmouth for Arsenal.

LADISLAS MAZURKIEWICZ: A Uruguayan of Polish parentage, Mazurkiewicz demonstrated his outstanding ability early in his career. Playing for Peñarol at the age of twenty-one in a World Club championship game against Real Madrid, he made seventeen saves and recorded a shutout against a team that featured such high-scoring forwards as Alfredo Di Stefano and Ferenc Puskas.

He was outstanding in his role as goalkeeper for Uruguay's national team and Pelé, who played against him many times, said, "No matter what move you tried to put on him you could be sure that somehow he would get himself into position to have a better than even chance of making a save. The stop of a shot he made against me in the 1970 World Cup was a classic example of a goalie maintaining his position and balance after having been initially faked out of position."

In addition to playing for Peñarol, Mazurkiewicz was the goalkeeper for the Brazilian club Atlético Mineiros.

LEV YACHIN: "The Octopus" and "the Black Spider" are just two of the affectionate nicknames Soviet fans bestowed on Lev Ivanovich Yachin during the two decades he filled the goalkeeper's position for Moscow Dynamo. A pioneer of the tactic of making the goalie an extra fullback, it was not unusual to see Yachin in his distinctive black uniform joining Dynamo's defenders outside the penalty area, heading and kicking the ball while his goal was left unguarded.

Yachin made seventy-eight appearances for the Soviet national team and was in the nets when the squad won the 1954 Olympic Games and the 1960 European Nations Cup. In 1963, Yachin was elected Europe's Soccer Player of the Year and the same year was an automatic choice as goalkeeper for the Rest of the World Team that played England in the Football Association's Centenary Match.

When he retired as a player in July of 1971, at the age of forty-one, over 100,000 spectators filled Moscow's cavernous Lenin Central Stadium to watch his farewell game. He had personally selected the opposition, which included such international stars as Eusebio, Gerd Müller, Bobby Charlton, and Giacinto Facchetti.

From the opening kickoff, Yachin displayed every bit of the flash and daring that had made him a legend. Against some of the world's best shooters, he thrilled the crowd with his extraordinary acrobatic finesse and his flawless sense of timing as he rejected shot after shot. After fifty-two minutes, with his team leading 2–0, Yachin was relieved by Vladimir Pilgui and walked off the field to a standing ovation.

RICARDO ZAMORA: When he was ten years old, Ricardo Zamora would skip school to watch Barcelona's Universitiari club practice. The year was 1911 and goal nets had not yet been adopted for use in Spain, so the boy would station himself a few yards behind the goalkeeper and much to the latter's embarrassment and consternation come up with spectacular saves every time a ball got by the goalie. His natural skill did not go unnoticed, and by the time he was fourteen this child prodigy was Universitiari's starting goalkeeper.

At the age of fifteen Zamora joined another Barcelona club, Español, and over the next three seasons he permitted a mere ten goals to be scored against his team. After a brief absence, when he abandoned soccer to resume his studies, Zamora returned to the game with a new club, Barcelona, whose fans quickly dubbed him "the Divine One." He soon became the toast of Spain's sports public and occupied a position of national prominence that had traditionally been reserved for bullfighters.

His reputation spanned the globe in 1923 when, with Zamora guarding its goal, Spain defeated England 4–3 in Madrid. It was England's first defeat at the hands of a European team.

In all, Zamora made forty-six appearances with Spain's national team, a record that stood until 1975 when it was broken by Iribar, Atlético Bilbao's outstanding goalkeeper.

In 1930 Zamora joined Real Madrid, where he remained for the last six seasons of his career. In 1964 the U.S.S.R. national team visited Barcelona and Lev Yachin asked to meet Zamora. When two of the greatest goalkeepers of all time met, Yachin kissed his Spanish colleague on the cheek and said, "Ever since I was a boy I've had dreams of meeting you and coming to Barcelona just to give you a hug of friendship."

DINO ZOFF: In the early 1970's, Zoff compiled the sort of record that any goalkeeper would envy. Through thirteen international matches, no team was able to score against Italy with Zoff in the nets. In the opening round of the 1974 World Cup finals, Sanon of Haiti managed to get a ball past Zoff and

Pat Jennings failed in this diving attempt for a save against
Manchester City in 1977.

The ball gets by Uruguayan goalkeeper Ladislas Mazurkiewicz during a 1966 World Cup match.

snap this remarkable string after it had run for 1,143 minutes of playing time.

Born in 1940 in the village of Mariano del Friuli, Zoff began his career with a local club before moving on to Naples in 1965. He was a member of the Napoli club through nine successful seasons and was then transferred to Juventus, where he became one of Italy's highest-paid athletes.

On three separate occasions he has been voted Italy's Player of the Year, and in 1973 finished second behind Johann Cruyff in the voting for Europe's Player of the Year. In 1978, at the age of thirty-eight, Zoff still remained a mainstay of the Italian national team.

The Defenders

FRANZ BECKENBAUER: Shock waves went rippling through the European soccer community in May of 1977 when it was revealed that Franz Beckenbauer, regarded by many experts to be the continent's outstanding player of the 1970's, had signed a $2.8 million contract to play for the Cosmos of the North American Soccer League.

An exceptionally elegant and inventive athlete, Beckenbauer almost singlehandedly changed the tactics of soccer by transforming what had been an essentially defensive position into a constant offensive threat. Functioning as a sweeper, Beckenbauer was the dominant force on his team's end of the field. With his uncanny positional sense, he seemed always to be in the right place at the right time to squelch an opponent's attack. When his team had the ball Beckenbauer patrolled the midfield line, always ready to swoop down and exploit a momentary crack in the opposition's defensive wall.

Born in 1945, Beckenbauer was the most sought-after youngster in West Germany's youth soccer program before he finally signed with Bayern Munich, a club he captained to three European championships.

He made his first World Cup appearance in 1966, when West Germany lost in the championship match to England; returned in 1970 when his team finished third; and then was captain of the 1974 championship squad. In all, Franz Beckenbauer has worn his nation's colors in 103 full international matches.

One of the most personable men ever to play the game professionally, Beckenbauer has said, "I play the game to win, but if I lose I accept defeat and begin planning for the next game. Soccer is a sport and not the end of the world."

GIACINTO FACCHETTI: When coach Helenio Herrera perfected the *catenaccio* with Inter-Milan in the 1960's, it was Facchetti who added offensive punch to this otherwise sterile formation with his swift overlapping runs down the left sideline.

Facchetti won his first full international cap when Italy faced Turkey in 1963 and subsequently played with the *azzurri* more than seventy-five times. In 1960, at the age of eighteen, he joined Inter-Milan and remained with the club throughout his career, becoming the most popular player in the team's

Lev Yachin makes a save against Bulgaria during the 1956 Olympic Games.

history. Many times Inter-Milan rejected lucrative transfer fees from other teams seeking his services for fear that Facchetti's fans would wreck the club's headquarters.

Standing five-foot-eleven, Facchetti had great range as a defender and was particularly effective when airborne and competing for headers.

BOBBY MOORE: "To me he is the ideal defender who cannot be fooled by anyone," said Pelé when asked his opinion of Bobby Moore. "I know he makes a mental note of everything you do against him so that if you revert to the same tactics the next time you face him Bobby is going to stop you—not by fouling but with his great technique. To me he is the greatest gentleman I have ever encountered on the soccer field."

That about sums up the general feeling concerning this outstanding fullback who was born in East London in 1941. Moore became a professional at the age of seventeen when he signed with West Ham United, a club he played for in 545 matches. He made his first appearance as a full international for England in 1962 and subsequently won a total of 108 caps, many of them as captain of the national team.

Moore was a complete ballplayer who did everything well and even at the age of thirty-five was still showing flashes of brilliance when playing for the NASL's San Antonio Thunder during the summer of 1976. Afterwards he returned to London and spent a season with Fulham before announcing his retirement as a player.

Ricardo Zamora goes high to knock the ball away during a match between Spain and England in 1931.

Italian goalkeeper Dino Zoff.

Italian defensive star Giacinto Facchetti.

GERSON: During his eighty-four appearances with Brazil's national team Gerson, born Nuñes de Oliveira Gerson, earned a reputation as one of the finest passers in the world. His accuracy with the ball, especially at distances of from thirty to fifty yards, often set up goals for the likes of Pelé, Garrincha, and Jairzinho.

When the opportunity arose Gerson was also capable of scoring himself. It was his goal that broke a 1–1 tie twenty minutes into the second half of the 1970 World Cup championship match against Italy. Taking the ball thirty yards from Italy's goal line, he eluded one defender, advanced five yards, and then fired a rocket past Albertosi, the Italian goalkeeper. Five minutes later Gerson sent a perfect forty-yard pass to Pelé that was headed to Jairzinho, who scored with ease. After that Italy was never in the game and eventually lost 4–1.

During his career Gerson played for five different Brazilian clubs, beginning with Canto do Rio, then going with Flamengo, Botafogo, São Paulo, and finally, before retiring because of an ankle injury in 1973, Fluminese.

DJALMA SANTOS: During the course of his career Djalma Santos played in more international matches than any other Brazilian player. He won his first cap in 1952 at the age of twenty-three and before retiring in 1969 had earned a total of 110, two more than Pelé.

With Djalma Santos at the right fullback position and his namesake Nilton Santos, who won eighty-one caps, at the left back Brazil had the kind of tenacious defense it needed to complement the wide-open 4–2–4 formation it employed to such success in the 1958 World Cup.

In the championship game Djalma Santos nullified the scoring threat presented by Sweden's talented winger

Franz Beckenbauer, playing for Bayern Munich, maneuvers with the ball.

Nacka Skoglund, while Nilton Santos completely outplayed the dangerous Kurre Hamrin on the opposite flank as Brazil won 5–2.

Djalma Santos provided one of the key plays as Brazil defeated Czechoslovakia 3–1 in the 1962 World Cup championship game. Recovering a loose ball near the right touchline, Santos allowed it to bounce just behind him and then hooked it powerfully downfield with his left foot. Sailing high into Santiago's bright afternoon sun it flew some forty yards downfield. Czech goalie Wilhelm Schroiff had been carefully watching the ball's progress, but at the last moment seemed to lose it in the sunlight. The ball bounced out of his hands and Vava, loitering nearby, never hesitated as he banged it home for Brazil's third goal.

During his career Santos played for three clubs, Portuguesa de Desportos, Palmeiras, and Atlético Paranaense.

The Midfielders

JOSEF BOSZIK: One of the keys to the success of Hungary's "Magical Magyars," Europe's dominant team in the early 1950's, was this attacking right half who, between 1947 and 1962, represented his country one hundred times in international matches. In many of those games he served as captain of the Hungarian team.

Functioning as the fifth attacker in Hungary's 3-3-4 formation, Boszik would overlap his right winger and pose an additional threat to the opposition. This on a squad that already had, until 1956, such devastating attackers as Zoltan Czibor, Sandor Kocsis, and Ferenc Puskas.

Boszik also played with Honved, the Hungarian army team, and for many years was a member of Hungary's National Assembly.

Bobby Moore and Pelé exchange jerseys following a 1970
World Cup game.

BILLY BREMNER: Although barely five-foot-six, size never hampered this combative Scotsman as much as the hair-trigger temper that matched his fiery red hair. "It is a constant mystery to all of us how he has been able to survive in the game," said Don Revie, who was Bremner's manager when he and fellow midfielder Johnny Giles formed the nucleus of Leeds United, one of the strongest clubs in English soccer from 1967 to 1972.

An energetic, hard-tackling defender, Bremner would brook no nonsense from an opponent and was always ready to retaliate with his fists when he thought he had been wronged. This trait endeared him to the Leeds fans who filled the terraces at Elland Road but often attracted the wrath of referees laboring to keep a match under control.

This same competitive instinct carried over to Bremner's appearances with Scotland. He captained the team in the 1974 World Cup finals and earned a total of eighty-six international caps before being dropped from the national squad, along with three other players, following a 1975 brawl in a Danish restaurant.

Never one to back off from an opponent, Bremner could, when he wanted to, control his temper. On those occasions he would respond to a foul by putting together a series of deft moves to bewilder the player who had fouled him.

JOHN CHARLES: Nearly six-foot-six, this Welshman played outstandingly well both as a center forward and as a center halfback, towering over both teammates and opponents alike. He began playing for Leeds United at the age of seventeen, but because of his unusual size and talent had little trouble gaining acceptance from more seasoned athletes.

In England Charles, a skillful and extremely mild-mannered player, was called "the Gentle Giant" and was never known to use his strength to intentionally harm an opponent, no matter how sorely he had been provoked. Later, when he played in Italy, his nickname became "Il Buon Gigante." In all Charles' Italian sojourn covered six and a half seasons, six in Turin with Juventus and a half season with Roma.

Because he spent so much time in Italy, Charles made only

Gerson (right) is hugged by a team official following Brazil's winning of the 1970 World Cup.

thirty-eight appearances with the Welsh national team. In 1958, he was instrumental in Wales' reaching the World Cup quarterfinals, but was then sidelined by an injury. Without his services Wales lost to Brazil 1–0 on a goal by Pelé.

Charles ended his playing career following three seasons with Cardiff City in his native land. He is remembered best as a scoring threat with his head (because of his height he had an immediate advantage over shorter players) and for his remarkable ability to launch a hard, accurate shot on goal with either foot.

BOBBY CHARLTON: One of the survivors of the 1958 air disaster that claimed the lives of eight Manchester United players, Bobby Charlton went on to become one of the most successful and popular athletes in English soccer history.

When he was still a mere lad of fourteen, Charlton was already creating a national stir as the midfield star of the East Northumberland Schoolboys in Newcastle. Virtually every First Division club in the English League sought his services before Manchester United Manager Matt Busby succeeded in getting his name on a contract.

After two years in United's reserve system, Charlton made his debut with the first team in 1957 at the tender age of seventeen and celebrated the event by scoring a pair of goals. One year later, Charlton's battered body was discovered about sixty yards from the wreckage of the Munich air disaster that destroyed most of what had been a great team.

His injuries were mental as well as physical and it was some time before he was able to play up to his capabilities. When he was finally fully recovered, Charlton had few peers in the world.

Serving sometimes as a forward and sometimes as a midfielder, Charlton played in 606 games for Manchester United and among the many honors he earned was his selection as Europe's Player of the Year in 1966. His ability to swerve and evade defenders and then launch a devastating shot with either foor caused crowds to buzz expectantly every time he gained possession of the ball.

Before retiring in 1973, Charlton won 106 caps for England and scored a record forty-nine goals with the national team. His play in the 1966 World Cup finals is regarded as one of the primary reasons for England's ultimate victory.

Brazil's Djalma Santos.

Bobby Charlton fights to retain his balance after a hard tackle.

ROBERTO RIVELINO: For many seasons Rivelino seemed to hover on the threshold of greatness, held back not by any lack of talent but by a fierce and volatile temper that always seemed ready to explode at the slightest provocation. After becoming captain of Brazil's national team in 1976, he appeared to at last have his emotions under complete control. Now his exceptional abilities could be exploited to their fullest potential.

One of the most dangerous dead-ball shooters in the game, his swerving free kick is one of the most difficult shots to defend against. Rivelino is also one of soccer's most creative players. Capable of making split-second adjustments to the flow of play, he distributes passes from his midfield position with both skill and assurance. Whenever Rivelino has the ball, the other team is in trouble. With his powerful left-footed shot, he can quite easily score from thirty yards out or send a perfect pass to an unmarked teammate fifty yards downfield.

For most of the early part of his career Rivelino played for the São Paulo club Corinthians. In 1977, he was transferred to Fluminense of Rio.

Forwards

PELE: Nobody, to paraphrase the popular song, did it better. His statistics alone are incredible, but they tell only half the story. Pelé began life on October 23, 1940 as Edson Arantes de Nascimento in the tiny village of Tres Coracoes in the Brazilian state of São Paulo, the son of a fairly good soccer player named Dondinho.

He received his nickname from childhood friends as they kicked an old sock stuffed with rags that served them as a makeshift soccer ball. At first he hated the name, often challenging boys who used it to fistfights. He and his friends played a form of street soccer called *pedala* and it was while running barefoot over cobblestoned alleys that Pelé began to perfect the form that would soon be world famous.

After starring with a youth team that won three consecutive junior championships, Pelé was given a tryout with the Santos FC, one of the richest and most powerful teams in the city of São Paulo. Although he was not yet sixteen, Pelé's thirty-minute performance at the audition brought practice to a

Billy Bremner (left) about to be tackled.

standstill. Members of the Santos team who had been working out on other parts of the field began to stop what they were doing and drift over to watch this marvelous child perform his magic. By the time Pelé was finished, all other activity had come to a halt. It was the first of his many captive audiences.

Within a year Pelé had cracked the Santos starting lineup and the legend began to grow. In 1958, although only seventeen years old, Pelé was one of twenty-two players named to Brazil's World Cup team. Hobbled by a knee injury, he sat on the sidelines through the first two games of the finals in Sweden. Then Pelé got his chance to start against the Soviet Union and earned an assist on a goal by Vava in a game Brazil won 1–0. A few days later Brazil faced Wales in the quarterfinal match, and Pelé got the game's only goal. Pelé scored again in the semifinal match against France and twice more in the 5–2 championship game victory over Sweden.

His international reputation was established and Santos was on its way to becoming the most traveled team in the world. Because soccer fans everywhere wanted to see Pelé perform, Santos received invitations to play from all parts of the globe. Before Pelé left Santos in 1974, the club played in sixty-five different nations.

When Santos visited Rome, Pope Paul VI told Pelé: "Don't be nervous, my son. I am more nervous than you because I have been wanting to meet Pelé personally for a long time." In Paris, Charles de Gaulle made Pelé a knight of the Order of Merit—and press critics of the regime said that the French president had done so to increase his popularity by having his name linked with Pelé's. When Santos visited Africa in 1970, the Biafran war was stopped for three days because both sides wanted to see Pelé play. The day after he left, fighting resumed.

In Brazil Pelé became known as *El Perola Negra* ("the Black Pearl"); in France, *Le Tulipe Noire* ("the Black Tulip"); in Chile, *El Peligro* ("the Dangerous One"); and in Italy, simply as *Il Re* ("the King").

Back home, the Brazilian government voted in 1960 to declare Pelé a national treasure so that he could not be sold to a club outside the country. Crowds had begun to expect greatnes from Pelé. A typical goal would raise a roar from the packed stands, an exceptional shot would bring forth a standing ovation. Then there were the special ones, goals that required such uncommon skill that they were called *gols de placa* ("plaque goals"), because every time Pelé scored one local fans would place a plaque in the stadium to commemorate the occasion.

John Charles of Wales (dark shirt) during a match against Bulgaria at the 1958 World Cup.

On November 19, 1969, 80,000 fans braved a torrential rainstorm to sit in Rio's Maracana Stadium and watch Santos play Vasco da Gama. They could have stayed home and watched the game on television, but all wanted to be on hand because Pelé entered the match with 999 career goals.

Several times Pelé came close to scoring his one-thousandth goal, but each time fate intevened. Once the Vasco goalie managed to push his shot over the crossbar. Late in the game there was a great roar as Pelé prepared to slam home a high center, but at the last moment the head of a Vasco defender came between Pelé and the ball. It went into Vasco's net and the defender was charged with an own goal—a score for Santos, not for Pelé.

As time ran out Pelé received one last chance. Splitting the Vasco defense he took the ball, slid past two defenders, and charged into the penalty area where he was tripped before getting off a shot.

Pelé took his time with the penalty kick. Andrada, the Argentine international who played goalie for Vasco, stood frozen trying to read the Great One's mind. Apart from the rain's noise there was no sound until the ball exploded off Pelé's right foot and curved untouched into the net. In seconds the field was covered with hundreds of people—fans, reporters, and photographers—who first kept Pelé imprisoned in Vasco's net and then carried him around the field on their shoulders in triumph.

Before Pelé concluded his twenty-two-year playing career he would score 1,281 goals in 1,363 games. In ninety-three of those matches he scored three goals, and in thirty-one games he scored four. In addition, he scored five goals six times and eight goals once.

Medical experts once examined Pelé for weeks in a Brazilian university laboratory. They wired, probed, and prodded him and when their tests were concluded, announced, "Whatever this man might have decided to do in any physical or mental endeavor, he would have been a genius."

But the experts' tests only measured Pelé's physical attributes—they did not reveal the inner man. Pelé has impressed thousands with his charming, gracious manner. He is a man who, despite the enormous pressures often placed upon him, never acts put-upon and has often demonstrated his willing-

Pelé in action during his first game with the Cosmos.

Plaque in Rio's Maracana Stadium that commemorates Pelé's one-thousandth goal.

ness to stand for hours signing autographs for children.

"I would like to be remembered," Pelé once said, "as a person who showed the world that the simplicity of a man is still the most important quality. Through simplicity and sincerity, you can put all humankind together."

GEORGE BEST: When Bob Bishop, Manchester United's scout for Northern Ireland, first saw him he sent a wire back to the home office that said simply, "I think I have found a genius." Not long after that ecstatic report was received, fifteen-year-old George Best found himself on a train to Manchester for a tryout. Two days later he was back in Belfast, the victim of homesickness, not failure.

"When I got home my father was furious," recalled Best, "he felt I had thrown away the chance of a lifetime." Manchester United Manager Matt Busby was not about to allow such a prize prospect to escape so easily, and with the aid of Best's father, a shipyard worker, persuaded George to return and join United's reserve squad. He spent two years there before receiving promotion to the first team in 1963, at the age of seventeen.

He was, recalled Bishop, "just a speck of a body," who weighed all of one hundred pounds. Frail and shy, Best had little to recommend him except his talent—which was prodigious. "He is possibly the greatest player on the ball I have ever seen," said Busby, who gave Best the opportunity to develop his individualistic style. Blossoming quickly, he developed into the best dribbler in European soccer and by 1966, when he was not yet twenty-one, Best had an international reputation as a goal scorer.

As Best's skills expanded, so did his personality. No longer a shy and inhibited young kid, he quickly gained an off-field reputation as a playboy and a businessman. Soon he was earning much more money from his two fashionable men's boutiques and his advertising endorsements than he was from playing soccer. Every month England's more sensation-

George Best in action.

al tabloids would carry a picture of Best and his latest amorous conquest. One month it would be a movie starlet, the next a model, and the next a beauty-contest winner. There seemed to be no end to the steady procession of attractive young women who found their way to his elbow while the flashbulbs popped.

Best paid a heavy price for all this acclaim. Opponents would call him a "long-haired twit" and often subject him to batterings unusual even by the rough-and-tumble standards of English League soccer.

After a match Best would stagger to United's dressing room, peel off his muddy jersey, and reveal shoulders black and blue from the pounding he had just received. His ankles would be swollen from the kicks they had sustained and his legs bloody from the cuts inflicted by opponents' studded shoes.

"I don't ask for special consideration for George," said Busby, "but in some respects he deserves it. I am convinced that some opponents have gone out to hurt him. He takes some knocks long after the ball is gone. No one in the game takes as much stick as George, and probably no one ever has."

After several brief retirements from the game Best, Europe's Soccer Player of the Year in 1968, called it quits in 1973 and vowed he would never play in England again. As things turned out, Britain's loss was the NASL's gain. After playing in South Africa and Australia, Best joined the Los Angeles Aztecs in 1976.

In his first season Best played in twenty-three games and scored fifteen goals. After missing the season's first four games in 1977, Best still managed to finish third among the league's scorers with eleven goals and eighteen assists for forty points. In June 1978, Best was traded to the Ft. Lauderdale Strikers.

JOHANN CRUYFF: Three times Europe's Player of the Year (in 1971, 1973, and 1974), this Dutch striker signed with Ajax of Amsterdam in 1964 at the age of seventeen and was the player most instrumental in making the club Europe's best before leaving to play for Barcelona in 1973.

A complete athlete, Cruyff can draw upon a wide variety of skills, not the least of which are his phenomenal ability to accelerate with the ball, his change of pace, and the absolute control he has of the ball whenever it is at his feet.

With Cruyff leading the way, Ajax won the European Cup three times and the Dutch national team reached the championship game of the 1974 World Cup before losing to host team West Germany 2–1. His transfer fee to Barcelona totaled $2.2 million, the highest in the world up to that time. Cruyff soon proved to be as great a star in Spain as he had been in the Netherlands.

ALFREDO DI STEFANO: After achieving stardom in both his native Argentina and Colombia, Di Stefano went to Spain in 1953 at the age of twenty-seven and was the key to making Real Madrid one of the greatest club teams of all time.

With Di Stefano leading the way, Real won five consecutive European Cups beginning in 1958. In all, he played 510 games for Real and scored 428 goals before leaving in 1964 to join another Spanish League team, Español. Two years later, at age forty, Di Stefano announced his retirement as a player and went on to become a successful coach, first in Argentina with Boca Juniors and then in Spain with Valencia.

If Di Stefano had a flaw as a player it was his personality. Cold and aloof, he never hesitated to openly criticize a

Johann Cruyff during the final game of the 1974 World Cup.

219

Hungarian goalkeeper Szentmihalyi grabs the ball from Eusebio's feet during a 1966 World Cup match.

teammate—even if his comments were unwarranted or uncalled for. As a result, many players of international stature found it impossible to play more than one or two seasons with him. Didi, the brilliant Brazilian midfielder, was one of those disgruntled stars who fell victim to Di Stefano's disdain and France's Raymond Kopa was another.

Those who did remain found themselves playing alongside one of the greatest all-around talents the game of soccer has ever produced.

EUSEBIO: He was born Eusebio da Silva Ferreira on January 25, 1942, in the city of Lourenço Marques in Mozambique—then known as Portuguese East Africa. At the age of seventeen, Eusebio signed with a local club and as a bonus received the first pair of soccer shoes he had ever owned. "To me this was worth more than money," he said years later. "I cried for hours as I walked around the streets with my new shoes shining."

His devastating right-footed kick was powerful without shoes, but with them he was able to knock goalkeepers down. His reputation spread quickly, and in 1961 Eusebio was called to Lisbon where he signed with Benfica. Soon after joining the club he was inserted as a substitute in a game against Santos, Pelé's club, and scored three goals.

Five times Portugal's leading scorer, Eusebio created a sensation at the 1966 World Cup finals where he led all scorers with nine goals in six games as the Portuguese national team finished third.

Near the end of the 1975 season Eusebio joined the NASL's Boston Minutemen. In 1976 he was traded to Toron-

Alfredo Di Stefano (white uniform) scores as Real Madrid defeats Eintracht Frankfurt 7–3 in 1960 for its fifth straight European Cup championship.

to, where he scored sixteen goals and had four assists to finish the season with twenty-six points in twenty-one games.

TOM FINNEY: Beginning in 1946 and continuing for the next fifteen years, Tom Finney played for Preston North End in England. Although the club never won either the league championship or the F.A. Cup, Finney was regarded as the equal of Stanley Matthews, the other great English forward of this era.

Finney, who usually operated as a right-wing forward, played seventy-six games for England and scored thirty goals, including four in a 1950 game against Portugal. An all-around player, Finney was effective with either foot and was an exceptionally accurate header and shooter.

JAIRZINHO: Born Jasir Ventura Filho in 1946, Jairzinho made his first appearance with Brazil's national team in 1964 and scored against Portugal. A natural right winger, he was forced to play on the left side throughout the early years of his career because his teammate was Garrincha, who had established himself on the right side with both their club team, Botafogo, and the national squad.

Jairzinho made his first World Cup appearance in 1966 playing on the left wing. During the 1970 finals, he replaced Garrincha at right wing and scored in each of Brazil's six games—finishing with a total of seven goals.

A flawless ball-control artist, Jairzinho is a devastating kicker whose cannonlike volleys coming at the conclusion of long runs have made him one of the most dangerous forwards in the world.

Brazil's Jairzinho.

Stanley Matthews (white shirt) launches one of his perfect passes in a 1948 match against Switzerland.

STANLEY MATTHEWS: No player has played so well for so long as "the Dribbling Wizard" whose professional career spanned thirty-five years and did not come to an end until he finally retired at the age of fifty.

Matthews's greatness was not as a goal scorer (in 698 English League games he only scored seventy-one goals) but as a player with an uncanny ability to set up goals for others. Matthews could control the ball as if it were attached to his foot with a string. Swerving and dodging through opponents he would attract defenders like a magnet, thus creating openings for his teammates. Whenever one got loose near the goal, Matthews could lay the ball at a teammate's feet or bounce it off his head and into the nets like a billiards shot.

The son of prizefighter Jack Matthews, who was known as "the Fighting Barber of Hanley," he made his debut as a professional with Stoke City in 1931 and remained with this club until England entered World War II. After the war, Matthews was transferred to Blackpool, where he played until 1961 when he returned to Stoke and helped that club gain promotion to the First Division. In 1956, at the age of forty-one, Matthews was named Europe's Player of the Year. He was British Footballer of the Year twice, first in 1948 and again in 1963. In 1965, one year after he retired as a player, Matthews was knighted by Queen Elizabeth and became Sir Stanley.

When asked about his incredible ability to get around defenders Matthews said, "Don't ask me to describe it. It just comes out of me under pressure."

GERD MULLER: He's not much on defense, there is nothing outstanding about the way he passes, and no one ever called him one of the game's outstanding dribblers. Just about all Müller can do is score, and score, and score. Short, with heavy thighs, stumpy legs, and a low center of gravity, Müller lurks near an opponent's penalty area and is always ready to pounce on a loose ball and hammer it home.

"I just know when the ball is coming," he once said, "it's like a radar sense in me. I often, they say, smell out the ball and the goal at the same time."

Playing for West Germany in the 1970 World Cup finals, Müller scored ten goals in six games as his team finished third. In the 1974 finals he scored four, including the go-ahead tally in West Germany's championship game victory against the Netherlands.

Before retiring from international competition following the 1974 World Cup, Müller played in sixty-two matches for West Germany and scored a total of sixty-eight goals. For his club team, Bayern Munich, Müller averaged nearly a goal a game.

FERENC PUSKAS: Born in Kispest, Hungary, in 1926, Puskas was good enough to begin playing for his national team at the age of seventeen. In all, he appeared in eighty-four games for Hungary and scored eighty-five goals.

A major in Hungary's army, Puskas was on tour with the army's soccer club, Honved, when Russian troops invaded Budapest in 1956 to crush the brief Hungarian Revolution. Puskas refused to return home, sought political asylum, and

West Germany's Gerd Müller launches a shot.

at the age of thirty began a new playing career in Spain with Real Madrid.

There he revealed a new talent, the ability to get along with Alfredo Di Stefano, team captain of Real and a man who hated to share the limelight with anyone else. Puskas spent five seasons with Real and during the first four won the Spanish League scoring title. He could have won five straight but elected to follow another path. Entering the final match of the 1961–62 season he and Di Stefano were tied for the scoring lead with twenty-six goals each.

Both scored in the first half and then with time running out Puskas slid through the defense and drew the goalkeeper out of position. He faked a shot and then passed the ball back to Di Stefano, who scored and won the title. After the match the normally cold and aloof Di Stefano grabbed Puskas in a bear hug and planted a kiss on his cheek.

After retiring as a player, Puskas became a successful coach. In 1971 he guided the Greek club Panathinaikos to the championship game of the European Cup. Even though the Greek team lost to Ajax 2–0, it was a remarkable feat just to get that far in this rugged competition. He has also coached the NASL's Vancouver Whitecaps and the Chilean club Colo Colo.

Ferenc Puskas as a member of a FIFA all-star team in the early 1960's.

HONORABLE MENTION

GOALKEEPERS
Peter Bonetti (England)
Cejas (Argentina)
Ubaldo Fillol (Argentina)
Iribar (Spain)
Bert Williams (England)
Pedro Zape (Colombia)
Ivo Viktor (Czechoslovakia)

DEFENDERS
Jimmy Armfield (England)
Orvar Bergmark (Sweden)
Paul Breitner (West Germany)
Brito (Brazil)
Jackie Charlton (England)
Hector Chumpitaz (Peru)
Puck van Hell (Netherlands)
Roger Marchie (France)
Ladislav Novak (Czechoslovakia)
Freddie Shields (U.S.A.)
George Young (Scotland)

MIDFIELDERS
Johnny Althouse (U.S.A.)
Osvaldo Ardiles (Argentina)
Alan Ball (England)
Danny Blanchflower (Northern Ireland)
Mario Coluna (Portugal)
Clodoaldo (Brazil)
Teofilio Cubillas (Peru)
Johnny Giles (Republic of Ireland)
Bill Gonsalves (U.S.A.)
Arie Haan (Netherlands)
Gerhardt Hanappi (Austria)
Enrique Marzolini (Argentina)
Josef Masopust (Czechoslovakia)

Vicky Mees (Belgium)
Igor Netto (U.S.S.R.)
Gunter Netzer (West Germany)
Johann Neeskens (Netherlands)
Gyorgy Orth (Hungary)
José Santamaria (Uruguay)
Valeri Voronin (U.S.S.R.)
Billy Wright (England)
Zito (Brazil)

FORWARDS
Florian Albert (Hungary)
Ivor Allchurch (Wales)
Josef Bican (Czechoslovakia)
Oleg Blokhin (U.S.S.R.)
Miguel Brindisi (Argentina)
Dixie Dean (England)
Dragan Dzajic (Yugoslavia)
Ralf Edströem (Sweden)
Hugh Gallacher (Scotland)
Garrincha (Brazil)
Lopez Francisco Gento (Spain)
Kevin Keegan (England)
Mario Kempes (Argentina)
Grzegorz Lato (Poland)
Denis Law (Scotland)
Tommy Lawton (England)
Nils Liedholm (Sweden)
Sandor Mazzola (Italy)
Michel Plantini (France)
Luigi Riva (Italy)
Giovanni Rivera (Italy)
Paolo Rossi (Italy)
Didier Six (France)
Allan Simonsen (Denmark)

14. THE DARK SIDE OF SOCCER

"Oh, we kicked him where he lives and we kicked him in the head . . . Bleedin' old Cockney, too bad he's dead."

If the words to the above song, sung by Manchester United fans during a game against Arsenal, sound inflammatory they are meant to be just that. Almost always the response will be in kind; another song or some abusive chant. But sometimes the reaction will go beyond words, and that is when the real trouble begins.

By its very nature soccer is a sport filled with tension. Often goals are few and far between and sometimes, as the passions of spectators are stirred to a fever pitch, they never come. For the most part this is a harmless enough effect, but when added to existing religious or political rivalries—or just plain bad feelings between two groups—it can and has led to violence, injury, and, in far too many cases, death.

In England this problem is referred to as "hooliganism" and its perpetrators are almost always young men between the ages of fifteen and twenty-five, who stand packed together in crowded terraces exchanging taunts and threats with fans of the rival club. On one not atypical Saturday in September of 1977, police arrested eighty-seven soccer fans at various matches throughout England. The worst incident occurred in Leeds, where fifty-four people were detained following a riot that interrupted a game with Manchester United.

The location of this brawl was not surprising, for in the 1970's Leeds' fans have earned the reputation for being among the most unruly in England. In January of 1978, the English League banned Leeds United from playing cup matches at home for the next three seasons because of a riot at a cup match earlier that month.

Celtic vs. Rangers

The most unenviable record for violence in Great Britain has been compiled not in Leeds, but to the north in the Scottish city of Glasgow where the supporters of two clubs—Celtic and Rangers—have been doing harm to each other for more than half a century.

Religious bigotry, pure and simple, is the root of the problem here. Almost to a man supporters of the Rangers come from Glasgow's 1,550,000 Presbyterian residents,

Police scuffle with unruly spectators during a match between Celtic and Rangers in Glasgow.

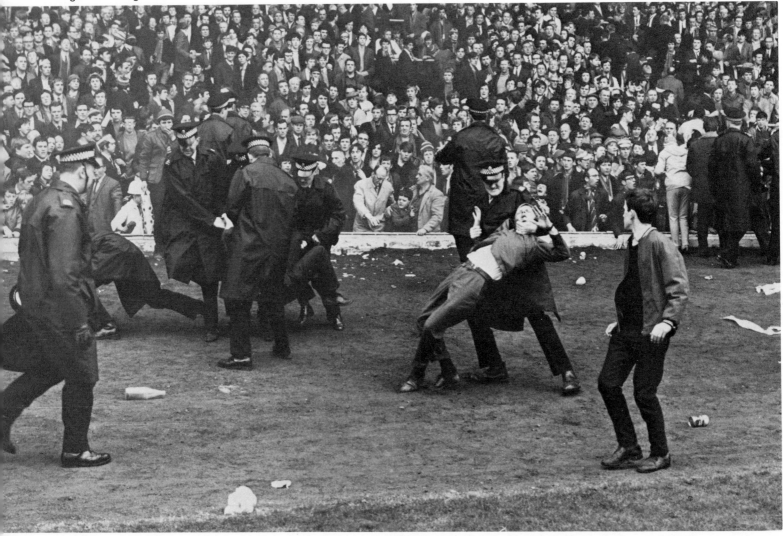

while Celtic's fans are drawn from the city's 330,000 Catholic inhabitants.

In 1931, Celtic acquired a martyr to the cause when goalkeeper John Thomson was kicked in the head while diving for a ball at the feet of a Rangers player. Thomson, only twenty-three years old, died from the blow.

During a Rangers-Celtic match in 1961, two fans suffocated during a melee in the stands, and since then hardly a game between these two clubs has gone by without some sort of violent incident.

Ironically the worst tragedy in the history of Scottish soccer had little to do with the long-standing animosity between supporters of the two clubs. On January 2, 1971, Celtic and the Rangers were battling it out in a scoreless tie before a packed house in Glasgow's Ibrox Stadium. With only three minutes left in the game Celtic scored and the Rangers' fans, believing their team had lost, began to file out of the stands.

Then, in the remaining seconds, the Rangers scored. Hearing a great roar, fans who had already left the stands came rushing back, colliding head-on with other spectators on their way out. There was panic, those in front were

An English referee hands a dart that was thrown on the field during a game to the police. In March of 1978, a fourteen-year-old boy was wounded by a similar missile thrown during a match between Burnley and Oldham. The dart penetrated two inches into the boy's skull, just missing his eyes.

Ibrox Stadium in Glasgow, where sixty-six people were killed following a Celtic-Rangers match in February of 1971.

A dry moat, like this one in Brazil's Maracana Stadium, surrounds the field in most large South American soccer stadiums.

trampled while others in the middle suffocated. To make matters worse, a steel barrier on one of the stairways collapsed and people tumbled down on top of each other forming a pile of bodies thirty feet high. By the time rescue workers got this mass of humanity untangled, 66 people had lost their lives and 108 were injured. Players from both clubs joined the efforts to pull people to safety, but when the two teams met again a few months later the old animosity resurfaced once again.

In 1977 the Rangers management announced it would discourage the singing of sectarian songs at games with Celtic. While most church leaders in Glasgow voiced their approval of this move, James McLean, a leader of the Loyal Orange Institution (the city's most militant Protestant organization), was quoted as saying, "I have no doubt some will stay away from the matches. People may be religious bigots, but that doesn't mean they are hooligans."

Disaster in Peru

By far the worst tragedy in soccer history occurred in May of 1964 at a game between the Olympic teams of Argentina and Peru. The match was played in Lima's National Stadium, before a full house of 53,000 spectators.

Tension built slowly through a scoreless first half and when Argentina drew first blood after sixty-eight minutes of play the highly partisan Peruvian crowd was tense and restless. Then, ten minutes before time ran out, the stands exploded with roars of delight as Peru tied the score.

But Uruguayan referee Angel Eduardo Pazos disallowed the goal, claiming that Peru had committed a foul in the process of scoring. Cries of joy turned to growls of anger. A spectator leaped over the fence separating fans and field and began chasing the referee. Then another joined the chase, and another, and another.

Within seconds a squad of police was on the field, bashing

Military police, armed with tear-gas guns, stood guard against violence at the 1978 World Cup in Argentina.

heads with their truncheons and firing tear-gas grenades. Panic filled the stands and thousands began to run toward the exits. Tunnels leading to the street filled quickly but those in front received a stomach-wrenching shock when they reached the gates.

Attendants guarding the exits had left their posts to watch the game's end. To prevent anyone from sneaking into the stadium they had locked the massive steel doors and now thousands were trapped in the tunnels, an immovable barrier at one end and terrified people crushing in to escape the tear-gas fumes at the other.

As pressure mounted the steel gates swelled outwards like balloons and finally burst, sending broken bodies tumbling out into the streets. The terror that engulfed the stadium quickly spread to the surrounding neighborhood. A full-scale riot was soon in progress as shop windows were smashed and cars overturned.

When it finally ended, hours later, 318 people had lost their lives, and more than 500 were hospitalized with injuries in a catastrophe that is unparalleled in sports history. Tempers remained hot for a long time, and as a safety measure the Peruvian government declared martial law in Lima—an edict that stayed in effect for a full thirty days.

Although there have been serious incidents elsewhere in Latin America and in Europe it makes little sense to catalogue these grim moments in soccer. Instead it seems best to conclude with a quote from a London newspaper editorial printed on the eve of the 1966 World Cup championship match between England and West Germany. Regarding a potentially explosive situation if the visitors defeated the home team in London's own Wembley Stadium the editorial noted: "If perchance on the morrow Germany should beat us at our national game, let us take consolation from the fact that twice we have beaten them at theirs."

LAWS OF THE GAME

The Laws of the Game that follow are reproduced with the special permission of the Fédération Internationale de Football Association (FIFA), and the text is the official text as published by FIFA.

Law I The Field of Play

Dimensions: The field of play shall be rectangular, its length being not more than 130 yards nor less than 100 yards and its breadth not more than 100 yards nor less than 50 yards. (In International Matches the length shall be not more than 120 yards nor less than 110 yards and the breadth not more than 80 yards nor less than 70 yards.) The length shall in all cases exceed the breadth.

Marking: The field of play shall be marked with distinctive lines, not more than 5 inches in width, not by a V-shaped rut, in accordance with the plan, the longer boundary lines being called the touchlines and the shorter the goal lines. A flag on a post not less than 5 feet high, and having a nonpointed top, shall be placed at each corner; a similar flagpost may be placed opposite the halfway line on each side of the field of play, not less than 1 yard outside the touchline. A halfway line shall be marked out across the field of play. The center of the field of play shall be indicated by a suitable mark and a circle with a 10-yard radius shall be marked round it.

The Goal Area: At each end of the field of play two lines shall be drawn at right angles to the goal line, 6 yards from each goalpost. These shall extend into the field of play for a distance of 6 yards and shall be joined by a line drawn parallel with the goal line. Each of the spaces enclosed by these lines and the goal line shall be called a goal area.

The Penalty Area: At each end of the field of play two lines shall be drawn at right angles to the goal line, 18 yards from each goalpost. These shall extend into the field of play for a distance of 18 yards and shall be joined by a line drawn parallel with the goal line. Each of the spaces enclosed by these lines and the goal line shall be called a penalty area. A suitable mark shall be made within each penalty area, 12 yards from the midpoint of the goal line, measured along an undrawn line at right angles thereto. These shall be the penalty-kick marks. From each penalty-kick mark an arc of a circle, having a radius of 10 yards, shall be drawn outside the penalty area.

The Corner Area: From each corner flagpost a quarter-circle, having a radius of 1 yard, shall be drawn inside the field of play.

The Goals: The goals shall be placed on the center of each goal line and shall consist of two upright posts, equidistant from the corner flags and 8 yards apart (inside measurement), joined by a horizontal crossbar the lower edge of which shall be 8 feet from the ground. The width and depth of the goalposts and the width and depth of the crossbars shall not exceed 5 inches (12 cm). The goalposts and the crossbars shall have the same width.

Nets may be attached to the posts, crossbars, and ground behind the goals. They should be appropriately supported and be so placed as to allow the goalkeeper ample room.

Goal Nets: The use of nets made of hemp, jute, or nylon is permitted. The nylon strings may, however, not be thinner than those made of hemp or jute.

Law II The Ball

The ball shall be spherical; the outer casing shall be of leather or other approved materials. No material shall be used in its construction that might prove dangerous to the players.

The circumference of the ball shall be not more than 28 inches and not less than 27 inches. The weight of the ball at the start of the game shall not be more than 16 ounces nor less than 14 ounces. The pressure shall be equal to 0.6-0.7 atmosphere, which equals 9.0-10.5 pounds/square inch(=600-700 gr/cm²) at sea level. The ball shall not be changed during the game unless authorized by the Referee.

Law III Number of Players

(1) A match shall be played by two teams, each consisting of not more than eleven players, one of whom shall be the goalkeeper.

(2) Substitutes may be used in any match played under the rules of an official competition at FIFA, Confederation or National Association level, subject to the following conditions:

(a) that the authority of the international association(s) or national association(s) concerned has been obtained;

(b) that, subject to the restriction contained in the following paragraph (c), the rules of a competition shall state how many, if any, substitutes may be used; and

(c) that a team shall not be permitted to use more than two substitutes in any match.

(3) Substitutes may be used in any other match, provided that the two teams concerned reach agreement on a maximum number, not exceeding five, and that the terms of such agreement are disclosed to the Referee before the match. If the Referee is not informed, or if the teams fail to reach agreement, no more than two substitutes shall be permitted.

(4) Any of the other players may change places with the goalkeeper, provided that the Referee is informed before the change is made, and provided also that the change is made during a stoppage in the game.

(5) When a goalkeeper or any other player is to be replaced by a substitute, the following conditions shall be observed:

(a) the Referee shall be informed of the proposed substitution before it is made;

(b) the substitute shall not enter the field of play until the player he is replacing has left, and then only after having received a signal from the Referee;

(c) the substitute shall enter the field during a stoppage in the game, and at the halfway line.

Punishment:

(a) Play shall not be stopped for an infringement of paragraph 4. The players concerned shall be cautioned immediately after the ball goes out of play.

(b) For any other infringement of this Law, the player concerned shall be cautioned, and if the game is stopped by the Referee to administer the caution, it shall be restarted by an indirect free kick, to be taken by a player of the opposing team, from the place where the ball was when play was stopped.

Law IV Players' Equipment

A player shall not wear anything that is dangerous to another player.

Footwear (boots or shoes) must conform to the following standards:

(a) Bars shall be made of leather or rubber and shall be transverse and flat, not less than half an inch in width, and shall extend the total width of the sole and be rounded at the corners.

(b) Studs that are independently mounted on the sole and are replaceable shall be made of leather, rubber, aluminum, plastic, or similar material and shall be solid. With the exception of that part of the stud forming the base, which shall not protrude from the sole more than one-quarter of an inch, studs shall be round in form and not less than half an inch in diameter. Where studs are tapered, the minimum diameter of any section of the stud must not be less than half an inch. Where metal seating for the screw type is used, this seating must be embedded in the sole of the footwear and any attachment screw shall be part of the stud. Other than the metal seating for the screw type of stud, no metal plates, even though covered with leather or rubber, shall be worn, nor studs that are threaded to allow them to be screwed on to a base screw that is fixed by nails or otherwise to the soles of footwear, nor studs that, apart from the base, have any form of protruding edge rim or relief marking or ornament should be allowed.

(c) Studs that are molded as an integral part of the sole and are not replaceable shall be made of rubber, plastic, polyurethane, or similar soft materials. Provided that there are no fewer than ten studs on the sole, they shall have a minimum diameter of 3/8 inch (10 mm). Additional supporting material to stabilize studs of soft materials, and ridges that do not protrude more than 5 mm from the sole and are molded to strengthen it, shall be permitted provided that they are in no way dangerous to other players. In all other respects they shall conform to the general requirements of this Law.

(d) Combined bars and studs may be worn, provided the whole conforms to the general requirements of this Law. Neither bars nor studs on the soles shall project more than 3/4 inch. If nails are used, they shall be driven in flush with the surface.

The goalkeeper shall wear colors that distinguish him from the other players and from the Referee.

Punishment: For any infringement of this Law, the player at fault shall be sent off the field of play to adjust his equipment and he shall not return without first reporting to the Referee, who shall satisfy himself that the player's equipment is in order; the player shall only reenter the game at a moment when the ball has ceased to be in play.

Law V   Referees

A Referee shall be appointed to officiate in each game. His authority and the exercise of the powers granted to him by the Laws of the Game commence as soon as he enters the field of play.

His power of penalizing shall extend to offenses committed when play has been temporarily suspended, or when the ball is out of play. His decision on points of fact connected with the play shall be final, so far as the result of the game is concerned. He shall:

(a) Enforce the Laws.

(b) Refrain from penalizing in cases where he is satisfied that by doing so he would be giving an advantage to the offending team.

(c) Keep a record of the game; act as timekeeper and allow the full or agreed time, adding thereto all time lost through accident or other cause.

(d) Have discretionary power to stop the game for any infringement of the Laws and to suspend or terminate the game whenever, by reason of the elements, interference by spectators, or other cause, he deems such stoppage necessary. In such a case he shall submit a detailed report to the competent authority, within the stipulated time, and in accordance with the provisions set up by the National Association under whose jurisdiction the match was played. Reports will be deemed to be made when received in the ordinary course of postal service.

(e) From the time he enters the field of play, caution any player guilty of misconduct or ungentlemanly behavior, and if he persists, suspend him from further participation in the game. In such cases the Referee shall send the name of the offender to the competent authority, within the stipulated time, and in accordance with the provisions set up by the National Association under whose jurisdiction the match was played. Reports will be deemed to be made when received in the ordinary course of postal service.

(f) Allow no person other than the players and linesmen to enter the field of play without his permission.

(g) Stop the game if, in his opinion, a player has been seriously injured; have the player removed as soon as possible from the field of play, and immediately resume the game. If a player is slightly injured, the game shall not be stopped until the ball has ceased to be in play. A player who is able to go to the touchline or goal line for attention of any kind shall not be treated on the field of play.

(h) Send off the field of play any player who, in his opinion, is guilty of violent conduct, serious foul play, or the use of foul or abusive language.

(i) Signal for recommendation of the game after all stoppages.

(j) Decide that the ball provided for a match meets with the requirements of Law II.

Law VI   Linesmen

Two linesmen shall be appointed, whose duty (subject to the decision of the Referee) shall be to indicate when the ball is out of play and which side is entitled to the corner kick, goal kick, or throw-in. They shall also assist the Referee to control the game in accordance with the Laws. In the event of undue interference or improper conduct by a linesman, the Referee shall dispense with his services and arrange for a substitute to be appointed. (The matter shall be reported by the Referee to the competent authority.) The linesmen should be equipped with flags by the club on whose ground the match is played.

Law VII   Duration of the Game

The duration of the game shall be two equal periods of 45 minutes, unless otherwise mutually agreed upon, subject to the folowing: (a) Allowance shall be made in either period for all time lost through accident or other cause, the amount of which shall be a matter for the discretion of the Referee; (b) Time shall be extended to permit a penalty kick being taken at or after the expiration of the normal period in either half.

At halftime the interval shall not exceed 5 minutes, except by consent of the Referee.

Law VIII   The Start of Play

(a) At the beginning of the game, choice of ends and the kickoff shall be decided by the toss of a coin. The team winning the toss shall have the option of choice of ends or the kickoff. The Referee having given a signal, the game shall be started by a player taking a place kick (i.e., a kick at the ball while it is stationary on the ground in the center of the field of play) into his opponents' half of the field of play. Every player shall be in his own half of the field and every player of the team opposing that of the kicker shall remain not less than 10 yards from the ball until it is kicked off; it shall not be deemed in play until it has traveled the distance of its own circumference. The kicker shall not play the ball a second time until it has been touched or played by another player.

(b) After a goal has been scored, the game shall be restarted in like manner by a player of the team losing the goal.

(c) After halftime, when restarting the game, ends shall be changed and the kickoff shall be taken by a player of the opposite team to that of the player who started the game.

Punishment: For any infringement of this Law, the kickoff shall be retaken, except in the case of the kicker playing the ball again before it has been touched or played by another player; for this offense, an indirect free kick shall be taken by a player of the opposing team from the place where the infringement occurred. A goal shall not be scored direct from a kickoff.

(d) After any other temporary suspension of play for any cause not mentioned elsewhere in these Laws, provided that immediately prior to the suspension the ball has not passed over the touchline or goal line, when restarting the game, the Referee shall drop the ball at the place where it was when play was suspended and it shall be deemed in play when it has touched the ground; if, however, it goes over the touchline or goal line after it has been dropped by the Referee but before it is touched by a player, the Referee shall again drop it. A player shall not play the ball until it has touched the ground. If this section of the Law is not complied with, the Referee shall again drop the ball.

Law IX Ball In and Out of Play

The ball is out of play:

(a) When it has wholly crossed the goal line or touchline, whether on the ground or in the air.

(b) When the game has been stopped by the Referee.

The ball is in play at all other times from the start of the match to the finish including:

(a) If it rebounds from a goalpost, crossbar, or corner flagpost into the field of play.

(b) If it rebounds off either the Referee or linesmen when they are in the field of play.

(c) In the event of a supposed infringement of the Laws, until a decision is given.

Law X Method of Scoring

Except as otherwise provided by these Laws, a goal is scored when the whole of the ball has passed over the goal line, between the goalposts, and under the crossbar, provided it has not been thrown, carried, or intentionally propelled by hand or arm by a player of the attacking side, except in the case of a goalkeeper who is within his own penalty area.

The team scoring the greater number of goals during a game shall be the winner; if no goals or an equal number of goals are scored, the game shall be termed a "draw."

Law XI Offside

A player is offside if he is nearer his opponents' goal line than the ball *at the moment the ball is played unless:*

(a) He is in his own half of the field of play.

(b) Two of his opponents are nearer to their own goal line than he is.

(c) The ball last touched an opponent or was last played by him.

(d) He receives the ball direct from a goal kick, a corner kick, a throw-in, or when it was dropped by the Referee.

Punishment: For an infringement of this Law, an indirect free kick shall be taken by a player of the opposing team from the place where the infringement occurred.

A player in an offside position shall not be penalized unless, in the opinion of the Referee, he is interfering with the play or with an opponent, or is seeking to gain an advantage by being in an offside position.

Law XII Fouls and Misconduct

A player who intentionally commits any of the following nine offenses:

(a) Kicks or attempts to kick an opponent;

(b) Trips an opponent, i.e., throws or attempts to throw him by the use of the legs or by stooping in front of or behind him;

(c) Jumps at an opponent;

(d) Charges an opponent in a violent or dangerous manner;

(e) Charges an opponent from behind unless the latter is obstructing;

(f) Strikes or attempts to strike an opponent;

(g) Holds an opponent;

(h) Pushes an opponent;

(i) Handles the ball, i.e., carries, strikes, or propels the ball with his hand or arm. (This does not apply to the goalkeeper within his own penalty area.);

shall be penalized by the award of a *direct free kick* to be taken by the opposing side from the place where the offense occurred.

Should a player of the defending side intentionally commit one of the above nine offenses within the penalty area he shall be penalized by a *penalty kick.*

A penalty kick can be awarded irrespective of the position of the ball, if in play, at the time an offensive within the penalty area is committed.

A player committing any of the five following offenses:

1. Playing in a manner considered by the Referee to be dangerous, e.g., attempting to kick a ball held in the hands of a goalkeeper;

2. Charging fairly, i.e., with the shoulder, when the ball is not within playing distance of the players concerned and they are definitely not trying to play it;

3. When not playing the ball, intentionally obstructing an opponent, i.e., running between the opponent and the ball, or interposing the body so as to form an obstacle to an opponent;

4. Charging the goalkeeper except when he
   (a) is holding the ball;
   (b) is obstructing an opponent;
   (c) has passed outside his goal area;

5. When playing as goalkeeper,
   (a) takes more than four steps while holding, bouncing, or throwing the ball in the air and catching it again without releasing it so that it is played by another player; or
   (b) indulges in tactics which, in the opinion of the Referee, are designed merely to hold up the game and thus waste time and so give an unfair advantage to his own team

shall be penalized by the award of an *indirect free kick* to be taken by the opposing side from the place where the infringement occurred.

A player shall be *cautioned* if:

(j) he enters or reenters the field of play to join or rejoin his team after the game has commenced, or leaves the field of play during the progress of the game (except through accident) without, in either case, first having received a signal from the Referee showing him that he may do so. If the Referee stops the game to administer the caution, the game shall be restarted by an indirect free kick taken by a player of the opposing team from the place where the ball was when the Referee stopped the game. If, however, the offending player has committed a more serious offense he shall be penalized according to that section of the Law he infringed;

(k) he persistently infringes the Laws of the Game;

(l) he shows by word or action dissent from any decision given by the Referee;

(m) he is guilty of ungentlemanly conduct.

For any of the last three offenses, in addition to the caution, an *indirect free kick* shall also be awarded to the opposing side from the place where the offense occurred unless a more serious infringement of the Laws of the Game was committed.

A player shall be *sent off* the field of play if:

(n) in the opinion of the Referee he is guilty of violent conduct or serious foul play;

(o) he uses foul or abusive language;

(p) he persists in misconduct after having received a caution.

If play be stopped by reason of a player being ordered from the field for an offense without a separate breach of the Law having been committed, the game shall be resumed by an *indirect free kick* awarded to the opposing side from the place where the infringement occurred.

Law XIII Free Kick

Free kicks shall be classified under two headings: "direct" (from which a goal can be scored direct against the offending side), and "indirect" (from which a goal cannot be scored unless the ball has been played or touched by a player other than the kicker before passing through the goal).

When a player is taking a direct or an indirect free kick inside his own penalty area, all of the opposing players shall remain outside the area, and shall be at least 10 yards from the ball while the kick is being taken. The ball shall be in play immediately after it has traveled the distance of its own circumference and is beyond the penalty area. The goalkeeper shall not receive the ball into his hands, in order that he may thereafter kick it into play. If the ball is not kicked direct into play, beyond the penalty area, the kick shall be retaken.

When a player is taking a direct or an indirect free kick outside his own penalty area, all of the opposing players shall be at least 10 yards from the ball until it is in play, unless they are standing on their own goal line between the goalposts. The ball shall be in play when it has traveled the distance of its own circumference.

If a player of the opposing side encroaches into the penalty area, or within 10 yards of the ball, as the case may be, before a free kick is taken, the Referee shall delay the taking of the kick until the Law is complied with.

The ball must be stationary when a free kick is taken, and the kicker shall not play the ball a second time, until it has been touched or played by another player.

Punishment: If the kicker, after taking the free kick, plays the ball a second time before it has been touched or played by anotyher player, an indirect free kick shall be taken by a player of the opposing team from the spot where the infringement occurred.

Law XIV Penalty Kick

A penalty kick shall be taken from the penalty mark, and when it is being taken, all players, with the exception of the player taking the kick and the opposing goalkeeper, shall be within the field of play but outside the penalty area, and at least 10 yards from the penalty mark. The opposing goalkeeper must stand (without moving his feet) on his own goal line, between the goalposts, until the ball is kicked. The player taking the kick must kick the ball forward; he shall not play the ball a second time until it has been touched or played by another player. The ball shall be deemed in play directly after it is kicked, i.e., when it has traveled the distance of its circumference, and a goal may be scored direct from such a penalty kick. If the ball touches the goalkeeper before passing between the posts when a penalty kick is being taken at or after the expiration of halftime or fulltime, it does not nulify a goal. If necessary, time of play shall be extended at halftime or fulltime to allow a penalty kick to be taken.

Punishment: For any infringement of this Law:

(a) by the defending team, the kick shall be retaken if a goal has not resulted.

(b) by the attacking team other than by the player taking the kick, if a goal is scored it shall be disallowed and the kick retaken.

(c) by the player taking the penalty kick, committed after the ball is in play, a player of the opposing team shall take an indirect free kick from the spot where the infringement occurred.

Law XV Throw-in

When the whole of the ball passes over a touchline, either on the ground or in the air, it shall be thrown in from the point where it crossed the line, in any direction, by a player of the team opposite that of the player who last touched it. The thrower at the moment of delivering the ball must face the field of play and part of each foot shall be either on the touchline or on the ground outside the touchline. The thrower shall use both hands and shall deliver the ball from behind and over his head. The ball shall be in play immediately after it enters the field of play, but the thrower shall not again play the ball until it has been touched or played by another player. A goal shall not be scored direct from a throw-in.

Punishment:

(a) If the ball is improperly thrown in, the throw-in shall be taken by a player of the opposing team.

(b) If the thrower plays the ball a second time before it has been touched or played by another player, an indirect free kick shall be taken by a player of the opposing team from the place where the infringement occurred.

Law XVI Goal Kick

When the whole of the ball passes over the goal line, excluding that portion between the goalposts, either in the air or on the ground, having last been played by one of the attacking team, it shall be kicked direct into play beyond the penalty area from a point within that half of the goal area nearest to where it crossed the line, by a player of the defending team. A goalkeeper shall not receive the ball into his hands from a goal kick in order that he may thereafter kick it into play. If the ball is not kicked beyond the penalty area, i.e., direct into play, the kick shall be retaken. The kicker shall not play the ball a second time until it has touched—or been played by—another player. A goal shall not be scored direct from such a kick. Players of the team opposing that of the player taking the goal kick shall remain outside the penalty area while the kick is being taken.

Punishment: If a player taking a goal kick plays the ball a second time after it has passed beyond the penalty area, but before it has touched or been played by another player, an indirect free kick shall be awarded to the opposing team, to be taken from the place where the infringement occurred.

Law XVII Corner Kick

When the whole of the ball passes over the goal line, excluding that portion between the goalposts, either in the air or on the ground, having last been played by one of the defending team, a member of the attacking team shall take a corner kick, i.e., the whole of the ball shall be placed within the quarter-circle at the nearest corner flagpost, which must not be moved, and it shall be kicked from that position. A goal may be scored direct from such a kick. Players of the team opposing that of the player taking the corner kick shall not approach within 10 yards of the ball until it is in play, i.e., it has traveled the distance of its own circumference, nor shall the kicker play the ball a second time until it has been touched or played by another player.

Punishment:

(a) If the player who takes the kick plays the ball a second time before it has been touched or played by another player, the Referee shall award an indirect free kick to the opposing team, to be taken from the place where the infringement occurred.

(b) For any other infringement the kick shall be retaken.

INTERNATIONAL DIRECTORY

The world organization of soccer, FIFA, is headquartered in Zurich, Switzerland. Its 142 members are divided into six continental confederations: Africa; North/Central America and the Caribbean; Asia; Europe; South America; and Oceania.

AFRICA
(The African Football Confederation)

Algeria: Fédération Algérienne de Football. Founded 1962.
Burundi: Fédération de Football du Burundi. Founded 1948.
Cameroon: Fédération Camerounaise de Football. Founded 1960.
Central African Republic: Fédération Centrafricaine de Football. Founded 1937.
Congo: Fédération Congolaise de Football. Founded 1962.
Dahomey: Fédération Dahoméenne de Football. Founded 1968.
Egypt: Egyptian Football Association. Founded 1921.
Ethiopia: Yeitiopia Football Federechin. Founded 1943.
Gabon: Fédération Gabonaise de Football. Founded 1962.
Gambia: Gambia Football Association. Founded 1952.
Ghana: Ghana Football Association. Founded 1957.
Guinea: Fédération Guinéenne de Football. Founded 1959.
Ivory Coast: Fédération Ivoirienne de Football. Founded 1960.
Kenya: Football Association of Kenya. Founded 1945.
Lesotho: Lesotho Sports Council. Founded 1932.
Liberia: The Liberia Football Association. Founded 1960.
Libya: Libyan General Football Federation. Founded 1963.
Madagascar: Fédération Malagasy de Football. Founded 1961.
Malawi: National Football Association of Malawi. Founded 1966.
Mali: Federation Malienne de Football. Founded 1960.
Mauritania: Fédération de Football de la République Islamique de Mauritanie. Founded 1961.
Mauritius: Mauritius Sports Association. Founded 1952.
Morocco: Fédération Royale Marocaine de Football. Founded 1955.
Niger: Fédération Nigérienne de Football. Founded 1967.
Nigeria: Nigeria Football Association. Founded 1945.
Rhodesia: Football Association of Rhodesia. Founded 1965.
Senegal: Fédération Sénégalaise de Football. Founded 1960.
Sierra Leone: The Sierra Leone Amateur Football Association. Founded 1967.
Somalia: Federazione Somalia Giuoco Calcio. Founded 1951.
South Africa: The Football Association of South Africa. Founded 1892.
Sudan: Sudan Football Association. Founded 1936.
Tanzania: Football Association of Tanzania. Founded 1930.
Togo: Fédération Togolaise de Football. Founded 1960.
Tunisia: Fédération Tunisienne de Football. Founded 1958.
Uganda: Federation of Uganda Football Association. Founded 1924.
Upper Volta: Fédération Voltaïque de Football. Founded 1960.
Zaïre: Federation Zaïroise de Football Association. Founded 1919.

NORTH AND CENTRAL AMERICA AND THE CARIBBEAN
(Confederation of North and Central American and Caribbean Association Football, or CONCACAF)

Antigua: The Antigua Football Association. Founded 1967.
Bahamas: Bahamas Football Association. Founded 1967.
Barbados: Barbados Football Association. Founded 1910.
Bermuda: The Bermuda Football Association. Founded 1928.
Canada: The Canadian Soccer Association. Founded 1912.
Costa Rica: Federación Costarricense de Fútbol. Founded 1921.
Cuba: Asociación de Fútbol de Cuba. Founded 1924.
Dominican Republic: Federación Dominicana de Fútbol. Founded 1953.
El Salvador: Federación Salvadorena de Fútbol. Founded 1964.
Guatemala: Federación Nacional de Fútbol de Guatemala. Founded 1950.
Guyana: Guyana Football Association. Founded 1902.
Haiti: Fédéracion Haïtienne de Football. Founded 1912.
Honduras: Federación Nacional Deportiva Extraescolar de Honduras. Founded 1951.
Jamaica: The Jamaica Football Federation. Founded 1910.
Mexico: Federación Mexicana de Fútbol Asociación. Founded 1922.
Netherlands Antilles: Nederlands Antilliaanse Voetbal Unie. Founded 1921.
Nicaragua: Federación Nacional de Fútbol. Founded 1968.
Panama: Federación Nacional de Fútbol de Panama. Founded 1951.
Puerto Rico: Federación Puertoriqueña de Fútbol. Founded 1940.
Surinam: Surinaamse Voetbal Bond. Founded 1920.
Trinidad: Trinidad Football Association. Founded 1906.
U.S.A.: United States Soccer Federation. Founded 1913.

SOUTH AMERICA
(Confederación Sudamerican de Fútbol, or CONMEBOL)

Argentina: Asociación del Fútbol Argentino. Founded 1893.
Bolivia: Federación Boliviana de Fútbol. Founded 1925.
Brazil: Confederação Brasileira de Desportos. Founded 1914.
Chile: Federación de Football de Chile. Founded 1895.
Colombia: Federación Columbiana de Fútbol. Founded 1925.
Ecuador: Asociación Ecuatoriana de Fútbol. Founded 1925.
Paraguay: Liga Paraguaya de Fútbol. Founded 1906.
Perú: Federación Peruana de Fútbol. Founded 1922.
Uruguay: Asociación Uruguaya de Fútbol. Founded 1900.
Venezuela: Federación Venezolana de Fútbol. Founded 1926.

EUROPE
(Union of European Football Associations, or UEFA)

Albania: Fédération Albanaise de Football. Founded 1932.
Austria: Oesterreichischer Fussball-Bund. Founded 1904.
Belgium: Union Royale Belge des Sociétés de Football-Association. Founded 1895.
Bulgaria: Fédération Bulgare de Football. Founded 1923.
Czechoslovakia: Ceskoslovenský Fotbalový Svaz. Founded 1901.
Cyprus: Cyprus Football Association. Founded 1934.
Denmark: Dansk Boldspil-Union. Founded 1889.
England: The Football Association. Founded 1863.
Finland: Suomen Palloliitto—Finlands Bollforbund. Founded 1907.
France: Fédération Française de Football. Founded 1919.
German Democratic Republic (East Germany): Deutscher Fussball-Verband der DDR. Founded 1948.
German Federal Republic (West Germany): Deutscher Fussball-Bund. Founded 1900.
Greece: Elliniki Podesfairiki Omospondia. Founded 1926.
Hungary: Magyar Labdarugok Szovetsege. Founded 1901.
Iceland: Knattspyrnusamband Islands. Founded 1947.
Ireland, Northern: Irish Football Association, Ltd. Founded 1880.
Ireland, Republic of (Eire): The Football Association of Ireland. Founded 1921.
Italy: Federazione Italiana Giuoco Calcio. Founded 1898.
Luxemburg: Fédération Luxembourgeoise de Football. Founded 1908.
Malta: Malta Football Association. Founded 1900.
Netherlands: Koninklijke Nederlandsche Voetbalbond. Founded 1889.
Norway: Norges Fotballforbund. Founded 1902.
Poland: Fédération Polonaise de Football. Founded 1919.
Portugal: Federacão Portuguese de Futebol. Founded 1914.
Romania: Federatia Romana de Fotbal. Founded 1908.
Scotland: The Scottish Football Association, Ltd. Founded 1873.
Spain: Real Federación Espanola de Fútbol. Founded 1913.
Sweden: Svenska Fotbollforbundet. Founded 1904.
Switzerland: Association Suisse de Football. Founded 1895.
Turkey: Türkiye Futbol Federasyonu. Founded 1923.
U.S.S.R.: U.S.S.R. Football Federation. Founded 1912.
Wales: The Football Association of Wales, Ltd. Founded 1876.
Yugoslavia: Fudbalski Savez Jugoslavije. Founded 1919.

ASIA
(The Asian Football Confederation)

Afghanistan: The Football Association of Afghanistan. Founded 1922.
Bahrain: Football Association of Bahrain. Founded 1951.
Brunei: Brunei State Amateur Football Association. Founded 1959.
Burma: Burma Football Association. Founded 1947.
China (Taiwan): Republic of China Football Association. Founded 1951.
Hong Kong: Hong Kong Football Association. Founded 1915.
India: All-India Football Federation. Founded 1937.
Indonesia: All-Indonesia Football Federation. Founded 1930.
Iran: Iranian Football Federation. Founded 1920.
Iraq: Iraq Football Association. Founded 1948.
Israel: Israel Football Association. Founded 1928.
Japan: The Football Association of Japan. Founded 1921.
Jordan: Jordan Football Association. Founded 1949.
Khmer (Cambodia): Fédération Khmère de Football Association. Founded 1933.
Korea (DPR): Football Association of the Democratic People's Republic of Korea. Founded 1945.
Korea (Republic of South Korea): Korea Football Association. Founded 1928.
Kuwait: Kuwait Football Association. Founded 1952.
Laos: Fédération Lao de Football. Founded 1951.
Lebanon: Fédération Libanaise de Football Association. Founded 1933.
Malaysia: Football Association of Malaysia. Founded 1933.
Nepal: All-Nepal Football Association. Founded 1951.
Pakistan: Pakistan Football Federation. Founded 1948.
Qatar: Qatar Football Association. Founded 1900.
Saudi Arabia: Saudi Arabian Football Association. Founded 1959.
Singapore: Football Association of Singapore. Founded 1892.
Sri Lanka: The Football Association of Sri Lanka. Founded 1939.
Syria: Fédération Arabe Syrienne de Foot-Ball. Founded 1936.
Thailand: The Football Association of Thailand. Founded 1916.
Vietnam: Association de Football de la République Démocratique de Viet-nam. Founded 1962.
Yemen (PDR): People's Democratic Republic of Yemen Football Association. Founded 1940.

OCEANIA
(The Oceania Football Confederation, or OFC)

Australia: Australia Soccer Federation. Founded 1961.
Fiji: Fiji Football Association. Founded 1936.
New Zealand: New Zealand Football Association, Inc. Founded 1891.
Papua-New Guinea: Papua-New Guinea Football Association. Founded 1962.

INTERNATIONAL TEAMS

ARGENTINA
National Colors: Light blue and white horizontal stripes, black shorts.
Principal Honors: South American champions: 1921, 1925, 1927, 1929, 1937, 1941, 1945, 1946, 1947, 1955, 1957, 1959; World Cup champions: 1978.
Leading Clubs: Independiente, River Plate, Boca Juniors, Estudiantes.
Recent League Champions

1958	Racing Club	1968	San Lorenzo
1959	San Lorenzo	1969	Chacarita Juniors
1960	Independiente	1970	Independiente
1961	Racing Club	1971	Independiente
1962	Boca Juniors	1972	San Lorenzo
1963	Independiente	1973	Huracán
1964	Boca Juniors	1974	Newells Old Boys
1965	Boca Juniors	1975	River Plate
1966	Racing Club	1976	Boca Juniors
1967	Estudiantes	1977	River Plate
		1978	Boca Juniors

AUSTRIA
National Colors: White shirts, black shorts, black stockings.
Principal Honors: Olympic Games: runners-up 1936.
Leading Clubs: Tirol-Svarowski Innsbruck, Rapid Vienna, Austria/WAC, Linz ASK, Voest Linz.
Recent League Champions

1958	Wiener SK	1968	Rapid Vienna
1959	Wiener SK	1969	FK Austria
1960	Rapid Vienna	1970	FK Austria
1961	FK Austria	1971	Wacker Innsbruck
1962	FK Austria	1972	Tirol-Svarowski
1963	FK Austria	1973	Tirol-Svarowski
1964	Rapid Vienna	1974	Voest Linz
1965	Linz ASK	1975	Tirol-Svarowski
1966	Admira-Energie	1976	Austria/WAC
1967	Rapid Vienna	1977	T.S. Innsbruck
		1978	Austria Wien

BELGIUM
National Colors: White shirts with tricolored (black, yellow, red) collar, white shorts, white stockings with tricolored tops.
Principal Honors: Olympic Games: winners 1920.
Leading Clubs: Anderlecht, Standard Liège, FC Bruges.
Recent League Champions

1958	Standard Liège	1968	Anderlecht
1959	Anderlecht	1969	Standard Liège
1960	Lierse SK	1970	Standard Liège
1961	Standard Liège	1971	Standard Liège
1962	Anderlecht	1972	Anderlecht
1963	Standard Liège	1973	FC Bruges
1964	Anderlecht	1974	Anderlecht
1965	Anderlecht	1975	Molenbeek
1966	Anderlecht	1976	FC Bruges
1967	Anderlecht	1977	FC Bruges
		1978	FC Bruges

BRAZIL
National Colors: Gold shirts, blue shorts.
Principal Honors: World Cup winners: 1958, 1962, 1970; runners-up: 1950.
South American champions: 1919, 1922, 1949.
Leading Clubs: Botafogo, Santos, Palmeiras, São Paulo, Fluminense, Atlético Mineiro, Cruzeiro, Flamingo, Vasco da Gama.
Recent League Champions

Rio League		São Paulo League	
1958	Vasco da Gama	1958	Santos
1959	Fluminense	1959	Santos
1960	America	1960	Santos
1961	Botafogo	1961	Santos
1962	Botafogo	1962	Santos
1963	Flamengo	1963	Palmeiras
1964	Fluminense	1964	Santos
1965	Flamengo	1965	Santos
1966	Bangu	1966	Palmeiras
1967	Botafogo	1967	Santos
1968	Botafogo	1968	Santos
1969	Fluminense	1969	Santos
1970	Vasco da Gama	1970	São Paulo
1971	Fluminense	1971	São Paulo
1972	Flamengo	1972	Palmeiras
1973	Fluminense	1973	Santos, Portuguese, and Palmeiras, co-champions
1974	Flamengo	1974	Palmeiras
1975	Fluminense	1975	São Paulo
1976	Fluminense	1976	Palmeiras
1977	Vasco da Gama	1977	Corinthians

CZECHOSLOVAKIA
National Colors: Red shirts, white shorts, blue stockings.
Principal Honors: World Cup: runners-up 1934, 1962; Olympic Games: runners-up 1964.
Leading Clubs: Dukla Prague, Slovan Bratislava, Banik Ostrava, Inter Bratislava, Slavia Prague.
Recent League Champions

1958	Dukla Prague	1968	Spartak Trnava
1959	Red Star Bratislava	1969	Spartak Trnava
1960	Spartak Hradec Kralove	1970	Slovan Bratislava
1961	Dukla Prague	1971	Spartak Trnava
1962	Dukla Prague	1972	Spartak Trnava
1963	Dukla Prague	1973	Spartak Trnava
1964	Dukla Prague	1974	Slovan Bratislava
1965	Sparta Prague	1975	Slovan Bratislava
1966	Dukla Prague	1976	Banik Ostrava
1967	Sparta Prague	1977	Dukla Prague

ENGLAND

National Colors: White shirts with red-and-blue stripes on sleeves, blue shorts with red-and-white stripes on the sides, which stockings with red-and-blue tops.
Principal Honors: World Cup champions: 1966
Leading Clubs: Arsenal, Aston Villa, Birmingham City, Chelsea, Derby County, Everton, Leeds United, Liverpool, Manchester City, Manchester United, Nottingham Forest, Tottenham Hotspur, West Bromwich Albion, Wolverhampton Wanderers.

Recent League Champions

Year	Champion	Year	Champion
1958	Wolverhampton Wanderers	1968	Manchester City
1959	Wolverhampton Wanderers	1969	Leeds United
1960	Burnley	1970	Everton
1961	Tottenham Hotspur	1971	Arsenal
1962	Ipswich Town	1972	Derby County
1963	Everton	1973	Liverpool
1964	Liverpool	1974	Leeds United
1965	Manchester United	1975	Derby County
1966	Liverpool	1976	Liverpool
1967	Manchester United	1977	Liverpool
		1978	Nottingham Forest

FRANCE

National Colors: Blue shirts, white shorts, red stockings.
Principal Honors: World Cup: third place, 1958.
Leading Clubs: Bastia, Lyon, Nancy, Nantes, Marseilles, St. Etienne, AS Monaco, Nice, Strasbourg.

Recent League Champions

Year	Champion	Year	Champion
1958	Stade de Reims	1968	St. Etienne
1959	OGC Nice	1969	St. Etienne
1960	Stade de Reims	1970	St. Etienne
1961	AS Monaco	1971	Marseilles
1962	Stade de Reims	1972	Marseilles
1963	AS Monaco	1973	Nantes
1964	St. Etienne	1974	St. Etienne
1965	Nantes	1975	St. Etienne
1966	Nantes	1976	St. Etienne
1967	St. Etienne	1977	Nantes
		1978	AS Monaco

HUNGARY

National Colors: Red shirts, white shorts, green stockings.
Principal Honors: World Cup: runners-up 1938, 1954; Olympic Games: winners 1952, 1964, 1968; runners-up 1972.
Leading Clubs: Ferencvaros, Vasas Budapest, Ujpesti Dozsa, Honved.

Recent League Champions

Year	Champion	Year	Champion
1958	MTK	1968	Ferencvaros
1959	Csepel	1969	Ujpesti Dozsa
1960	Ujpesti Dozsa	1970	Ujpesti Dozsa
1961	Vasas Budapest	1971	Ujpesti Dozsa
1962	Vasas Budapest	1972	Ujpesti Dozsa
1963	Ferencvaros	1973	Ujpesti Dozsa
1964	Ferencvaros	1974	Ujpesti Dozsa
1965	Vasas Budapest	1975	Ujpesti Dozsa
1966	Vasas Budapest	1976	Ferencvaros
1967	Ferencvaros	1977	Vasas Budapest
		1978	Ujpesti Dozsa

ITALY

National Colors: Blue shirts, white shorts, blue stockings with white tops.
Principal Honors: World Cup: winners 1934, 1938; runners-up 1970.
Leading Clubs: Juventus, Torino, AC Milan, Inter-Milan, Lazio, Fiorentina.

Recent League Champions

Year	Champion	Year	Champion
1958	Juventus	1968	AC Milan
1959	AC Milan	1969	Fiorentina
1960	Juventus	1970	Cagliari
1961	Juventus	1971	Internazionale Milan
1962	AC Milan	1972	Juventus
1963	Internazionale Milan	1973	Juventus
1964	Bologna	1974	Lazio
1965	Internazionale Milan	1975	Juventus
1966	Internazionale Milan	1976	Torino
1967	Juventus	1977	Juventus
		1978	Juventus

THE NETHERLANDS

National Colors: Orange shirts, white shorts, blue stockings.
Principal Honors: World Cup: runners-up, 1974, 1978.
Leading Clubs: Ajax, Feyenoord, PSV Eindhoven, Twente Enschede, AZ 67 Alkmaar.

Recent League Champions

Year	Champion	Year	Champion
1958	DOS Utrecht	1968	Ajax
1959	Sparta	1969	Feyenoord
1960	Ajax	1970	Ajax
1961	Feyenoord	1971	Feyenoord
1962	Feyenoord	1972	Ajax
1963	PSV Eindhoven	1973	Ajax
1964	DWS Amsterdam	1974	Feyenoord
1965	Feyenoord	1975	PSV Eindhoven
1966	Ajax	1976	PSV Eindhoven
1967	Ajax	1977	Ajax
		1978	PSV Eindhoven

POLAND

National Colors: White shirts, red shorts, white and red stockings.
Principal Honors: World Cup: third place 1974; Olympic Games: winners 1972.
Leading Clubs: Ruch Chorzow, Stal Mielec, Gornik Zabrze, Slask Wroclaw.

Recent League Champions

Year	Champion	Year	Champion
1958	LKS Lodz	1968	Ruch Chorzow
1959	Gornik Zabrze	1969	Legia Warsaw
1960	Ruch Chorzow	1970	Legia Warsaw
1961	Gornik Zabrze	1971	Gornik Zabrze
1962	Polonia Bytom	1972	Gornik Zabrze
1963	Gornik Zabrze	1973	Stal Mielec
1964	Gornik Zabrze	1974	Ruch Chorzow
1965	Gornik Zabrze	1975	Ruch Chorzow
1966	Gornik Zabrze	1976	Stal Mielec
1967	Gornik Zabrze	1977	Slask Wroclaw
		1978	Wisla Krakow

PORTUGAL

National Colors: Red shirts, white shorts, green stockings.
Leading Clubs: Benfica, Sporting Lisbon, Porto, Boavista Porto.
Recent League Champions

1958	Sporting Lisbon	1968	Benfica
1959	FC Porto	1969	Benfica
1960	Benfica	1970	Sporting Lisbon
1961	Benfica	1971	Benfica
1962	Sporting Lisbon	1972	Benfica
1963	Benfica	1973	Benfica
1964	Benfica	1974	Sporting Lisbon
1965	Benfica	1975	Benfica
1966	Sporting Lisbon	1976	Benfica
1967	Benfica	1977	Benfica
		1978	FC Porto

SCOTLAND

National Colors: Blue shirts with white stripes on sleeves, white shorts, red stockings.
Leading Clubs: Celtic, Rangers, Heart of Midlothian, Dundee, Dundee United, Aberdeen, Partick Thistle.
Recent League Champions

1958	Heart of Midlothian	1968	Celtic
1959	Rangers	1969	Celtic
1960	Heart of Midlothian	1970	Celtic
1961	Rangers	1971	Celtic
1962	Dundee	1972	Celtic
1963	Rangers	1973	Celtic
1964	Rangers	1974	Celtic
1965	Kilmarnock	1975	Rangers
1966	Celtic	1976	Rangers
1967	Celtic	1977	Celtic
		1978	Rangers

SPAIN

National Colors: Red shirts, dark blue shorts, black stockings.
Principal Honors: European Nations Cup: winners 1964; Olympic Games: runners-up 1920.
Leading Clubs: Real Madrid, Barcelona, Atlético Madrid, Atlético Bilbao.
Recent League Champions

1958	Real Madrid	1968	Real Madrid
1959	Barcelona	1969	Real Madrid
1960	Barcelona	1970	Atlético Madrid
1961	Real Madrid	1971	Valencia
1962	Real Madrid	1972	Real Madrid
1963	Real Madrid	1973	Atlético Madrid
1964	Real Madrid	1974	Barcelona
1965	Real Madrid	1975	Real Madrid
1966	Atlético Madrid	1976	Real Madrid
1967	Real Madrid	1977	Atlético Madrid
		1978	Real Madrid

SWEDEN

National Colors: Yellow shirts with blue stripes on sleeves, blue shorts, yellow stockings with blue tops.
Principal Honors: World Cup: runners-up 1958; Olympic Games: winners 1948.
Leading Clubs: Malmö, Atvidaberg, AIK Stockholm.
Recent League Champions

1958	IFK Gothenburg	1968	Oester Vaexjoe
1959	Djurgaarden	1969	IFK Gothenburg
1960	IFK Norrköping	1970	Malmö
1961	IF Elfsborg	1971	Malmö
1962	IFK Norrköping	1972	Atvidaberg
1963	IFK Norrköping	1973	Atvidaberg
1964	Djurgaarden	1974	Malmö
1965	Malmö	1975	Malmö
1966	Djurgaarden	1976	IFK Halmstad
1967	Malmö	1977	Malmö
		1978	Malmö

USSR

National Colors: Red shirts, white shorts, red stockings.
Principal Honors: European champions: 1960; Olympic Games: winners 1956.
Leading Clubs: Dynamo Kiev, Moscow Torpedo, Moscow Dynamo, Moscow Spartak.
Recent League Champions

1958	Spartak Moscow	1968	Dynamo Kiev
1959	Moscow Dynamo	1969	Spartak Moscow
1960	Torpedo Moscow	1970	CSKA Moscow
1961	Dynamo Kiev	1971	Dynamo Kiev
1962	Spartak Moscow	1972	Saria Voroshilovgrad
1963	Moscow Dynamo	1973	Ararat Erevan
1964	Dynamo Tbilisi	1974	Dynamo Kiev
1965	Torpedo Moscow	1975	Dynamo Kiev
1966	Dynamo Kiev	1976	Torpedo Moscow
1967	Dynamo Kiev	1977	Moscow Dynamo

URUGUAY

National Colors: Light blue shirts, black shorts, black stockings with light blue tops.
Principal Honors: World Cup: winners 1930, 1950; South American champions: 1916, 1917, 1920, 1923, 1924, 1926, 1935, 1942, 1956, 1959, 1967.
Leading Clubs: Peñarol, Nacional, Defensor.
Recent League Champions

1958	Peñarol	1968	Peñarol
1959	Peñarol	1969	Nacional
1960	Peñarol	1970	Nacional
1961	Peñarol	1971	Nacional
1962	Peñarol	1972	Nacional
1963	Nacional	1973	Peñarol
1964	Peñarol	1974	Peñarol
1965	Peñarol	1975	Peñarol
1966	Nacional	1976	Defensor
1967	Peñarol	1977	Nacional

WEST GERMANY

National Colors: White shirts, black shorts, white stockings.
Principal Honors: World Cup: winners 1954, 1974; runners-up 1966; European Championship: winners 1972; runners-up 1976.
Leading Clubs: Bayern Munich, Borussia Mönchengladbach, FC Cologne, SV Hamburg, Eintracht Frankfurt, Schalke 04, Eintracht Brunswick.
Recent League Champions

1958	FC Shalke 04	1968	Nuremberg
1959	Eintracht Frankfurt	1969	Bayern Munich
1960	Hamburg	1970	Borussia Mönchengladbach
1961	Nuremberg	1971	Borussia Mönchengladbach
1962	FC Cologne	1972	Bayern Munich
1963	Borussia Dortmund	1973	Bayern Munich
1964	FC Cologne	1974	Bayern Munich
1965	Werder Bremen	1975	Borussia Mönchengladbach
1966	Munich 1860	1976	Borussia Mönchengladbach
1967	Eintracht Brunswick	1977	Borussia Mönchengladbach
		1978	FC Cologne

YUGOSLAVIA

National Colors: Blue shirts with red and white stripes on sleeves, blue shorts, red stockings with blue-and-white tops.
Principal Honors: Olympic Games: winners 1960.
Leading Clubs: Red Star Belgrade, Partizan Belgrade, Hajduk Split, Sloboda Tuzla.
Recent League Championships

1958	Dynamo Zagreb	1968	Red Star Belgrade
1959	Red Star Belgrade	1969	Red Star Belgrade
1960	Red Star Belgrade	1970	Red Star Belgrade
1961	Red Star Belgrade	1971	Hajduk Split
1962	Red Star Belgrade	1972	Zeljeznicar
1963	Red Star Belgrade	1973	Red Star Belgrade
1964	Red Star Belgrade	1974	Hajduk Split
1965	Partizan Belgrade	1975	Hajduk Split
1966	Vojvodina Novi Sad	1976	Partizan Belgrade
1967	Sarajevo	1977	Red Star Belgrade
		1978	Partizan Belgrade

GLOSSARY OF SOCCER TERMS

Advantage rule: The referee will not call a foul or an offside violation if, in his opinion, it would create an advantage for the offending team.

Backs: The fullbacks or defenders.

Bye: When there is an uneven number of teams in a tournament, one or more may be selected to skip the opening round of the competition.

Caution: When giving an official caution, the referee will write the player's name in his notebook and will hold up a yellow card. If a player receives a second caution, he is automatically ejected from the game and the referee will hold up a red card.

Center: To pass the ball from a wide position on the field into the penalty area; also called a cross.

Charge: Legally pushing an opponent off balance with shoulder-to-shoulder contact.

Clear: To kick or head the ball away from the goalmouth.

Dribble: A method of advancing the ball past defenders by means of a series of short taps with one or both feet.

Half volley: Kicking the ball just as it is bouncing off the ground.

Hands, or hand ball: The illegal act of touching the ball with the hands or arms.

Linkman: Another name for a midfielder or halfback.

Lob: A high, soft kick taken on the volley that lifts the ball over the head of the opponents.

Marking: Guarding an opponent.

Obstruction: To prevent an opponent from going around another player by standing in his path.

Offside: A player is offside if he is nearer his opponent's goal line than the ball at the moment the ball is played unless: (a) he is in his own half of the field; (b) there are two of his opponents nearer to their own goal line than he is; (c) the ball last touched an opponent or was last played by him; or (d) he receives the ball directly from a goal kick, a corner kick, a throw-in, or when it is dropped by the referee. In the NASL, an attacking player is not offside until he is within thirty-five yards of his opponent's goal. Under international rules, the midfield line also serves as the offside line.

Offside trap: The defenders move upfield behind an opponent so that if the ball is played to him he will be whistled offside.

Overlap: The attacking play of a defender going down the touchline past his own winger.

Penalty kick: A direct free kick taken at the penalty mark twelve yards in front of the goal. All players except the kicker and the goalkeeper must be at least ten yards from the ball until the kick is taken.

Pitch: Another name for the field of play.

Running off the ball: When a player moves into an open space, ready to receive a pass from a teammate who has the ball. Also, when a player draws off a defender with him in order to create a gap in the defense.

Save: The goalkeeper stopping a potential goal by catching or deflecting the ball away from the goal.

Screen: Obstructing an opponent's view of the ball.

Shootout: The tie-breaking procedure used in NASL games when teams are tied after playing two sudden-death overtime periods. Teams are given five alternating shots at opposing goalkeepers in a one-on-one situation.

Sudden death: Playing after regulation time until one team scores a goal to break the tie.

Sliding tackle: Attempting to take the ball away from an opponent by sliding on the ground.

Striker: A central forward position with a major responsibility for scoring goals.

Sweeper: A defender who roams either in front of or behind a team's rear defensive line.

Tackling: Attempting to tackle or tackling the ball away from an opponent when both players are playing the ball with their feet.

Touchline: The sideline.

Trap: Controlling the ball with the feet, thighs, or chest.

Volley: Kicking the ball while it is in flight.

Wall pass: A pass to a teammate, followed by a first-time return pass on the other side of a defender—similar to basketball's give-and-go pass.

Wing: An area of the field near the touchlines.

Winger: Name given to the left and right outside forwards.

Zone defense: A defense that requires defenders to guard a specific area of the field rather than a specific opponent.

Index

Acknowledgments

The author wishes to thank Ted Slate, Lynn Seiffer and the staff of the Newsweek Library for their invaluable assistance in the preparation of this book. He would also like to express his appreciation to David Barnes of West & Nally, Ron Ahrens of Syndication International, Cherry Young of the Football Association, Ken Jones of the London *Sunday Mirror,* Peter Robinson of *Onze,* Terry Venables of the Crystal Palace FC, Johnny Hollins of the Queen's Park Rangers, the management of Arsenal and the NASL's Cosmos for their advice, assistance, and cooperation.

Picture Credits

The following abbreviations are used:
    FA—The Football Association, London
    MC—Mansell Collection, London
    SI—Syndication International, London

FRONTISPIECE Adidas.

CHAPTER 1   **6–8** All: MC.   **10** top and bottom, FA.   **11** SI

CHAPTER 2   **12–17** All: SI.   **18** left, SI; right, Peter Robinson.   **19–21** All: SI.   **22** Peter Robinson.   **23–24** Both: SI.   **25** Tampa Bay Rowdies.   **26–29** All: SI.   **30** George Tiedemann.   **31** left, Peter Robinson; right, L.A. Aztecs. **33** Peter Robinson.   **34–36** All: SI.   **37** FA   **38–40** All: SI.   **41** left and below, SI; above, Popperfoto.   **42–43** Both: SI.

CHAPTER 3   **50** Popperfoto.   **51** SI.   **52** Popperfoto.   **53** left, Popperfoto; right, Keystone.   **54–57** All: Keystone. **58** SI.   **59** Popperfoto.   **60** Both, FA.   **61** Keystone.   **62** left, Keystone; right, Popperfoto.   **63–65** All: Popperfoto. **66–68** All: FA.   **69** SI.   **70–71** both, SI.   **72** Central Press Photo.   **73–79** All: SI.   **80** Popperfoto. **81** Central Press Photo.   **82–83** Both: Popperfoto.

CHAPTER 4   **88** SI.   **89** Peter Robinson.   **91** top, Peter Robinson; below, SI.   **92** SI.   **93** top, SI; below, Peter Robinson.   **94–95** both: FA.   **96** top, FA; below, SI.   **97** FA.   **98** Popperfoto.   **99** Both: Peter Robinson.   **100** SI. **101–02** Both: Peter Robinson.   **103** left and right, SI; below, Peter Robinson.

CHAPTER 5   **104** Both; FA.   **105** Both: FA.   **106** SI.   **107** FA.   **108** The Press Association.   **109** FA.   **110** SI. **111** Both: SI.   **112** The Press Assocation.   **113** SI.

CHAPTER 6   **120–33** All: Peter Robinson.

CHAPTER 7   **136** Peter Robinson.   **137** SI.   **138** Peter Robinson.   **140–44** All: SI.

CHAPTER 8   **146–53** All: Peter Robinson.   **159** Witters.   **160–61** Both: Peter Robinson.

CHAPTER 9   **163** Peter Robinson.

CHAPTER 10   **164–67** All: Peter Robinson

CHAPTER 11   **168** New York Daily News.   **169–71** All: Richard Pilling.   **172–73** Both: Peter Robinson.   **174** Richard Pilling.   **175** Peter Robinson.   **176** George Tiedemann.   **177** Peter Robinson.

CHAPTER 12   **181–83** All: George Tiedemann.   **184** Dallas Tornado.   **185** Both: George Tiedemann.   **186** top, Minnesota Kicks; bottom, George Tiedemann.   **187** Judy Griesedieck.   **188–89** Both: Richard Pilling.   **190** left, Ursula Seeman; right, Dallas Tornado.   **191** Portland Timbers.   **192** left, Peter Robinson; right, Dallas Tornado.   **193** Ursula Seeman.   **194** Dallas Tornado.   **195–97** All: George Tiedemann.

CHAPTER 13   **204–05** Both: SI.   **206** FA.   **207** Both: SI.   **208–09** Both: FA.   **210–11** All: Peter Robinson. **212–15** All: SI.   **216** Popperfoto.   **217–19** All: Peter Robinson.   **220** left, SI; right, Wide World.   **221** left, Peter Robinson; right, Popperfoto.   **222–23** Both: SI.

CHAPTER 14   **225** SI.   **226** top, Peter Robinson; bottom, SI.   **227–28** Both: Peter Robinson.